Charles Cayley B.

The Psalms in Metre

Charles Cayley B.

The Psalms in Metre

ISBN/EAN: 9783744774895

Printed in Europe, USA, Canada, Australia, Japan

Cover: Foto ©Lupo / pixelio.de

More available books at **www.hansebooks.com**

THE
PSALMS IN METRE.

BY

C. B. CAYLEY, B.A.,

TRANSLATOR OF "DANTE'S DIVINE COMEDY;" AUTHOR OF

"PSYCHE'S INTERLUDES."

LONDON:
LONGMAN, GREEN, LONGMAN, AND ROBERTS.
1860.

[ENTERED AT STATIONERS' HALL.]

THE PSALMS IN METRE.

PREFACE.

It is a common theory, and almost, perhaps, a national one, that the Psalms cannot be well translated—no, not for any purpose—except in prose; and that our authorized prose translation should enable us to dispense, except for occasional reference, with all others that are likely to be brought forward. In practice, however, this fine version remains, among state-churchmen, unopened and unfingered in the midst of the sacred volume, while a rendering of far inferior correctness and insight is employed in their established Liturgy—in part, no doubt, because it assimilates the ancient Word to modern and Christian thoughts and feelings, and adapts its rhythm to the received forms of our usual congregational responses. Then there are translations, not only in verse, but in the most modern and national forms of verse, and sometimes, as in the case of the Scotch rendering, in the most rude and homely, though not vigor-lacking diction; and parts of such versions, in their popular liturgic application, have no doubt been found practically effective and influential, though unsuccessful, perhaps, with those classes among which luxury or education has introduced a refined sense of elegance and dignity, such as in Levantine climates was apparently a gift of simple nature. So a version designed more expressly for the upper classes, and aiming to gratify them by a superficial polish, has been found convenient for their use, if not brilliantly effective—although the language was generally defective in force and in directness.

In theoretical estimation, again, the authors of the national versions are very generally decried and slighted with great abandonment, which might be moderated, I think, if it were remembered that even men of undoubted genius, like Milton and Sidney, have failed egregiously to attain the perfections—nay, the very proprieties—which, in a literary or æsthetic view, can be desiderated in the psalmodies we are familiar with. But there is, as I believe that I can show, an inherent insuperable obstacle to anyone's writing a really poetic version of the Psalms (or most of them) that shall also be a serviceable liturgic rendering—at least, until the composer of psalm-tunes shall be controlled by the versifier, instead of controlling him, as hitherto, and shall apply some undeveloped resources of his art to produce accompaniments for such couplets or stanzas as are at first adopted, in deference to the structure of the Hebrew, without consulting him. Till this be done, men of very unequal talent and acquirements will compete, with almost equal ill-success, in the problem not legitimately propounded to them; and the true critic will abstain from personal censures and invidious comparisons (among not a few, but a legion of experimenters) which the general circumstances of the case render as unnecessary as they would be odious. Meantime candor and common sense, which already tolerate, nay approve, the simultaneous usage among us of at least three versions, in most places and most circles, may make room, I trust, for a fourth kind of version, which attempts a special function, without pretentiously derogating from the functions of the rest—that is, a version aiming, in the first place, at that truth and propriety in poetic *form* and diction which we commonly demand in translations of modern classic authors, for the free pursuit of which qualities it declines the ceremonious exactness of prose-renderings, and also the modernizing paraphrastic or conglomerative licence of those made to sing in church or chapel.

I will review and analyze the above observations more explicitly. We readily dispense, most of us, with prose translation for Homer or for Tasso, because we hope, notwithstanding all technical difficulties, to realize the charm and power of their compositions more effectually where they are not quite divested of all connatural form and euphony. And not only our heart and imagination, but our understanding even, is not slightly interested in people's imitating the original shape of great poetic writings; for the understanding fears to be misled by poetic utterances presented to her under the mask of prose, and to take as materially true that which is only true in sentiment and spirit. Yet it would be most ridiculous to derogate in a general way from the value of a prose version of any part of the Bible; for prose only can give that high material accuracy which must be demanded where we have recourse so confidently, as regards every detail, to deduce all the principles of morality and of religion. Still, the practical exposition of the Bible must demand some recognition of the dissimilarity of its diction in prose and poetry, and this even, as could be demonstrated, to prevent gross errors and sophistications. And on this ground, an occasional reference to a poetic version of the Psalter, or other Scriptures, may be useful even to those who, by nature or by training, are most insensible or indifferent to poetry in a general point of view. But here an objection to my argument will be readily started by many who are acquainted, if even slightly, with the Hebrew language. "The poetry of your originals," they will say, "is not verse in our modern sense: the prose of your authorized version is not, in the fullest sense, prosaic; the Hebrew form and the Elizabethan are not so incompatible as you pretend. We find no rhymes in Hebrew—no regular accentual metres—not even those quantitative verses which we recognize in Greek or Latin, but which we generally despair of seeing imitated in a modern language. The cadences of parallel clauses, the equality or the simple proportions which we observe in their length, give the Hebrew text a poetic character that we feel, but are incapable of defining; yet the same cadences, the same symmetry, seem to come of themselves, by the grace of nature, into a literal prose version: a little art, at most, is requisite to bring them into strong relief, as we see by the translations of Herder, or by some of the chants and anthems used in our own worship." This objection I can only in part hope to overcome. I will remark, however, that, despite the general resemblance between Hebrew poetry and what we call measured prose in English, the former is distinguished by a remarkable brevity and compactness (so that not half as many words, perhaps, go to a verse in the Hebrew as in the most literal prose English), as likewise by great freedom in grouping the leading words—not in the order of the logical sentence, but in any that may suit the feeling of the writer. And the necessity of preserving such a brevity is the greater, because it generally implies a simple breadth and vagueness, though without equivocalness, in the import of a phrase, that cannot but be sorely injured by those continual fillings-up, qualifications, and limitations which we know so little how to dispense with in modern languages. This conciseness, this compactness and simplicity, this comeliness of well-grouped words, cannot be at all imitated in English without sometimes using such ellipses and inversions as we are not accustomed to tolerate in prose, though a simple rhyming metre renders them familiar and acceptable, while it tends to strengthen the cadences, and the correspondences of term to term, that might otherwise be lost or weakened through the inevitable multiplication of words in English.

It may, indeed, seem idle to talk of concentration, or the nice arrangement of pause and period, when we know, by repeated experience, what a continued sacrifice of these points seems required by the ballad-metre that the psalm translators have so generally taken to. Where, it may be asked, can concentration be, if you have five words given you to spin into four verses? or even three words, as in that ill-fated chorus, ki lolam chasdo, "for his mercy is everlasting" (Psalm cxxxvi.) which it has been found necessary, in the usually brief Scotch version, to extend to—

> "For certainly
> His mercies dure,
> Both firm and sure,
> Eternally."

Do we not find vicious paraphrase even in that passage which is considered the most happy in Sternhold's version, and which was so elaborately commended in one of the youthful lucubrations of Kirke White?—in which he broke, indeed, the head of the Angelic Doctor by the distinction he drew between the two plural nouns in line 5—

> "The Lord descended from above,
> And bow'd the heavens high,
> And underneath his feet he cast
> The darkness of the sky.
> On *cherubs and on cherubims*
> Full royally he rode,
> And on the wings of mighty winds
> Come flying all abroad."

Or can we better reconcile with the imitation of a sententious style such intercalations as this in Tate and Brady—

> "The heavens declare thy glory, Lord,
> *Which that alone doth fill*" (Ps. xix.)—

less pleonastic, certainly, but not more calculated to edify the mind, or to assist the march of fancy. But if, on the other hand, the Scotch version is mostly elegiac couplets. I do not say I have used the same kind of couplet all through the Psalter, but most of my metres spring from very simple variations of that in Psalm i. I have not, however, been so despitefully minded to the quatrain as not to admit it in many places where the predominant heavy structure of the verse seemed to make it suitable, as witness part of Psalm xliv., in which I have often followed the Scotch version. I may be excused for dwelling on these metrical experiments, because our English literature is rather poor in first-rate lyrical models—at least in comparison with its standing in other high provinces of the poetic art; so that one who would cultivate this style in various forms, and especially such as may lie within a brief compass, must be to a great extent an innovator.

As for attempting to expound the Psalms, whether by direct comments or by implication in the language of my versions, I have thought it allowable, in a literary undertaking like the present, to confine myself within very narrow limits. It has been a maxim with me, that when a psalm is reputed to contain some *unconscious* foreboding, or some figure unintended by the immediate writer, which Inspiration or Providence shall have overruled to bear witness to an event not methodically predicted in the context, or to a mystery that transcended the simple theology of the ancient world, then I am not bound to comment on this reputed import; for I should thus be making myself a commentator, not any longer on David or on the Asaphs, but on the Divine government in general. I should be affecting the theologian rather than the critical student. But common sense will urge upon me that the passage has some more direct and obvious signification, which was sufficient to make it profitable to the countrymen and contemporaries of the writer, and conciliate such respect for it as is imported by our now finding it, perhaps unsheltered by any great name, in the canon of the Scriptures.

As for the views to which I have been guided on the direct interpretation of the Psalter, I will not here attempt to characterize them, because their connexion with special criticisms on various passages renders it likely that they will be better supported by reference to the notes I have annexed. Suffice it to say, that I have not endeavoured to define the meaning of my original as strictly in the text as in the notes; so that, in construing my verses, the reader will have, I hope, every reasonable latitude, but none such as to involve a downright *équivoque*. Not that I have hoped, through my own studies of the Hebrew text, to merit any considerable confidence from the reader, or to add much to his material knowledge as regards the Psalms. I have sought more to avoid the conscience of any wilful negligence in endorsing such renderings as I might, at any time hereafter, think erroneous or imperfect. It is to free a poetic version from any gross errors, not to work up, on a subject presenting so many obscurities, a prose commentary that might *per se* merit the attention of the public, that I have pursued the researches by which this work is illustrated; and it is not the primary object of the versifier to explain obscure passages to the understanding, but to restore to familiar ones a form in which they may promptly and vividly impress the feelings and imagination.

I need only add to these observations, that the difficulty I have felt in thus far dwelling on the nature of my own enterprise, adds much to my indebtedness to those kind friends and respected sympathizers who have patronized it, after no other preface than a few specimens, and thus enabled me to fulfil a plan long cherished, and several times laid down in diffidence.

C. B. CAYLEY.

5, *Montpelier Row, Blackheath, S.E.*

NAMES OF SUBSCRIBERS.

Allingham, W., Esq., Ballyshannon, Ireland.
Baines, Mrs. C. A., Little Marlow, Bucks.
Barham, Mrs., Trecwm, Haverford West, 3 copies.
Bayley, Misses, Newbury, Berks, 5 copies.
Borradaile, Mrs., Blackheath, 2 copies.
Bowen, Mrs., Blackheath.
Bowen, Mrs. J., Blackheath, 2 copies.
Brett, J. Esq., Temple, London.
Bulard, Mme de, Paris, 10 copies.
Busk, Mrs. G., London.
Chichester, the Right Rev. the Lord Bishop of, 3 copies.
Carr, W., Esq., Blackheath, 2 copies.
Cayley, E. S., Esq., M.P., London, 2 copies.
Cayley, E. Esq., Stamford.
Cayley, Mrs., Brookhurst, 5 copies.
Cayley, Mrs. H., Blackheath, 6 copies.
Cayley, Miss M. E., Southwell, 3 copies.
Cayley, Miss S., Blackheath, 2 copies.
Cayley, Miss H., Blackheath.
Cayley, A., Esq., Lincoln's Inn, London, 6 copies.
Cazalet, L. Esq., London, 5 copies.

NAMES OF SUBSCRIBERS.

Christie, H. J., Esq., London, 2 copies.
Clarke, Rev. J., Blackheath.
Cope, Rev. E. M., Trinity College, Cambridge.
Cozens, Miss E., London.
Cramer, C., Esq., Eastmount, Isle of Wight,
Douglass, Rev. C., Brighton.
Duroure, Mrs., Blackheath.
Ebury, the Right Hon. Lord, London.
Edes, F. H., Esq., London, 2 copies.
Ferguson, S. Esq., Dublin.
Gamble, I. C. C., Esq., Lee, S.E.
Gardner, C., Esq., London.
Gillum, Major, London.
Gower, E., Esq., Lee, S.E., 3 copies.
Gray, Mrs., British Museum, 3 copies.
Griffiths, C., Esq., Temple, London.
Heimann, Dr. H., University College, London.
Hunt, W. Holman, Esq., London.
Ince, W., Esq., London.
James, Miss, London.
Kirby, J. J., Esq., Dublin.
Lambert, Miss, Farnham Royal, Bucks.
Latham, Dr. R. G., Greenford, London, W.
Leifchild, F., Esq., London, 10 copies.
Leifchild, H. S., Esq., London, 5 copies.
Leifchild, Miss, London, 5 copies.
Macgregor, Misses, London.
Mitchell, Rev. T., London, 2 copies.
Moberly, Dr. G., Winchester, 3 copies.
Moline, Mrs. Greenwich.
Moline, Miss, Greenwich.

NAMES OF SUBSCRIBERS.

Munro, A., Esq., London, 4 copies.
Narishkin, Madame N., St. Petersburg, 3 copies.
Norris, Rev. J. P., Rowley Bank, Staffordshire, 2 copies.
North, Rev. I. W., Blackheath.
Oliver, Mrs. A., London, 4 copies.
Ormesby, J., Esq., Inner Temple.
Patmore, Coventry, Esq., Finchley.
Pitman, I., Esq., Bath.
Pocock, Rev. N., Clifton.
Polidori, Miss C., London.
Reed, T. A., Esq., London, 2 copies.
Rossetti, Mrs., London, 4 copies.
Rossetti, W., Esq., London, 3 copies.
Sedgwick, Prof. A., Trin. Coll., Cambridge, 2 copies.
Shadwell, C., Esq., London, 4 copies.
Smith, Mrs. G., Liverpool.
Smith, Miss Emma, Leeds.
Smith, H., Esq., Morden College, Blackheath, 2 copies.
Soames, Rev. W. A., Greenwich.
Stevens, Mrs., Edinburgh, 2 copies.
Stokes, Mrs., Dublin.
Stokes, Whitley, Esq., Lincoln's Inn, London.
Sylvester, Prof. J., London, 2 copies,
Taylor, Tom, Esq., London, 2 copies.
Tooke, C. C., Esq., East Grinsted, 2 copies.
Touchet, Mrs., London.
Venables, Rev. E., Bonchurch, Isle of Wight.
Voase, Mrs., Hull.
Volpe, G., Esq., London, 3 copies.
Watts, Miss S., Pontefract, Yorkshire.
Weatherdon, B. F., Esq., Sydenham.

NAMES OF SUBSCRIBERS.

White, Rev. T. R., Finchley.
Wilson, E., Esq., Blackheath, 2 copies.
Worsley, Rev. T., Downing College, Cambridge, 2 copies.
Wyer, N. W., Esq., Leamington Priors, 3 copies.
Young, J., Esq., London.

THE PSALMS IN METRE.

Psalm I.

1 He's blessed who no counsel hath pursued
  Of wicked men, nor stood
  Upon the paths of sinners, nor hath e'er
  Sat in the scoffer's chair;
2 But who doth in the Lord's law take delight
  By day, and muse by night.

3   Like by the waters of the rills a tree
  Planted, that man shall be;
  His leaf shall fade not, and success shall all
  Works of his hand befall.

4   Not so the wicked. As the chaff the breath
  Of the wind scattereth,
5 The wicked in the judgment shall not stand,
  Nor sinners with the band
  O' th' just men. For the Lord the just men's way
  Avoweth; but the wicked's shall decay.

Psalm II.

1 Why storm the nations, why are compassing
  The Gentiles a vain thing?
2 Against the Lord the kings of earth have set
  Themselves; the chiefs have met
3 Against the Lord's anointed. "Break their bands,
  Loose from their cords our hands."
4 He that in heaven is thronèd shall contemn,
  The Lord shall sneer at them.
5 Soon he in wrath shall speak unto them, yea,
  With fury them dismay.
6 "Nay, I've on Zion, on my holy hill,
  My King anointed still."
7 Thus saith the Lord (I speak from his decree),
  "My Son thou art: this day begat I thee.

8 Ask of me, and o'er nations thou shalt sway:
  Thee shall earth's ends obey.
9 Thou shalt with iron rod them rule, and break
  Like that which potters make."

10 Ah, now be wise, ye kings; be counselled, ye
  That guides of nations be!
11 And serve the Lord with fear, and joy before him,
  While trembling you adore him.
12 Homage the Son, lest him you move to wrath,
  And perish from your path,
13 If his anger is but kindled. Blest are those
  Who trust in him repose.

Psalm III.

1 How increased are my enemies! many are those
  Who confront me, O Lord, as my foes.
2 Many, many there are of my soul that have said,
  That in God there is for it no aid. *Selah.*

3   But my covering shield and my glory art thou:
  By thee, Lord, is exalted my brow.
4 To the Lord has my voice been uplifted, and he
  From his holy hill answereth me. *Selah.*

5   To my rest I lie down, slumber, wake up again;
  For me ever the Lord doth sustain:
6 I am not for the myriads of people afraid,
  That against me in arms are arrayed.
7 O Lord, stand thou up in thy might now, and be
  A deliv'rer, my God, unto me.
8 For thou smit'st all my foes on the cheek; by thy stroke
  Have the jaws of the wicked been broke.
9 Of the Lord's is deliverance; his blessing on those
  Dwelleth, whom for his people he chose.

Psalm IV.

1 O God, my righteous God, when unto thee
  I call, give ear to me.
  Thou'st given me room in my distress; O spare
  Me thou, and heed my prayer.
2 Children of men, how long will you disdain
  My glory, and to vain
  Delusions cleave, and how long after fraud
  Will you go seek abroad?

3   But know, in me the Lord sets by alone
    A votary of his own;
    For me the Lord will hear, when I implore.
4   Tremble, do wrong no more;
    Commune within your chambers, and apart
    In stillness with your heart.

5   Go, offer righteous sacrifice: then let
    Your hearts tow'rd God be set.
6   "Who is there," many say, "that will of weal
    Aught more to us reveal?"
7   Lord, lift on us thy aspect's light; be thou
    Mine heart's rejoicer now,
    More than in times when corn abounds, and when
    The new wine gladdeneth men.
8   I lay me down in peace, and straightway sleep,
    Because thou singly, Lord, wilt safe me keep.

Psalm V.

1   Incline unto my words, O Lord, thine ear:
    My fervent utterance hear.
2   My king, my God (for unto thee pray I),
    Heed the voice of my cry.
3   Thou'lt hear my voice, Lord, early; at dawn I'll set
    My face tow'rd thee, and wait.
4   For thou'rt no God by ill deeds gratified:
    No wrongs dare thee abide,
5   Presumption bears thy face not: doers of fraud
    Thou hatest, O my God.
6   Thou quellest liars; men of perfidy
    And blood are loathed by thee.

7 But I, Lord, will approach thy dwelling-place
　I' th' fulness of thy grace ;
　Thee fearing, tow'rd thy temple's halidom
　To worship will I come.
8 Lord, lead me (for thou seest how foes me press),
　After thy righteousness ;
9 A plain path of thine make me. For no sound
　Word in their mouth is found ;
　Hearts have they set on rapine, throats which crave
　Like a wide open grave ;
10 Smoothed are their tongues. O doom them, God; by all
　Their counsels let them fall.
　They 'gainst thee have rebelled ; confound them in
　The plenitude of their sin.
11 So shall all those who trust in thee rejoice,
　And aye lift a glad voice,
　Thou guarding them ; so all who love thy name
　Shall thee with joy proclaim ;
12 For thou the upright wilt bless, and round him wield
　Thy favour, like a shield.

Psalm VI.

1 Rebuke not in thy anger ; chasten me,
　O Lord, not furiously.
2 Spare, Lord, for I am faint ; my pangs allay ;
　For my bones with dismay
3 Are seized, Lord, and my soul with terrors strong ;
　And thou, Lord, wilt how long ?
4 Lord, turn thee in thy mercy, and my soul
　Deliver, and make whole.

5 For in death none remembers thee; by whom
   Art thou prais'd in the tomb?
6 I weary with my groans; each night I steep
   My pillow whilst I weep;
7 I flood my couch with tears; mine eye dim grows
   For wo amid all my foes.
8   Back, all perfidious doers! back from me keep;
   For my voice raised to weep
9 The Lord has heard; he's heard my prayer; the Lord
   Will grant what I implored.
10 Now let my enemies be ashamed; be they
   Now covered with dismay.
   Let them be put to flight; let them all be
   Dismayed right suddenly.

Psalm VII.

1 O Lord, my God, from all my foes set free,
   And save me, trusting thee;
2 Else, lion-like, he'll prey on me, and rend,
   When none can me defend.
3 O Lord, my God, if I have done this, and
   With guilt defiled my hand,
4 Or wronged my friend, or taken spoil from those
   Who causeless are my foes;
5 After my soul then let my haters make
   Pursuit, and overtake,
   And trample on the ground my life, and thrust
   Mine honor low in dust.
6   Arise, Lord, in thy wrath, and of my foes
   The outrages oppose;

7 Up for me, thou that judgment dost decree,
   And let encompass thee
   The throng of nations, and thou over it
   Return on high to sit.
8 The Judge of nations is the Lord : be thou
   My Judge, O Lord God, now,
   After the truth I cleave to, and the right.
9 I pray, let their despite
   Be overthrown, who put in crime their trust,
   And stablish thou the just.

10 The righteous God, he searches out the mind
    And the heart of mankind;
11 Thou, God, wilt shield me : thou a Saviour art
   Unto the pure of heart.
12 God is a just Judge, and incessantly
   An angered God is he.
13 If man will go not back, his sword he'll whet :
   His bow is drawn and set ;
14 He fits the instruments of death ; he takes
   Shafts which as fire he makes.
15 Lo, one who fraud conceives, and bears delusion,
   And teems his own confusion.
16 He digs and delves a pit, and he is caught
   In the mischance he wrought.
17 His mischief on his head, his malice all
   Back on his crest shall fall.
18 But I will praise the Lord, I'll Him confess
   After his righteousness.
19 I will sing praises to Him, and record
   His name, " the most high Lord."

Psalm VIII.

1 O Lord, our Lord, what dread
Renown of thy name through the world is spread!

Thou hast beyond the height
Of heaven set up the splendor of thy might.
2 Thou dost a basis raise,
From lips of babes and sucklings, for thy praise.
To put to shame the foe,
To still the enemy and avenger so.

3 When by thy fingers made
I see heav'n, and the moon, the stars, arrayed.
4 What is man, that in mind
Thou bear'st him, or the child of humankind
5 For thy regards? Thou makest him not far
Below what angels are.
6 With honor and glory thou hast him arrayed;
A sovereign thou hast made
Him over all thy creatures. Thou has put
All underneath his foot—
7 All flocks and herds, all beasts wold-wandering,
Fowls, that the welkin wing,
And fishes of the sea, and all that strays
Thorough the watery ways.

8 O Lord, our Lord, what dread
Renown of thy name through the world is spread!

Psalm IX.

1 With all my heart I will thee praise, O Lord,
   And thy great deeds record.
2 I will joy in thee, triumph, and proclaim,
   O highest One, thy name,
3 When back mine enemies turn them, when they fly
   Thy face, and stumble and die.
4 For thou maintain'st my right and cause; thou dost
   Sit thron'd, an umpire just.
5 The nations thou rebukest; thou dost slay
   The wicked, and wipe away
   Their names for evermore. The enemy dies:
6 Desolate for ever lies
   His dwelling. Thou hast cities overthrown;
   They and their fame are gone.

7   But the Lord sitteth, judgment to deliver,
   Upon his throne for ever,
8 And the world justly, and the nations he
   Thence judges righteously.
9 A tower the Lord is to the poor; a tower
   Of strength in the evil hour:
10 Hence all that know thy name will trust in thee;
   Thy seekers, Lord, deserted shall not be.

11 Praise ye the Lord, who in Zion dwells; His great
   Deeds in the lands narrate.
12 He, tracing blood, regards the poor; He hath not
   This plaint of their's forgot;
13 Have mercy on me, Lord; regard the wo
   I suffer from my foe.

May'st thou me from the gates of death upraise
To show forth all thy praise
14 I' th' gates of Zion's daughter: my delight
Be in thy saving might.

15 The heathen sink i' th' pit they dug; they've set
Foot in their own hid net.
16 They judgments, Lord, are shown. The wicked is caught
By that his hands have wrought.
17 Down to the grave the wicked shall be brought—
All that have God forgot.
18 The poor shall not be aye cast out of mind;
The humble shall not find
19 Their patience lost for ever. Up, Lord, and yield
No more to man the field.
20 Arraign the nations: make them quake, Lord, so
That each to be but man himself may know.

Psalm X.

1 Why standest Thou far off, and turn'st away
Thy face, Lord, in the troublous day?
2 The wicked in his pride the poor pursues;
He snares them by the plots he strews.
3 The wicked boasts to work his will, disdains
The Lord, and blesses evil gains.
4 Presumption saith in all the wicked's thought,
God will not question, God is nought;
5 Corrupt are all his ways. Thy judgments lie
Beyond his prospect and on high.
6 He mocks at all his foes: he tells for sure
His heart, unmoved I shall endure

From age to age, through which I shall not see
Disaster that can come near me.
7 His mouth is full of cursing, fraud and wrong;
Guile and despite are under his tongue.
8 He crouches in the by-ways, in the still
Dark places, innocent men to kill;
9 He watches for the feeble with fix'd eyes;
As a lion in the thicket lies,
So waits he to devour the poor; he falls
Upon them, when his nets he hauls.
10 He stoopeth, he is meek; and lowly men
Fall by his talons; he says then
11 To his heart; God hides his face, God hath forgot;
For ever and aye God sees it not.

12   Up. Lord, and raise thy arm, O God; let not
The poor man always be forgot.
13 Why should the wicked say, who God defies
In his heart, God will not scrutinize?
14 Thou seest it, for thou mark'st oppression, and
Treachery, to note it on thy hand.
15 The poor to thee commits himself; thou art
The taker of the orphan's part.
Break the fell wrongful arm, and thou'lt explore,
And find its evil work no more.
16 Lo! the Lord reigns for ever and for aye;
The heathen from his land shall die.
17 Thou the desire, Lord, of the poor man hearest;
Thou lend'st him ear; his heart thou cheerest.
18 The weak and orphan thou wilt judge, lest men
Should scare them from their dwelling-place again.

Psalm XI.

1 In the Lord have I trusted: how bid then you me,
   As a bird, to your mountain to flee?
2 For the wicked the bow draw; their arrows they put
   On the string, at the righteous to shoot
3 In the dark; for the pillars of order in dust
   Being levelled, what help has the just?

4 Nay, the Lord in the temple of his holiness reigns,
   In the heavens his throne he maintains.
5 And his eyes overlook them—the children of man
   Are his eyelids directed to scan.
6 And the righteous he proves; but the wicked and those
   Who in violence delight are as foes
7 To his soul. For the wicked a rain he prepares,
   Fire and brimstone, and whirlwind and snares,
8 As their portion. The just are the just Lord's delight,
   And his aspect will glad the upright.

Psalm XII.

1 Lord, save me, for the pious dwindle away,
   The true men from the earth decay:
2 Each with his neighbour talketh falsehood, each
   Smooth-lipp'd and double-hearted speech.
3 The Lord the smooth, false lips will extirpate,
   The tongues that in pretence are great,
4 Those men that say, We'll with our tongues prevail;
   Our lips are ours: what master shall we hail?

5   When the poor is forlorn, the weak man sighs—
    Then saith the Lord, I will arise,
    And from his scorner I will him secure.
6   The words o' th' Lord are words right pure,
    As silver by the earthen furnace tried,
    As silver seven times purified.
7   Thou, Lord, wilt save the poor, thou wilt deliver
    Them from this evil brood for ever.
8   At large the wicked walk on all sides, when
    Vile things are highest among the sons of men.

Psalm XIII.

1 How long, Lord, wilt forget me? Wilt thou thy
   Face turn away for aye?
2 How long shall I with cares each day my brain
   Feed, and my heart with pain?
   How long triumphant shall my enemies be?
3 Look down and answer me,
   O Lord, my God; with life mine eyes illume,
   Before I sleep in tomb,
4 Lest my foes ever cry, We have prevailed—
   Lest, if my foot have failed,
5 They boast. But on thy grace my hopes are set,
   Mine heart will triumph yet
   In thy salvation. To the Lord I will
   Sing praise, when my deliverance he'll fulfil.

Psalm XIV.

1 In his heart the fool saith, God is nought;
   And corrupt and abhorred is all they have wrought.
2 There is none that doth right. From on high

Has the Lord upon men looked down to descry
If one faithful among them be seen.
If by any among them God sought for has been.
3 But they all are polluted, they've run
Is corruption together: none doth well, not one.

4   Shall the workers of evil, that eat
Thy people, as bread, with no chastisement meet?
5 On these have they not called. With fear
Shall they tremble, for God to the righteous is near.
? Will ye mock the defence of the poor, though in God
Be his trust? O that safety to Israel were showed
Out of Zion: then joy would there be
Their back, and triumph should Israel see.

Psalm XV.

1 Lord, who shall dwell within thy precincts, and
Upon thine holy mountain stand?
2 Who walketh purely and the right will do,
And from whose heart the words flow true.
3 Whose tongue no falsehood carries, and who hath
To his companion wrought no scath.
He hath not borne abroad his neighbour's shame:
4 Whose in his eyes no vile man claim:
Who fears the Lord he honours. Though he take
Oaths to his hurt, yet none he'll break.
5 He hath not lent to usury his gold:
The innocent blood he hath not sold
For guerdon. Whoso'er thus liveth, he
For ever and aye unmoved shall be.

Psalm XVI.

1 O God, whom I have trusted, save thou me!
2 My soul hath said to thee,
  Thou art my God, thou art more dear than all
  Weal that can me befall.
3 Thy saints on earth are noblest in my sight,
  These make my whole delight.
4 But their afflictions they shall multiply
  That haste to go awry:
5 Whose drink-offerings of blood I will not make,
  Nor names on my lips take.
6 My cup the Lord is, and my portioned share;
  My weal thou dost upbear.
7 Right goodly is mine heritage: my bounds
  Are fallen in pleasant grounds.
8 I'll praise the Lord, who guards me: and by night
  My reins me warn aright.
9 I keep on him mine eyes: he takes my side:
  I shall unmov'd abide.
10 Hence shall my glory exult, my heart shall leap,
   My flesh in trust shall sleep:
11 For thou'lt my soul not leave to death, nor have
   Thy votary see the grave.
12 Thou'lt show me paths of life: joy dwells before
   Thy face, and at thy right hand pleasures evermore.

Psalm XVII.

1 Do thou the righteous hear,
  O God, and at my call incline thine ear.

2 Unto my prayer give heed.
   Which doth not out of feigning lips proceed.
3 Send judgment from before
   Thy face, and let thine eyes the right explore.
4 Thou hast mine heart surveyed,
   Hast in the night-hour proved it, and assayed.
   Thou findest there no wrong;
   Fixed am I to offend not with my tongue.
5 In mens' affairs, the way
   Of rapine shunning, I'll thy hests obey.
6 Do thou my footsteps guide,
   Upon thy path, and let my feet not slide.
   Thee have I call'd. O Lord,
   For thou wilt answer; O bend and hear my word.
7 Show thy great mercy, how those
   Who trust thee, saves thy right hand from their foes.
8 As the apple of thine eye
   Keep me; in thy wing's shadow let me lie,
9 From the wicked to repose,
   Who would destroy me; yea, from deadly foes,
   Who compass me about.
10 From bloated men whose lips throw proud words out.
11 Our path, lo! they surround;
   Their eyes keep watch to bring us to the ground:
12 As a lion bent on prey,
   As a lion's whelp they lurk beside our way.
13 Arise, prevent them, Lord;
   From th' evil men preserve me by thy sword:
14 From men that by thy hand
   Raised up, the world and pomp of life command:
   Whose bosoms evermore
   Thou fillest with thy metal's hidden store.

Whose children thence receive
   Their fill, and heirlooms to their offspring leave.
15 But I thy face in righteousness will see;
   Thy aspect, when I wake, will satiate me.

Psalm XVIII.

1 I love thee, Lord, my strength: thee, Lord, my fort,
2 Safeguard and strong resort;
   My God, the rock I trust, mine horn to yield
   Rescue, my tower and shield.
3 I cry to the Lord, whom praise beseems, and he
   From my foes rescues me.
4 The snares of death encompassed me, the tide
   Of wrong me terrified:
5 The grave her snares begirt me; with the net
   Of death I was beset.
6 I called in my distress unto the Lord,
   Yea, I my God implored.
   My voice he did out of his temple hear,
   My orison reached his ear.
7 Earth quaked and trembled, roots of mountains shook
   And swayed at his rebuke.
8 Smoke rose before him; from his mouth there came,
   Enkindling brands, a flame.
9 He made the heavens lour, and came down; he spread
   Darkness beneath his tread.
10 He rode the cherub's flight; on wings of wind
11 He flew; he was enshrined
   In darkness; the dark vapors round him went,
   The storm-clouds were his tent.

c

12 The brightness from his face the clouds disperst,
   Hailstones and fire outburst.
13 Thundered in heaven the Lord; the most high God
   His thunders launched, hailstones and fires, abroad.
14 He showered his arrows, and my foes dispelled—
   His fires, and them he quelled.
15 Then were the channels of the floods disclosed,
   The roots of earth exposed,
   At thy rebuke, O Lord, across the path
   Of the blast of thy wrath.
16 He sent to save me from on high, to free
   My soul from swallowing sea.
17 He snatched me from who sought to do me wrong,
   From foes grown overstrong.
18 They troubled me in my distress, but he,
   The Lord God, rescueth me.
19 He brings me forward to an open place,
   He frees me by his grace.
20 He guerdoneth my righteousness, the Lord
   Shall honest hands reward.
21 For I have kept the Lord's ways, nor have I
   Gone from my God awry.
22 Before me all his judgments stood; my hands
   Were held by his commands.
23 Toward him I have been incorrupt; what ill
   I wrought, that loathed I still.
24 The Lord to my uprightness deals a prize,
   To hands pure in his eyes.
25 To the gracious thou art gracious, to the upright
   Thou show'st thyself upright:
26 Thou'rt pure unto the pure, and austere when
   Thou deal'st with crooked men.

27 For thou the humble wilt preserve, and thou
   Wilt lower the lofty brow.
28 'Tis thou dost light my lamp, the Lord God will
   With light my darkness fill.
29 In thee I have rushed against a host, and leapt
   The trench; for God me kept.
30 His ways are perfect; well proved is his word:
   All those who trust the Lord
31 He shields. For who, beside the Lord, is God?
   Or a rock, except our God?
32 The God who girdeth me with might, and hath
   Unerring made my path;
33 Who makes my feet as feet of harts, to light
   On rampart tops upright.
34 He trains my hands to war, mine arms shall make
   A bow of steel to break.
35 Thy succor shields, thy hand upholds me, thy
   Grace lifteth me on high.
36 Thou makest my path under me full wide,
   Thou let'st my feet not slide.
37 I chase and overtake, I turn not, no,
   Till I root out my foe.
38 I strike them, and they shall not stand; I beat
   Them down beneath my feet.
39 Thou girdest me with strength for war; my foe
   Thou lay'st beneath me low.
40 Thou mak'st mine enemies turn their backs, and they
   That hate me, are swept away.
41 They cry, and none delivers; yea, the Lord
   Unheeded they've implored.
42 I scatter them, like dust before the blast,
   Like mire in street upcast.

43 Thou from the strife of nations dost me free,
   O'er Gentiles liftest me;
   Thou mak'st a race I knew not, bend their knee.
44 The sons of strangers serve me; they revere
   At the hearing of the ear.
45 The sons of strangers wither, and are made
   In their strongholds afraid.
46 May the Lord live, my rock, and be thou blest,
   God, that me rescuest.
47 Be God exalted, mine avenger, he
   That puts realms under me,
48 That saves me from my foes, that makes me strong
   Against the hand of wrong:
   That doth me above all adversaries raise:
49 Therefore I will thee praise
   I' th' gates of Zion's daughter, and proclaim
   By sound of song thy name.
50 "He mighty things to help his king hath done;
   To his anointed one,
   To David and his seed perpetually
   Great mercy showeth he."

Psalm XIX.

1 The heavens declare his majesty; the art
  Of God the spheres impart.
2 Day by day lore they utter, and recite
  Wisdom from night to night.
3 There is no speech among them, and no word;
  Howbeit their voice is heard.
4 Their burden through the world, their lore has forth
  Gone to the bounds of earth.

5 Thou hast in them the sun's pavilion spread.
  As a bridegroom from his bed
  Thence doth he rise, and giant-like delight
  To run his course with might.
6 His going forth is from the verge, his round
  Is to the welkin's bound;
  There is no place of shelter from his ardor found.
7 The Lord's law is a perfect law; the soul
  Thereby is rendered whole.
  The Lord's behests are true; the simple mind
  Therein doth wisdom find.
8 The ordinances of the Lord are right;
  They give the heart delight.
9 Pure are the Lord's commandments, and the eye
  Recovereth light thereby.
  The Lord's fear is without pollution, and
  Perpetually shall stand.
10 The judgments of the Lord are truth; they are
  Righteous throughout, and far
  More sweet than comb-drawn honey; precious more
  Than gold and richest ore.
11 Thy servant they enlighten; they afford
  Their doers a great reward.
12 What man can tell his lapses? from unseen
  Transgressions make me clean.
13 Guard, too, thy servant from the proud, lest they
  Their yoke on him should lay.
14 So shall I live unblemished; I shall be
  From grave transgressions free.
  O let the musings of mine heart, and all
  Words from my lips that fall,
  Be in thy sight accepted, Lord, mine own
  Saviour and rock alone.

Psalm XX.

1 The Lord in troublous day give ear to thee;
   The name thy rescue be
2 Of Jacob's God. From his holy place God yield thee
   Strength, and from Zion shield thee:
3 Remember thine oblations; recognize
   Thy large burnt sacrifice,
4 Grant thee thy heart's desire, and prosperous end
   To all thy counsel send.
5 May we extol thy triumph, and proclaim
   Of our own God the name,
   Borne on our banners: may the Lord thee still
   Hear, to grant all thy will.
6 Now know I that the Lord will succor bring
   To his anointed King,
   From heavenly shrine will hear him, and his right
   Hand fill with rescuing might.
7 Some trust in chariots, and in horses some:
   The Lord, our God, we come
8 Naming. They fall, they are down-beaten, and
   We rise, and upright stand.
9 Save us, Lord; may our king that day reply,
   When unto him we cry.

Psalm XXI.

1 Lord, how the king rejoiceth in thy might;
   Great in thine help is his delight.
2 Thou giv'st him all his heart's desire, and nought
   Withholdest, that his lips have sought.

3 Thou meet'st him with thy gracious blessings: thou
  Encirclest with pure gold his brow.
4 He asked thee life, and thou dost him supply
  With length of days for ever and aye.
5 His glory in thy safeguard is made great:
  Thou puttest on him pomp and state.
6 For ever thou hast him with blessings clad;
  Thou by thy countenance mak'st him glad.
7 For the king trusteth in the Lord: he shall,
  Since high God helps him, never fall.
8   Thy hand will find out all thy foes; thy right
  Hand will thine adversaries smite.
9 Thou shalt them as in fiery furnace lay;
  Thou, Lord, wilt in thy visiting day
  Confound them, and the fire shall on them prey.
10 Their fruit shall perish from the earth, their race
  Among mankind shall have no place.
11 For they've devised against thee, and an ill
  Plot laid, which they could not fulfil;
12 So thou to flight shalt bring them, and thy dread
  Before their faces wilt thou shed.
13 Lord, lift thee in thy might, let us thy strong
  Arm praise with music and with song.

Psalm XXII.

1 My God, my God, why hast forsaken me,
  And far withdrawest thee,
  To hear not my imploring, nor my saviour be?
2 I call unanswered thee, my God, by day
  And by night without stay.

3 And thou art holy, that of Israel
  Dost in the praises dwell.
4 Our fathers in thee trusted; thee they gave
  Their trust, and thou didst save.
5 They called thee, and were succored; in thee they
  Hoped, and had no dismay.
6 But I, a worm, not man, by men am scorned,
  And by the people spurned.
7 All those who see me scoff at me; they shake
  Their heads, and mouths they make.
8 They say, Trust God! let God him save and free,
  If pleased with him he be.
9 Thou led'st me from the womb; thou wast my stay
  When on the breasts I lay.
10 From birth I was cast on thee; from my mother—
  Thou art my God, no other.
11 Be thou not far; for trouble stands hard by;
  For none to help is nigh.
12 For many bulls beset me; a Bashan herd
  Of tyrants me begird.
13 They ope at me their jaws, as lions may
  That roar and rend the prey.
14 Like waters I am poured out, and all
  My bones in sunder fall;
  Mine heart is like to wax within me, yea,
  Melts in my breast away.
15 My strength is dried up like a shard; my tongue
  Hath to my palate clung;
  Thou bring'st me down the sands of death among.
16 For hounds encompass me, the doers of wrong
  Banded against me throng.
17 My hands and feet they pierced; my bones I may

Count now—so bare are they.
18 They stare and watch me; they my vesture share,
Cast lots my robes to bear.
19 But thou, O Lord, my strength, be not far hence,
Haste thee to my defence.
20 Do thou my soul deliver from the glaive,
From hounds my darling save.
21 Snatch me from jaws of lions; thou hast borne
Me safe from wild bull's horn.
22 So to my brethren I'll declare thy name,
Thy praise I will proclaim
23 In the great gathering. Cause him praise to hear,
Ye that the Lord God fear.
Let Jacob's race him worship; let his dread
All Israel overspread.
24 He scorns not, he doth not abominate
The poor man's low estate.
His face he hides not; he gives ear, when they
To him with loud call pray.
25 In the great gathering I'll him praise; I will
Mine uttered vows fulfil
26 Before his fearers. Then the poor shall eat;
They shall be filled with meat;
The seekers of the Lord shall triumph then;
Your hearts shall bound again.
27 Let earth's ends him remember; let them all
Turn, on the Lord to call.
28 For the dominion is the Lord's; 'tis he
That rules in heathenry.
29 The rich on earth shall feast, and shall adore him;
They too shall kneel before him
Who in the dust were sinking; whose endeavor

Could not their lives deliver.
30 A future race shall serve him, whom the Lord
Shall for his own record.
31 They shall go forth, and shall his righteousness
To tribes unborn express;
Lo, how the Lord hath done! they shall confess.

Psalm XXIII.

1 Jehovah is my shepherd; there shall be
Nought wanting unto me.
2 He'll in green meadows couch me, and beside
Refreshing waters guide;
Revive my soul, and in his righteous ways
Guide me for his name's praise.
3 Hence will I through the valley of the shade
Of death walk undismayed;
For thou'lt be with me, and thy staff and rod
Shall comfort me, O God.
4 Thou wilt in my foes' front my table spread,
And plenteously mine head
5 Anoint with oil, and make my cup o'erflow.
Goodness and grace, I know,
Shall follow me through life; I shall appear
In God's house every year.

Psalm XXIV.

1 To the Lord the fullness of the earth belongs,
The world and all her throngs.
2 For he hath founded on the seas her place,
Built o'er the floods her base.

3   Who shall ascend the Lord's hill? who inside
His halidom shall bide?
4 The clean of hands, the pure of heart, whose mind
To fraud hath not inclined,
Who hath not sworn, his neighbour to deceive;
5 Blessing shall he receive
From God his sure defender, and from the Lord
The righteous man's reward.
6 These after Jacob's God enquire; the race
Are such, who seek his face.

7   Lift up your heads, ye gates; be lifted you
Perpetual doors; the King of glory will go through.
8 Who is the King of glory? 'tis the Lord,
The powerful and the mighty, that strong warrior, the Lord.

9   Lift up your heads, ye gates; be lifted you
Perpetual doors; the King of glory will go through.
Who is the King of glory? 'tis the Lord,
The mighty God of hosts; that King of glory is the Lord.

Psalm XXV.

1 Aye lifted is my soul, O Lord, to thee;
There is no trust in me
2 But on my God. O cause not me to fail,
While my glad foes prevail.
3 Confound thy trusters not; let shame belong
To who doth causeless wrong.
4 Direct me in thy path, Lord; teach me so
That I thy ways may know.

5 Expose to me thy ways; thy truth impart,
   Who God my safeguard art.
   For in thee day by day my trust I set;
   O do thou not forget,
6 God, thy compassion and thy grace, which hold
   Firm from the days of old.
7 Have not my youthful sins and faults in mind;
   Regard me to be kind
8 In thy great mercy. Gracious is the Lord;
   And just in his award.
   Jehovah teacheth those who went astray,
   Leads the meek in his way,
9 Keeps in the paths of equity the meek,
   Guides them, his ways who seek.
10 Loving and just are all ways of the Lord,
   When men observe his word.
11 My sin, O Lord, for thy name-sake remit,
   For deep and foul is it.
12 Name me the fearers of the Lord; lo! each
   To choose his paths he'll teach.
13 On such will blessings wait their lifetime; and
   Their seed shall hold the land.
14 Preserved is God's communion, and his law
   Known, where men stand in awe.
15 Quit him shall not mine eyes; 'tis he doth set
   My feet free from the net.
16 Return, and show me mercy; I am left
   A feeble man, bereft.
17 Sorrows my heart beleaguer; do thou me
   Set from my trouble free.
18 Turn thee, my grief and trouble to perceive,
   And all my faults forgive.

19 Upon my foes look down; how many are there
  Who toward me fierce hate bear.
20 Visit my soul and rescue; let not me
  Be shamed, who trust in thee.
21 Worth and uprightness shall me guard; for I
  Always on thee rely.
22 Yea, Lord, so may'st thou Israel redeem
  From all who trouble him.

Psalm XXVI.

1 Judge me, Lord; for in mine integrity
  I walk, I trust in thee,
2 And falter not; Lord, prove me and survey;
  My reins and heart assay.
3 For I keep ever in my sight thy grace,
  Thy paths of truth I trace.
4 With no false men I sit; nor walk amid
  Those whose intents are hid.
5 The gathering of the unjust and the debate
  Of wicked men I hate.
6 I wash mine hands in innocence; and so,
  Lord, to thine altar go,
7 That I may make resound the voice of praise,
  And speak thy righteous ways.
8 I love the precincts of thy house, O God—
  Thy majesty's abode.
9 Snatch not my soul with sinners, nor my life
  With men of blood and strife,
10 Whose hand is full of treasons, and in their
  Right hand a bribe they bear.

11 But I'll in mine uprightness walk; O save,
And mercy on me have.
12 My foot stands fast i' th' right; I will thy praise,
Lord, in the assemblies raise.

Psalm XXVII.

1 My light and safeguard is the Lord;
Whom therefore shall I dread?
The Lord is of my life the strength;
Who maketh me dismayed?
2 My foes and haters, evil men,
When toward me they come on,
As if they would devour my flesh—
They stumble and fall prone.
3 Against me though a host encamp,
Yet will my heart not quail;
And though a battle be drawn out,
Still shall my trust not fail.
4 One thing I'll ask the Lord and crave it,
To sit, while life is mine,
In the Lord's house, to see his pomp,
And to frequent his shrine.
5 For with his shelter he'll me screen
Throughout the troublous days,
And hide me in cover of his tent,
And me on rock upraise.
6 And now mine head shall be upreared
Above my foes all round,
And in God's tabernacle I
Will offer with glad sound;
And to the Lord make melody.

7 Give audience when I cry
 To theeward; be compassionate,
 O Lord God, and reply.
8 My heart has told me of the Lord;
 Seek you my face, saith he:
 Yea, Lord, and I will seek thy face;
 Turn not thy face from me.
9 Throw not thy servant off in wrath;
 Thou wast mine help long since:
 Forsake me not, desert me not,
 Lord God of my defence.
10 Father and mother may desert;
 The Lord will shelter me.
11 Teach me thy path, and from my foes
 Do thou, Lord, set me free.
12 To my foes' will resign me not;
 For lying witnesses
 Have risen against me, breathing out
 Malignant lawlessness.
13 I trust i' th' world of living men
 The Lord's grace to behold.
 O bide the good time of the Lord,
 Be strong of heart and bold.

Psalm XXVIII.

1 O Lord, my rock, I call out unto thee;
 Keep silence not with me.
 If thou keep silence, I am numbered then
 Amongst pit-entering men.

2 Do thou to mine imploring voice attend,
  When prayers to thee I send,
  When toward thine holy temple I mine hands extend.
3 Destroy not me with godless men, among
  Those who do fraud and wrong,
  Who speak unto their neighbours peace, the while
  Their hearts are filled with guile.
4 Deal with them after their own works; as they
  Do wrong, so them repay.
  Return them what their hands have wrought, O Lord;
  Requite them their reward.
5 Since lightly they regard the Lord's ways, and
  The dealings of his hand,
  So let him overthrow, not make them stand.
6   The Lord hath hearkened, blessed be the Lord,
  To that my voice implored.
7 On him, my shield and strength, my heart relied,
  And succors he supplied.
  Thence shall mine heart exult, and with my lays
  I will resound his praise.
8 Strength to his people and a strong aid will he
  To his anointed be.
9 Save, Lord, thy people, and bless thine heritage,
  And pasture them and prosper them, age after age.

Psalm XXIX.

1 Ascribe unto the Lord, O sons of light,
  Ascribe worship and might.
2 The glory of his name confess;
  Worship to the Lord address,
  In solemn pomp with holiness.

3 The Lord's voice on the waters broad !
   Thunders of the glorious God
   Across the mighty waters rode.

4   The Lord his voice was heard with sov'reignty,
   His voice with majesty.
5 The Lord his voice hath cedars bent,
   Yea, the boughs of cedars rent
   Adown from Lebanon he sent.
6 A-dancing by his voice were thrown
   Like a bullock Lebanon,
   Like a roebuck Sirion.

7   The Lord his voice betwixt the lightnings flew,
   In pangs the waste it threw.
8 Throes did the waste of Kadesh seize.
9 The Lord's voice the tall fir-trees
   Cleft, and laid bare the bushy leas.
10 All in his temple praises cry ;
    The Lord o'er the flood sat high ;
    A King the Lord sits ever and aye.

11   The Lord will give his people strength, and bless
    With peace his chosen race.

Psalm XXX.

1 Thee, Lord, I'll praise, for thou'st delivered me,
   Not made my foes to be
2 Glad through my downfall. Thou didst heal me, Lord
   My God, when I implored.
3 Thou'st lifted from the grave my soul, and stayed
   My life from low being laid.

4 Praise him with psalms, O ye that trust the Lord:
His holiness record;
5 Whose wrath a moment lives, and for the space
Of life endures his grace.
Though for an evening we abide with sorrow,
Yet gladness comes the morrow.
6 When I said in my welfare, I shall be
Unmoved perpetually;
7 Thou'st made mine hill so firm, Lord, in thy grace—
Then didst thou hide thy face;
8 I was dismayed. To thee I cried, O Lord:
Yea, I my God implored.
9 I said, What profiteth my blood, when low
Beneath the sods I go?
10 Shall the dust render praise to thee, and how
Faithful thou art avow?
11 Lord, hear me, and have mercy, Lord, and be
A rescuer unto me.

12 Thou'st changed my mourning into dancing now:
My sackcloth garb hast thou
Unloosed, and girded me with gladness round.
13 For this thy fame shall sound,
And ne'er be silent. Lord my God, I thee
Will praise perpetually.

Psalm XXXI.

1 In thee, Lord, have I trusted; let not me
For ever ashamèd be;
2 But free me, as thou'rt righteous. O give heed,
And toward my rescue speed.

Be thou my rock of strength and fortress sure,
Whither I may flee secure.
3 For thee my fastness and stronghold I make;
Guide me for thy name's sake;
4 Yea, draw me from the net which they have laid :
For thou art my strong aid.
5 Lord God of truth, I trust my soul to thee,
For thou deliverest me.
6 Votaries of idols vain I have abhorred,
But thee I trust, O Lord.
7 Let me be glad and joyful in thy grace;
For mine afflicted case
Thou dost behold; my soul how much of woe
Oppresseth, thou dost know.
8 Thou giv'st me not into my foes' hands bound,
But set'st my feet upon wide-open ground.

9   Be gracious, Lord, for troubles on me press :
Mine eye with heaviness
Consumes ; my spirits and my thews decay ;
10 My life is worn away
With trouble, and my years in moaning spent
Under my chastisement.
My strength is staggered, and my bones forworn.
11 I am become a scorn
Of foes, a marvel of the dwellers near,
A thing to strike with fear
All my familiar friends ; yea, those I meet
Flee from me in the street.
12 I am as the dead, to whom none have regard,
Forgot, like vessels marred.
13 For I have heard the crowd's despiteful sound;
And terror is all round,

While they against me muster, and to snare
My life while they prepare.
14 Yet trust I, Lord, in thee; to thee mine heart
Hath said, "My God thou art;"
15 Mine hours are in thy hand; my rescuer be
From those that hunt for me.
16 O make upon thy servant shine thy face,
Deliver me according to thy grace.

17   Lord, let me not be put to shame, for I
Have made to thee my cry.
18 Let evil men be shamèd; let them keep
In the Grave silence deep.
Let lying lips be stilled, which of the upright
Speak in hate, scorn, and spite!
19 O what great mercy hast thou treasured
For whosoe'er thee dread!
What works thou dost, that all mankind may see,
For those who trust in thee!
20 Thou givest them from men's cabals a place
Of refuge 'neath thy face.
Thou hast them from contentious tongues amid
Thy tabernacle hid.
21 Blest be the Lord, whose mercy wondrously
Makes a strong tower for me.
22 Yet I said in my terror, I am quite
Disparted from thy sight;
But yet thou heard'st my voice, when I implored,
When thee I called, O Lord.
23 Love ye the Lord, O all ye saints of his;
For he the guardian is
Of the true-hearted; yet requiteth he

The proud abundantly.
24 Be strong, and let your heart be fortified,
 All ye that trusting in the Lord abide.

Psalm XXXII.

1 Blessed the man, whose sin is pardoned,
 Whose guilt is covered;
 Blessed, in whom the Lord no blame shall find,
 Nor falsehood in his mind.
2 When I was silent, then with plaints all day
 My bones consumed away;
3 Night and day pressed on me thy hand, and brought
 Me down like summer's drought.
4 Then I declared my sin to thee; I did
 My trespass not keep hid.
 I said, To the Lord I will my guilt avow;
 Then my sin pardonedst thou.
5 For this shall every saint implore thee, when
 Thou may'st be found by men;
 But when the mighty flood prevaileth, we
 Have no access to thee.
6 Thou art my shelter in my hour of need;
 Thou for me takest heed.
 Thou makest me to hear on all sides round
 Songs of triumphant sound.
7 Come, I will teach ye, and point out to you
 The path ye should pursue;
8 Mine eye shall tend you. Be not void of mind,
 As mule and horse we find;
 Since bit and bridle must control their jaw,
 Lest they too near thee draw.

9 For wicked men full many plagues are stored;
But those who trust the Lord
10 Shall mercy compass. In the Lord rejoice,
Ye just, and lift your voice
In gladness. All you upright-hearted, raise
With triumph-songs his praise.

PSALM XXXIII.

1 Rejoice i' th' Lord, ye just; for to recite
Thanks well beseems the upright.
2 Hymn you the Lord with harp, and with tenfold
Lyre let his praise be told.
3 Sing a new song before him; let ring out
Your strains to him with a shout.
4 For just his word is, and his works are done
In faithfulness each one.
5 Judgment and right he loves; he fills the face
Of the world with his grace.
6 The heavens and all their host his word hath made,
The breath of his mouth arrayed.
7 He gathers the sea's waters in a heap,
Lays up in stores the deep.
8 Let all earth fear him, let his dread on all
The world's inhabiters fall;
9 Because he speaks, and it is done; he gives
Commandment, and it lives.
10 The counsels of the nations void he makes,
The Gentile's purpose breaks.
11 The counsels of the Lord for ever endure,
From race to race his heart's intents are sure.
12 O race, whose God the Lord is; blest are ye
Chosen out his own to be.

13 The Lord looks down from heaven, and all the sons
   Of man surveys at once;
14 He vieweth from his high enthronement forth
   All dwellers on the earth.
15 He shapeth all their hearts at once, his view
   Pierces through all they do.
16 No king is safe by armies, no strong wight
   Secure through bodily might.
17 A vain help to rely on is the horse;
   Nought booteth his great force.
18 Behold, the Lord regards his fearers, those
   Whose trusts in him repose,
19 To rescue from the death their souls, to give
   In dearth whence they may live.
20 Our souls upon the Lord wait; he doth yield
   Us help, and is our shield.
21 Our hearts in him rejoice, for on his just
   And holy name we trust.
22 O let the mercy of the Lord God be
   Upon us, as we trusting rest on thee.

Psalm XXXIV.

1 I'll ever bless the Lord: his praises aye
   Shall my mouth occupy.
2 My soul in him shall triumph; with glad cheer
   Thereof the poor shall hear.
3 Praise you with me the Lord: we will his name
   Exalt with one acclaim.
4 I sought the Lord, and he gave ear, and me
   From all my fears set free.

5 They that look toward him shall take heart; their brow
   Shall shame no longer bow.
6 Lo! the poor called him, and the Lord gave heed,
   And from all straits him freed.
7 The angels of the Lord keep watch for ever
   His fearers to deliver.
8 How kind the Lord is, taste and see: they're blest
   Their hopes on him who rest.
9 Fear aye the Lord, ye saints of his: them all
   Who fear, no need shall gall.
10 Young lions lack and pine: but they who've sought
   The Lord, shall want for nought.
11 Come, hearken to me, children: the Lord's fear
   To you I'll render clear.
12 Who is there covets life, and length of days
   Desires, on weal to gaze?
13 Guard thou thy tongue from evil, and thy lip
   From uttering falsehood keep.
14 Depart from evil, and do good: pursue
   Peace, and give chase thereto.
15 The Lord's eye watches o'er the just: his ear
   Is to their calling near.
16 Against ill-doers he hath set his face,
   To root from earth their trace.
17 Who call upon the Lord are heard, and freed
   By him from all their need.
18 The Lord is near the bruised heart, and whole
   He makes the wounded soul.
19 Though on the just full many troubles fall,
   The Lord him frees from all.
20 The Lord is his protection; not a limb
   Shall there be hurt of him.

21 Disaster shall the wicked slay, and all
   That hate the Lord shall fall.
22 The Lord his servants' lives redeems, and who
   Revere him shall not rue.

Psalm XXXV.

1 Strive, Lord, with my gain-strivers: at war be
   With those who war with me.
2 Lay on the buckler and the shield thy hand,
   And forth to save me stand.
3 Poise in thine hand the lance, and shut the way
   On my pursuers, and say,
4 I am thy rescue, to my soul. Let them
   Be foiled, be put to shame,
5 That seek my life. Confounded may they flee,
   Who scath devise for me.
6 As chaff i' th' wind, let them be driv'n abroad
   Before the angel of God.
   Let dark and slippery be their ways, and let
   God's angel them beset.
7 Since causeless for my life the net they've laid,
   The deadly pitfall made,
8 So may destruction take them unawares,
   Caught in their own hid snares.
9 And let my soul rejoice i' th' Lord, and be
   Gladdened, he rescuing me.
10 Let all my limbs, There is none can compare
   With thee, Lord God,—declare.
   Thou sav'st the weak from mastery of the strong,
   The poor from ravenous wrong.
11 False witnesses against me rise, and sue

Me for what ne'er I knew.
12 For all my benefits they return me ill,
Make fruitless my good will.
13 But I, when they were sick, in sackcloth dressed,
Fastings my soul depressed:
Turn back my prayer for them to mine own breast.
14 I walked and mourned, as for a friend or brother,
Drooped, as who mourns a mother.
15 But when I stumbled, they rejoiced: they flocked
Around me all, and mocked,
Before I knew it: yea, they cast out ill
Words, and would not be still.
16 With these profanest feast-buffoons were found,
Their teeth at me they ground.
17 How long wilt thou be looking on, Lord? keep
My soul from their fell sweep,
18 From lions my dear life. Thee, Lord, i' th' great
Concourse I'll celebrate;
I'll give thee praise before the throngs of men.
19 Let my false haters then
Not triumph o'er me; let not wink his eye
That hates me causelessly.
20 For peace they proffer not, but slanders speak
Of those who quiet seek.
21 They shoot at me their lips—Ha! ha! they cry,
That sight contents our eye.
22 Thou seest, Jehovah; be not silent: be,
O Lord, not far from me.
23 Rise to my judgment, Lord my God; and wake,
My cause in hand to take.
24 Judge me, thou just one; and to them accord
No boasts, my God and Lord.

25 Let them not say at heart, We have beheld
　　Our wish, our enemy quelled.
26 Let them not say thus. Bafle and shame them all,
　　The exulters in my fall;
　　Shame and confusion make to clothe them, who
　　Against me bold things do.
27 But let who love my righteous cause rejoice,
　　Saying ever with glad voice,
　　Great is the Lord, who always to requite
　　His servants hath delight.
28 Then shall thy justice on my tongue, thy praise
　　Dwell with me all my days.

Psalm XXXVI.

1 The words mine heart frames in me, to express
　　The unjust man's wickedness.
2 There is no fear of God before his eyes;
　　For in his own surmise
　　Himself he flatters, that his wrongful bent
　　And hate he may content.
3 His words are guile and fraud; he no more tries
　　To do well and be wise.
4 He meditates guile upon his couch; he lays
　　His course on evil paths; no malice he gainsays.

5 　Thy bounty, Lord, is like the heavens, and thy
　　Truth ample as the sky.
6 Like the strong hills thy justice, like the sea's
　　Deep ground thy judgment is.
　　Lord, man and beast are both preserved by thee.
7 How rich in clemency

Art thou, God, that in thy wing's shade all sons
Of men repose at once!
8 Out of thy mansion they partake rich meats:
They quaff thy flowing sweets.
9 In thee reside the founts of life; the light
That glads us is thy light.

10 Be gracious unto them that know thee; do
Well by the just and true.
11 Let not the foot of pride me reach, nor let
The ungodly hand beset.
12 Lo! now the unjust are routed, fall down, and
No more have power to stand.

Psalm XXXVII.

1 Repine not at the wicked, nor against
Wrong doers be incensed.
2 They soon will like the grass be mowed away,
Like the green herb decay.
3 Trust in the Lord, do right, and live secure,
And in the land endure.
4 Delight thee in the Lord; and what thy heart
Desires, he will impart.
5 Commit to the Lord thy way; on him believe,
And he will all achieve.
6 Thy truth, like daylight, he will make appear,
Thy faith as noontide clear.
7 Wait silent on the Lord, and him adore;
Let not thine heart be sore
At men who prosper in their path, at those
Who crafty plots compose.

8 Leave anger, cease to envy and repine.
　Lest thou to guilt incline.
9 For out the wicked shall be rooted, and
　God's trusters keep the land.
10 Yet a little, and the wicked are no more;
　Thou shalt their place explore,
11 And find none; and the poor shall hold the earth,
　And of peace taste no dearth.
12 Against the upright the ungodly set their mind;
　Their teeth at him they grind.
13 The Lord derides them, for he sees that they
　Draw near their reckoning day,
14 The ungodly have drawn out the sword; the bow
　They've bent, to overthrow
　The poor man and the feeble, and to slay
　The perfect in his way.
15 Their sword shall into their bosom go;
　Broken shall be their bow.
16 A little to the upright availeth more
　Than many a bad man's store.
17 For broken shall the wicked's arms be, and
　By the true the Lord will stand.
18 The good man's days the Lord knows, and secure
　Their heritage shall endure.
19 In th' evil hour they shall not faint: he will
　In days of dearth them fill;
20 While wicked men shall be destroyed, and they
　That hate the Lord decay,
　As when the fat of lambs consumeth, yea,
　As smoke fadeth away.
21 The wicked borrow, and from payment flee:
　The just give bounteously.

22 For who by Him is blest the land shall own ;
　Who curst, shall be o'erthrown.
23 'Tis of the Lord to guide a man's feet right,
　Whose course shall him delight.
24 Though falling, he shall not be quite downcast ;
　His hand the Lord holds fast.
25 I have been young, and I am now grown old ;
　Yet did I ne'er behold
　The righteous man forsaken, nor his seed
　Begging their daily bread.
26 He lendeth every day, and showeth grace,
　And blest shall be his race.
27 Depart from wrong, do well, and occupy
　The land for ever and aye.
28 For the Lord loveth right; he'll cast aside
　None that in him confide.
　These aye shall be preserved, while bad men, they
　And theirs, are swept away.
29 The righteous in the land, by them possest,
　For ever and aye shall rest.
30 The lips o' th' righteous wisdom exercise ;
　Judgment his tongue replies.
31 The laws of God within his heart abide,
　His feet shall never slide.
32 The ungodly for the just an ambush lay,
　And ever him seek to slay.
33 The Lord will not surrender him to them,
　No, nor his cause condemn.
34 Wait on the Lord in patience, keep his ways ;
　And he will thee upraise
　The land to inherit; thou shalt look on when
　He roots out evil men.

35 Strong have I seen the wicked, branching forth
   Like trees in native earth.
36 But soon he past, and was not, and I sought
   His place, and there was nought.
37 Mark thou the guileless, and the upright scan,
   For peace betides that man.
38 And the bad at once shall fall; the wicked's race
   Shall die, and leave no trace.
39 The true men's help is from the Lord; 'tis he
   Their strength at need will be.
40 He will assist them and preserve; he will
   Be their deliverer still.
   And rescue he will send them from the unjust,
   Because in him they trust.

Psalm XXXVIII.

1 Lord, in thy wrath rebuke not; in thy hot
   Fury chastise me not.
2 For upon me thy hand lays heavy weight,
   Thy shafts me penetrate.
3 No part of all my flesh is free from scath,
   By reason of thy wrath;
   In all my bones no respite I can win
   By reason of my sin.
4 For my transgressions over my head swell,
   A burthen unbearable.
5 My wounds are loathsome grown and purulent,
   My folly's chastisement.
6 I stagger, I am made to stoop down low,
   All day deprest I go.
7 My body fever ransacketh; no sound
   Part in my flesh is found.

8 I faint, I am sore smitten; loud I groan,
  Ever mine heart makes moan.
9 And my desire thou dost, O Lord God, see;
  My groans escape not thee.
10 My heart throbs; of my strength I am bereft;
  Mine eyes their light has left.
11 My friends and mates the plague upon me shun;
  My kinsmen far off run.
12 But all who seek my life, lay snares; and they
  That plot for my decay,
  Join in debate against me, and devise
  Each day fresh perfidies.
13 But like the deaf I hear not; I become
  Tongue-tied, and as the dumb;
14 As one that hears not, and from all reproof
  Whose mouth is held aloof;
15 For in thee, Lord, I trust: O Lord God, thou
  Wilt my defence avow.
16 O let them not boast o'er me, I have cried;
  For if my foot but slide
17 They glory. But to halt I am full nigh;
  My plagues confront me aye.
18 Lo! I confess my sinfulness; I do
  Mine own transgressions rue.
19 But my foes live and thrive, and they grow great
  That bear me causeless hate;
20 Those that for benefits requite me ill,
  And hatred, when good-will
21 I bore to them. O Lord, forsake not me,
  My God, nor far off be.
22 Make haste, for my deliverer art thou,
  O Lord, and save me now.

Psalm XXXIX.

1 I will observe, I said, my ways, lest wrong
  I utter with my tongue;
  My mouth, as with a curb, I will refrain
  In sight of the profane.
2 I kept me silent; I was mute and still
  From both good words and ill;
3 But more my grief was stirred. Mine heart became
  Within my breast as flame;
  Till in my anxious thought the fire outbroke,
  And with my tongue I spoke.

4 Teach me mine end, Lord; my days' length disclose:
  How frail I am, expose.
5 Lo! Thou hast made mine age a span: my days
  Are as nought in thy gaze.
  Sure all men are like phantoms, when in best
  Established weal they rest.
6 Sure man in shadows walks, and on a vain
  Show spends his toil and pain.
  He gathers riches, and whose profit they
  Shall turn to, cannot say.
7 But now, Lord, whom do I confide in? sure
  In thee mine hopes endure.
8 Save me from all my guilt; make thou not me
  The scorn of fools to be.
9 I hold my peace: I do my lips not part,
  Since thou my chastener art.
10 Remove from me thy plague: I am brought low
  By thy hand's heavy blow.

11 When with rebukes for sin thou chast'nest men,
   Their comely semblance then
   Thou frettest like the moth: so vain a show
   Are all men here below.

12   Hear, Lord, my prayer; give heed, when I implore;
   Keep silence not before
   My tears; for a pilgrim and a wanderer,
   As all my fathers were,
13 I walk before thee: hold, and grant me peace,
   Ere I go hence, and cease.

Psalm XL.

1 I watched and waited on the Lord, and he
   Gave ear and answered me
2 Imploring. When in blusterous gulf I lay,
   In sinking mire and clay,
   He reared my feet on rock; my steps he made
   On firm base to be laid,
3 And put a new song in my mouth, whereby
   Our God to glorify.
   This many saw and feared, and have adored
   And trusted in the Lord.
4 Blessed the man that doth on God rely,
   And turneth not his eye
   Toward vain pretenders; and to those who, fraud
   Devising, walk abroad.
5 Great are thy deeds, O Lord, our God; toward us
   Thy counsels marvellous.
   None can with thee compare; if I should seek
   Them to recount, or speak,

6 They pass all reckoning. 'Tis not sacrifice
　　Nor incense glads thine eyes;
7 Mine ear thou'st opened.　Thou dost not require
　　Sin-offering nor by fire.
　Then, said I, Lo, I come! (thus for me it
　　In the book's roll is writ),
8 To do thy will, O Lord; this love I best;
　　Thy law is in my breast.
9 Behold, I do thy righteousness i' th' great
　　Assembly promulgate;
　My lips do I withhold not, Lord, and thou
　　This knowest well enow.
10 I hide not in mine heart thy righteousness;
　　Thy saving faithfulness
　I show forth, nor conceal thy truth and grace
　　From all the people's face.
11 Do thou thy love, Lord, not withhold from me;
　　But let thy clemency
12 And truth support me aye.　When numberless
　　Disasters round me press,
　When chastisements have gathered over me,
　　Till I no bourne can see,
　When they exceed the hairs upon mine head,
　　When my heart sinks dismayed,
13 Vouchsafe, Lord, my deliverance; hasten thee
　　O Lord, to rescue me.
14 Let shame together seize them and dismay,
　　Who seek my soul to slay.
　Driven backward and confounded let them be,
　　That harm devise for me.
15 Let shame and consternation on them fall,
　　Who triumph in my fall.

16 Let those be glad who seek thee ; let their voice
　　Be lifted to rejoice.
　　Let them who love thy rescue, promulgate
　　Aye that the Lord is great.
17 And I am poor and lowly, but the care
　　Of the Lord God I share ;
　　Thou art my saviour and my champion strong ;
　　My God, withhold not long.

Psalm XLI.

1 Blessed the man, who to the poor takes heed ;
　　The Lord in day of need
2 Shall save him. He shall guard him living, and
　　Well prospering in the land.
3 He shall not let his foes their wish attain.
4 The Lord shall him sustain
　　Upon the couch of sickness. Thou wilt spread
　　Smooth ever his sick bed.

5 　I said, Lord, heal my soul, have pity on me.
　　Though I have sinned by thee.
6 My foes against me talk. When shall he die
　　And his name cease? they cry.
7 And if one visits me, his words are guile ;
　　His heart collects the while
　　Malignant thoughts, which, when abroad he goes,
　　Full soon he will disclose.

8 　Against me all conspire who bear me hate,
　　My harm they meditate.
9 " The foul doom pass against him ; whence he lies
　　Let him no more arise."

10 Yea, too, my friend, in whom my trust I set,
    And of my bread who eat,
    Is turned against me, and is great in zeal
    To catch me by the heel.

11   But have thou mercy; set me, Lord, upright,
    That I may them requite.
12 I know thy good will hence; thou dost not grant
    My foes o'er me to vaunt.
13 Thou wilt in right sustain me, and before
    Thy face keep evermore.

14   Blessed the Lord, the God of Israel, be
    Blest everlastingly.

Psalm XLII.

1 As pants the hart for water-brooks,
    My soul to thee, God, looks.
2 My spirit is athirst for God,
    Yea, for the living God.
    O shall I never more draw near
    In face of God to appear?
3 My tears have been my drink by night
    And day, while in despite
    They asked me, late and early, where
    Is that God of thy prayer?
4 Now when I think on this, I pour
    My soul forth to deplore.
    For erst with multitudes I went,
    Lord, to thy temple bent,
    And led forth loud in thanks and praise
    Those that keep holy days.

5   Why art thou full of heaviness,
My soul, and sore distress?
For what is thy disquietness?
O trust in God nathless.
His light and help he will restore,
And I give thanks once more.

6 O God, my soul is vexed in me;
I will remember thee
Out of the land of Jordan still,
From Mizar and Hermon hill.

7 One deep unto another shouts
With sound of waterspouts.
Thy waves and tempests over me
Have crowded all the sea.

8 Yet did in bygone times the Lord
His gracious help afford;
My song to thee by night I've made,
God of my life, and prayed.

9 O God, my strength, I've said to thee,
Why hast forsaken me?
And why must I in heaviness
Walk, while my foes oppress?

10 My bones are smitten mortally:
My foes in scorn of me
Demanding, late and early, where
Is that God of thy prayer?

11   Why art thou full of heaviness,
My soul, and sore distress?
For what is thy unquietness?
O trust in God nathless.
His light and help he will restore,
And I give thanks once more.

Psalm XLIII.

1 Judge for me, strive the strife that's mine.
Lord, with a race malign.
Against the arms of perfidy
And outrage rescue me.
2 For why, O God, my strength, art thou.
No more on my part now?
And why must I in heaviness
Walk while my foes oppress?
3 O send thy light and truth, that they
May guide me on my way,
4 Till to thy mountain's halidom
And thy abodes I come.
Then to the altar of God shall I
With joy and triumph hie,
And with the sound of harp shall laud
Thy name, O God, my God.
5   Why art thou full of heaviness,
    My soul, and sore distress?
    For what is thy unquietness?
    O trust in God nathless.
    His light and help he will restore,
    And I give thanks once more.

Psalm XLIV.

1 O God, we have heard it with our ears,
Our fathers have us told
The work thou wroughtest in their days,
In yonder days of old.

2 Thou drovest nations out, and they
 Were planted by thy hand;
 Thou shatteredst and threwest out
 The heathen from the land.
3 For land they won not by their sword,
 Nor safe their arm them kept;
 But thy right hand, arm, countenance;
 For thou didst them accept.
4 Lo, thou'rt my king; bid victory, Lord,
 To Jacob to return;
5 Our enemies we thrust back by thee,
 Our foes in thy name spurn.
6 Behold! I trust not in my bow,
 My sword no help I rate:
7 Thou sav'st us from our foes; thou foil'st,
 Lord, them that bear us hate.
8 Our God we daily boast; his name
 At all time celebrate.

9 But thou abhor'st and shamest us; thou go'st
 No more out with our host.
10 Thou turn'st us backward from our foes, and they
 That hate us, grasp our prey.
11 Thou makest us like sheep for slaughter fed,
 Through all the heathen spread.
12 Thou sell'st us all for nought; thou tradest in
 Thy tribes, no wealth to win.
13 Thou sett'st us for our neighbours to deride,
 For a mock on every side.
14 To grow the nation's byword, and to make
 The Gentiles their head shake.
15 All day my shame confronts me; my disgrace

Cloaks every hour my face,
16 To hear the scorner's contumelies, to see
The avenger's cruelty.

17 All this we suffer, and we do not forsake
Thee, nor thy covenant break.
18 Our heart hath not gone back, our steps astray
Have not gone from thy way;
19 Though us thou drive to jackals' haunts, and spread
Death-shadows round our head.
20 If we forgot God's name, or raised our hands
To a God of alien lands,
21 Would God not see, to whom are manifest
All secrets of the breast?
22 Nay; we're for thee slain daily, we're like sheep
That men for offerings keep.
23 Up, Lord, why slumberest thou? let us not be
Aye counted vile by thee.
24 Why dost thou hide thy face, and our distress
Forget, and abjectness?
25 Our soul is humbled to the dust, our shame
Bends to the ground our frame.

Psalm XLV.

1 Out of mine heart glad words distill;
My song, made for my king, I will
Rehearse; my tongue is a ready writers's quill.

2 Thou art more fair than all the sons
Of woman; grace thy mouth o'er-runs,
And shows thou wearest aye God's benisons.

3   Gird thou the sword thy flank upon ;
    Warrior, thy pomp and splendor don ;
    To conquest in thy majesty ride on.

4   Ride on for truth, for mercy and
    For righteousness, and thy right hand
    Shall cause thee fearful things to understand.

5   Sharp are thine arrows, traversing
    The hearts of enemies of my king ;
    Thou shalt low down the Gentile armies bring.

6   Thy throne for ever shall remain ;
    O God, the sceptre of thy reign
    Is such a sceptre as doth right maintain.

7   Thou lovest right, hast wrong abhorred,
    Therefore on thee thy God, the Lord,
    Above thy peers hath oil of gladness poured.

8   Thy vesture is all fragrances
    Of cassia, myrrh, and aloes ;
    Thine ear shall harps from halls of ivory please.

9   King's daughters are thy pensioners ;
    At thy right hand the queen appears ;
    Of gold of Ophir seemeth all she wears.

10 List, daughter, list, thine ear incline,
    Forget that native land of thine ;
    Yea, for thy father's house no longer pine.

11 Let by the king thy beauties be
    Desired, for thy lord is he,
    And thou before him shouldest bend the knee ;

12   That out of Tyre the virgin may
       Before thy feet her tribute lay,
       The people's wealthiest may thee homage pay.

13   The daughter of the king is she,
       That quite within, so gloriously,
       Sits, all arrayed in gold embroidery.

14   In robes of various woof they bring
       Her toward the presence of the king;
       The virgins, her companions, following.

15   All to thy presence they are led,
       With joy and exultation sped;
       Within the palace of the king they tread.

16   Behold, in place of parents thou
       Shalt children of thy own have now,
       Whom through the lands with princedoms to endow.

17   From race to race thy name will I
       Record, that thee for ever and aye
       The nations of the world may glorify.

Psalm XLVI.

1 Our trust and might is God; in troubles He
   Full nigh for aid will be.
2 Therein, therein, we shall not fear, though hurled
   Be from its place the world.
   Nought shall we dread, though mountains be among
   The depths of Ocean flung:

3 Nought, though his waters boom, and seethe, and make
In their pride mountains quake.
4 But the Lord's city they shall glad for ever—
The branchings of a river,
That by the sacred tabernacle's side
Of the most High shall glide.
5 God is in the midst of her: no shock shall bend her:
God shall betimes defend her.
6 The Gentiles raise alarms, the realms are stirred:
The Lord his voice is heard,
7 And the earth melts. Thy strength, O Lord of powers.
O Jacob's God, is ours.
8 Come now, behold, what marvels he hath wrought,
On earth what havoc brought!
9 He stills the rage of wars; he breaketh under
All heaven the bow in sunder:
He knaps the spears in pieces, and of war
He burns in fire the car.
10 Then hold, he saith, your peace, and be this known
That I am God alone.
I will be o'er the Gentiles glorified,
Over the Kingdoms wide.
11 Our help is Jacob's God: the strength is ours
Of the Lord God of powers.

Psalm XLVII.

1 Clap hands, O all ye people, let ring out
To God your jocund shout.
2 For supreme is the Lord, a dreadful and
Great King o'er every land.

3 He bowed the nations to our feet, he broke
  The Gentiles to our yoke.
4 He chose us out an heritage, his most
  Beloved Jacob's boast.
5   Up has God with a shout, the Lord has gone
  With voice of clarion.
6 Sing ye, make music unto God : yea, sing
  With music to our King.
7 For God is king of all the earth ; awake
  Your hymn, and music make.
8 God o'er the heathen rules ; He sits upon
  His hallowed holy throne.
9   The princes of the nations with the bands
  Of Abraham's God join hands ;
  For God is lord of those who shield the earth ;
  Right glorious he goes forth.

Psalm XLVIII.

1 Great is Jehovah, worthy of great laud
  I' th' city of our God,
2 In His holy hill. Full fair in seat and place,
  The joy of all earth's face
  Is Zion hill, where runneth to the north
  The great King's city forth.
3 God in the palaces thereof is known,
  Our sure salvation.
4 For lo ! the kings have mustered, and come thither,
  And are gone by together.
5 They saw and were confounded ; there did they
  Catch panic and dismay.

6 There they were seized with shudders, like to those
  Of women in their throes;
7 Like ships of Tarsus, when asunder cast
  By thy Levantine blast.
8 Ah! city of the Lord of Hosts, as we
  Have heard it, so we see.
  City of our God, He has thee rooted fast
  For ever and aye to last.

9   We meditate, O God, upon thy grace
  Within thy hallowed place.
10 Like as thy name, O God, thy praise goes forth
  To all the bounds of earth.
11 Justice thy right hand filleth. Let rejoice
  Mount Zion, let the voice
  Of Judah's daughters lift itself, to praise
  Ever thy righteous ways.
12 Go, compass Zion, and observe her; tell
  Her bastions' number well,
13 Regard her muniments, her mansions sum,
  To inform the times to come.
14 This God is our God ever and aye; 'tis he
  Till death our guide shall be.

Psalm XLIX.

1 Hear this, O all ye people; hearken well,
  All in the world who dwell—
2 Ye sons of lofty and of low estate,
  The poor man with the great.
3 My mouth shall utter wisdom, and my heart
  Shall prudent thoughts impart.

4 I'll give ear to dark lessons, and profound
  Lore with mine harp expound.

5 Why should I fear in evil days, when steals
  Encroachment round my heels?
6 Who that in riches trusts, and plumes himself
  Upon abounding pelf,
7 His brother can redeem, or ransom give
  To God, that he may live—
8 (Nay, men's deliverance is too dear, and he
  For aye must let that be),
9 That he may live for ever, and his sight
  Escape the mortal night?
10 For we behold them perish by one rule,
  Wise man, and boor, and fool,
11 Leaving their heirs their wealth; yet fancy they
  Their houses firm shall stay,
  Their homes endure from race to race; they claim
  To give the lands their name.
12 Man cannot rest in greatness; like the beast
  He dies, and all has ceast.

13 They trust in this their way, and by their talk
  Their comers-after walk.
14 They go down to the grave like sheep, and death
  Over them shepherdeth.
15 The righteous in the passing of a day
  Shall tread above their clay.
16 Their substance and their glory shall the tomb,
  Their latest home, consume.
17 But God my soul, which he accepts, will save,
  Yea, from the grasping grave.

18 Misdoubt not, when a man is rich, and great
    The glory of his estate.
19 For in death nought can he reserve, nor bear
    His riches with him there.
20 Though blest in life he thought himself; though praise
    Have those, who taste good days:
21 Yet must he, where his fathers went before,
    And see the light no more.
22 Man, being unwise in greatness, like the beast
    Dieth, and all hath ceast.

Psalm L.

1 The Lord, yea God, high God.
   He speaks, and calls, from where the sun goes forth
   To where it sinks, the earth.
2 From Zion, beauty's consummation, God
   Outbeams his light abroad.
3 Our God comes not in silence; flames devour
   Before his face, and tempests round him lour.
4 He calls the earth beneath and heaven on high,
   His people's cause to try.
5 "Assemble me my plighted, who through ties
   Are mine of sacrifice."
6 Lo! now shall heaven his righteousness applaud;
   For judge himself is God.
7 "Hear, people mine; I will my charges tell
   Against thee, Israel.
8 I blame thy offerings not; thy sacrifice
   Ever confronts mine eyes.
9 No bullock from thy stalls, no goat I crave
   Out of thy flocks to have.
10 Because all beasts in wood, the herds upon

A thousand hills I own.
11 All fowls in air I know, all deer on lea
  Are manifest to me.
12 Must thou know if I hunger? I have earth
  And all she bringeth forth.
13 That flesh of oxen I will eat, or drink
  Of goat's blood dost thou think?
14 Nay, offer to God praises, and redeem
  Thy vows to the Supreme;
15 And call me in the troublous hour, and be
  Saved, and give thanks to me."

16 To the wicked eke saith God;—
  "What dost thou to declare my law, and keep
  My covenant on thy lip.
17 When admonition thou dost loathe, and hast
  My words behind thee cast?
18 Thou seest a thief and hail'st him, and thy share
  Dost with the adulterer bear.
19 Thy mouth to evil is let loose, and strung
  With falsehood is thy tongue.
20 Thou sittest down and slanderest thy brother;
  Thou the child of thy mother
21 Backbitest. Thou hast done all this, while I.
  Saith God, stood silent by;
  Thou deemedst me what thou art; but I'll thee
  Correct, and make to see.
22 Mark this, O all that God forget, lest you,
  Ravening, I should pursue,
23 And none could save. Who offereth to me praise,
  Who ordereth right his ways,
  He gives me honor, and to him God's aid
  Apparent shall be made."

Psalm LI.

1 Spare me, God, in thy grace;
In thy compassion's floods my guilt efface.
2 Wash, wash iniquity
From off me, and from trespass cleanse thou me.
3 Because I know my crime,
Because my sin confronts me at all time.
4 Before thee, thee alone,
I sinned, and my offence thine eyes have known.
Therefore thy word hath been
Upright, and in thy judging thou art clean.
5 Lo, I was fashion'd in
Defect, my mother me conceived in sin.
6 But thou lov'st in our hearts
Truth, and set'st wisdom in our inmost parts.
7 Sprinkle me, wash me; so
Shall I be clean, I shall be white as snow.
8 Of comfort and joy make
Me hear, and glad the bones which thou didst break.
9 Hide from my sins thy face,
And all my wrongful acts do thou erase.
10 God! a clean heart create,
And a right spirit in me renovate.
11 Cast me not from thy sight,
Nor from thy holy spirit shut me quite.
12 Thy help, thy peace again
Grant, and let thy free spirit me sustain.
13 Then I shall teach thy way
To the sinner; I shall lead back them that stray.

14 Save me, God of my weal,
   God, from blood-guiltiness, and my tongue shall peal
15 Thy praises. Unbar, Lord,
   My mouth, and from these lips shall thanks be poured.
16 For thou dost not require
   Offering (else I would give it), nor desire
   Burnt sacrifice of mine.
17 A wounded soul is a holocaust of thine;
   Thou, God, the sacrifice
   Of a broken wounded heart wilt not despise.
18 May Zion prosper through
   Thy righteousness; build thou the walls anew
19 Around thy city; and then
   Shall sacrifices, brought by righteous men.
   Propitiate thee. Lo, they
   Shall sacrifices and burnt offerings pay,
   And undivided bullocks on thy altar lay.

Psalm LII.

1 Why boast of wrongs, thou mighty man, when each
   Day doth God's goodness teach?
2 Thy tongue contriveth scath; thy slander's made
   Wounding as whetted blade.
3 Thou dost in evil more than good delight,
   In false words than upright.
4 Thou lov'st, O tongue perfidious, every word
   Whence havoc may be stirred;
   And therefore likewise God shall overthrow
   For ever, and lay thee low,
5 And pluck thee from thy tent, and from the sphere
   Of life thy roots uptear,

6 The righteous shall behold, and fear God—yea,
 Shall mock at thee, and say,
7 " So fares it with the man who has not made
 God his defence, but laid
 His trust upon his gain's increase, and strong
 Has kept himself by wrong.
8 But I meantime like a green olive-tree
 I' th' house of God shall be ;
 Yea, on the bounty of the Lord will I
 Through all my days rely.
9 I will for ever praise thee in the thought
 Of that which thou hast wrought,
 And serve thy name, (for therein's my delight),
 In thy true people's sight.

Psalm LIII.

1 In his heart the fool saith, God is nought;
 Yea, corrupt and abhorred is all they have wrought;
2 There is none that doth right. From on high
 Has the Lord upon men looked adown, to descry
 If one prudent among them be seen—
 If by any among them God sought for has been.
3 But they all are polluted; they run
 After falsehood together; none doth well, not one.
4 Shall the workers of evil that eat
 My people as bread, with no chastisement meet?
5 On thee have they not called. With fear
 Shall they quake, no occasion of dread being near.
 For the bones God will scatter of those
 Who besieged you. To flight shall be turned your foes.

For the Lord hath defied, and in scorn
6 Has them held. O that rescue to Israel were born
Out of Zion; for joy would there be
Unto Jacob, and triumph would Israel see.

Psalm LIV.

1 For thy great name protect me, and my right
Judge, O God, in thy might.
2 Hear, God, my prayer, and to those words give heed
That from my lips proceed.
3 For aliens up against me rise, and men of violence who
Have set not God before their eyes, my life pursue.

4   Lo! God is my defence, and thou, Lord, art
A champion of my part.
5 Thou turnest back his malice on my foe;
In thy truth lay them low;
6 That free-will sacrifices I may offer, Lord, to thee,
And glorify thy name; for this delighteth me.
7 When thou hast me from all my foes delivered, and mine eye,
Fulfilled on those that hate me, shall my wish descry.

Psalm LV.

1 Hearken, O God, unto my prayer, and shun
Thou not mine orison.
2 Give ear, and answer me; for to and fro
In sorrow and wail I go,
Vexed by the enemies' voice, the cruelty
Of men's iniquity.

3 For they cast on me calumnies; they nurse
  Against me hatred fierce.
4 My heart is racked within me, and the dread
  Of death is o'er me shed.
5 Dismay and terror seize on me, and cold
  Tremblings my frame enfold.
6 Give me, I said, the dove's wing; I would flee
  Forth, and at peace would be.
7 Behold! I would fly far, and take my rest
  Out in the desert waste.
8 I would make speed to fly, and shelter find
  From tempest and loud wind.

9   Destroy them, O Lord God, their tongues divide,
    For strife I have descried,
10 And violence in the city; around her they
   Walk the walls, night and day.
   Within there woe and ruin make their stay;
11 Within there foulest guilt; wrongs and deceits
   Depart not from her streets.
12 For not my foe has put me thus to scorn—
   Nay, that I would have borne.
   Or if so much mine adversaries did,
   From them I would have hid.
13 But it was thou, mine own compeer, my tried
   Associate, and my guide;
   With whom I took sweet counsels, and along
   To God's house walked in throng.

14 Let death come on them swooping; let the tomb
    Them in their prime consume.
15 For there is wickedness amongst them, in
   Their homes and hearts within.

16 I cry against them unto God; and he,
    The Lord, will hark to me.
17 At morning, and at noontide, and at eve,
    I make my plaint and grieve.
18 But he will hear my voice, he will release
    My soul to taste of peace.
    Although against me war he raised, tho' foes
    Full numerous me oppose,
19 Me shall God hear, and answer, who the throne
    Of ages sits upon.

    For in them are no changes, and the fear
    Of God they will not hear.
20 Each one lays hand upon his peaceful mates,
    His covenant violates.
21 His mouth is smooth as curds are, and amid
    His bosom war is hid.
    Altho' more soft than oil may be his words,
    Yet are they very swords.

22   Cast thou thy burden on the Lord, and he
    Will all perform for thee.
    He will not let for ever be down-trod
23 The righteous. Nay, thou, God,
    Wilt bring down to the grave, (nor shall they live
    Half their days to achieve,)
    The men of perfidy and blood; but I
    Will ever on thee rely.

Psalm LVI.

1 Thy mercy on me show,
    O God, for men pant for my overthrow.

2 All day with warfare they
　Oppress me; my foes pant for me all day;
3 Many are at war with me,
　High God! but in my peril trust I thee.
4 In God I make my boast;
　I trust in God; I fear not, though flesh do its most.
5　Daily my words they wrest;
　Their thoughts to do me scath are all addrest.
6 They lurk, they congregate,
　They dog my heels; to snatch my life they wait.
7 Shall they in doing fraud
　Escape? Destroy the people in thy wrath, O God!
8 Cast up my wanderings,
　Put by my tears; doth not thy book record these things?
9　Then shall they turn and flee,
　When I implore; I know it; is not God with me?
10 I make in God my boast,
　Yea, in the Lord my boast;
11 I trust in God; I fear not, though flesh do its most.
12　Thy vows, God, are on me;
　I will perform thanksgivings unto thee.
13 Thou didst my soul preserve
　From dying; wilt not thou forbid my feet to swerve,
14 That I before God then
　May walk in daylight such as gladd'neth living men.

Psalm LVII.

1 Show mercy, mercy on me,
　O God, for I entrust my soul to thee.
　I take in thy wings' cover
　My refuge till these troubles be past over.

2 To God, to the God most high,
  Who justice will perform for me, I cry.
3 Send out of heaven, and save
  Me from their pride, who pant my life to have.
  Let God send forth his grace
  And truth; my soul is in the lions' place.
4 I lodge among the stern
  Sons of the Gentiles, who in rancor burn;
  Who spears and arrows have
  For teeth, whose tongue is like a whetted glaive.
5   Set thyself, O God, forth
      Above the heavens; thy glory above all earth.
6 They for my steps have laid
  A net; my life to stagger they have made.
  Before my feet a pit
  They've dug; let them fall in the midst of it.

7   My heart is ready with praise;
  My heart is ready, O God, I will song with harmony
    raise.
8 Awake up, O my delight;
  Psaltery, wake up and harp; I will up with the morn-
    ing's light;
9 I will utter, Jehovah, thy praise
  To the Gentiles; I will to the heathen my harmony
    raise,
10 For thy mercy beyond heaven rears
  Her stature; thy truth is exalted above the spheres.
11   Set thyself, O God, forth
      Above the heavens, thy glory above all earth

Psalm LVIII.

1 Do ye speak righteousness? do ye judge forsooth,
  O sons of men, the truth?
2 Nay, wrongs ye cherish in your hearts; your hand
  Deals violence o'er the land.
3 The wicked from the womb are swervers; yea,
  From birth toward falsehood stray.
4 Their venom is like that of snakes: they clasp
  Their ear, deaf as the asp
5 That will not hear the charmer's voice, though he
  Charm ne'er so cunningly.

6   Break, Lord, their teeth i' th' jawbone; dash abroad
  The lion's teeth, O God.
7 As running waters let them waste; let all
  Their arrows pointless fall.
8 Let, like a snail, each, as he moves, consume;
  Like that which falls from womb
  Untimely, let them sunlight ne'er behold.
9 Sooner than cauldron cold
  Can feel your kindled thorns, let strong and fierce
  God's tempest them disperse.
10 Then shall the righteous be rejoiced to see
  The vengeance; then shall he
  Dip in the ungodly's blood his footsteps; then
11 Shall it be said by men,
  In truth there is an harvest-day for worth,
  A God to judge the earth.

Psalm LIX.

1 Save me, God, from my foes ; my refuge be
From those who war with me.
2 Save me from evil doers ; for me withstand
The men of bloody hand.
3 For lo, they meet together to waylay me,
The stern of hand, to slay me—
For no offence of mine, O Lord ; nor sin,
Nor blame, have I therein.
4 They muster, they against me rush ; awake,
And watch, Lord, for my sake.
5 For art not thou Jehovah, God of Hosts,
The God whom Israel boasts ?
Rise, visit all the heathen ; spare thou none
Who traitorous wrong have done.
6 Let them return at evening, whine like hounds,
And walk the city's rounds.
7 Behold, their mouths foam out, their lips are swords :
For who doth hear their words ?
8 But thou dost mock at them ; thou dost deride,
Lord, all the heathens' pride.
9 Thou art my strength ; toward thee I look abroad,
For my strong tower is God.

10   Let God me guard, my gracious God, and show
Me vengeance on my foe.
11 Still for my people's sake destroy them not,
Lest they be soon forgot.
O Lord, our shield, disperse them with thy power,
And cause them low to cower.

12 Let their lips' word, their sinning mouth, and their
    Own pride become their snare,
    Yea, their own uttered curses and deceit.
13 Let wrath complete, complete
    Their doom, till they no more be found, and then
    Shall it be known by men,
    There is a God in Jacob rules and forth
    To the limits of the earth.

14   Let them return at evening; whine like hounds,
    And walk the city's rounds.
15 Let them go range for meat, and growl, if they
    By night unsated stay.
16 But I thy power will sing; I will thy grace
    Chant in the morning's face,
    For thou my refuge in the troublous hour,
    And thou art my strong tower.
10 Thou art my strength; I'll harp to thee, O God;
    For thou art my strong tower, and thou my gracious
        God.

Psalm LX.

1 Thou, God, hast thrown us off and scattered; thou
    Wast wroth; restore us now.
2 Thou rentest, thou didst make the land to reel;
    She quakes; her breaches heal!
3 Thou gav'st hard lessons; thou didst make thy nation
    Quaff wine of consternation.
4 Thou show'st an ensign to thy fearers, whither
    For truth's sake they may gather,
5 For thy beloved their rescue. O save us, and
    Answer with thy right hand.

6   God's holy word is given me; I will shout,
    And Shechem portion out,
7 And share the field of Succoth; Gilead's mine;
    Manasseh's land is mine.
    Ephraim, be thou my strong-hold; Judah, be
    Lawgiver under me.
8 Shout for me, Philistim; let th' Edomite
    Serve me and Moabite.
9 Who'll lead me into the city fortified?
    Who'll into Edom guide?
10 Thou, Lord, who didst reject us? thou that go'st
    No more out with our host?
11 O grant us help in trouble; for to gain
    The help of man is vain.
12 Through God shall we do mighty deeds; our foe
    He'll for us beat down low.

Psalm LXI.

1 Hear, Lord, my cry; let mount my prayer before thee;
    From earth's ends I implore thee,
2 When my heart sinks; O guide me, a rock to scale,
    For which my force would fail.
3 For thou against my foes art my defence,
    Strong tower and confidence.
4 Would I might always in thy tent abide,
    In thy wings' shadow hide.

5   For thou, God, hear'st my vows; I have from thee
    An heritage granted me,
6 With those who fear thy name. Thy king may'st thou
    With days on days endow,

And years on years, from race to following race ;
7 That he before God's face
May sit for ever, and the guardians of
His life be faith and love.
8 Then thy name hymning always, I will pay
My vows from day to day.

Psalm LXII.

1 Ay! my soul doth on God repose, and from
God shall my rescue come.
2 He is my rock, rescue, and tower of might ;
Through God I fail not quite.
3 How long will you infest a man ? ye rush
All forward him to crush,
As at a bowing fence, a tottering wall.
4 How they may make one fall
From his degree, is all that they devise.
They take delight in lies ;
They carry blessings on their lips, and nurse
Within their hearts a curse.

5 Ay! let my soul on God repose, and thence
Be all my confidence.
6 He is my rock, rescue, and tower of might,
By whom I stand upright.
7 God is my succor and my glory ; he
A strong rock is to me.
8 God is my refuge; trust him evermore,
Ye people, and outpour
In prayer to him your hearts ; at all times let
Our trust in God be set.

9   Ay! all reliance on the mean man fails;
    The great man in the scales
    Flies up; against him vanity prevails.
10 Trust ye not in oppression; take no vain
    Thoughts from ill-gotten gain:
    If pelf increase, be not your hearts too fain.
11 Once hath God uttered it; yea, I have heard
    Once and again his word.
    That power is God's; yea, power is of the Lord.
12 And thine, O Lord, is't mercy to display;
    For thou to each man wilt his works repay.

Psalm LXIII.

1 Lord, thou 'rt my God, sought early out by me;
   My soul thirsteth for thee,
   And my flesh pineth, like a parched-up and
   Faint water-lacking land,
2 To view thee in thy holy place, to see
   Thy power and majesty.
3 For dearer is thy grace than life. Now will
   My lips extol thee still,
4 Now will I bless thee while I live, and raise
   My hands, thy name to praise,
5 My soul with lushness, and with praise my tongue
   Filling, and my lips with song.
6 For taking rest I mind thee, and upon
   Thee muse, while night slips on.
7 How thou hast been my help; I have joyed in thee,
   Thy wings o'ershadowing me.
8 My soul hath leaned upon thee, and thy right
   Hand hath me held upright,

9 But those who seek my life with murder, low
   Beneath the ground shall go.
10 Let them be given to riving swords, to the beast
   Of carrion made a feast.
11 And let the king rejoice in God; let all
   Glory on his name who call.
   And let the lips be sealed up fast of those
   Who calumnies compose.

Psalm LXIV.

1 Hear the voice of my plaint, and guard my head,
   O God, from enemies' dread.
2 Hide me from bad men's councils, from the throng
   Of those intent on wrong,
3 Who whet their tongues like swords, who shoot forth each
   Arrows of deadly speech,
4 To smite the just in secret; unawares
   They strike, and have no fears.
5 They frame their evil plot, commune to lay
   Snares, and, Who sees? they say.
6 They compass subtle wrongs; they have devised
   Devices well disguised.
   Deep is the heart and inward mind of each.
7 Them shall God's arrows reach
   Wounding with sudden stroke; confusion o'er
   Their counsels he shall pour.
8 Then shall be fear-struck all who see them: yea
   All men shall catch dismay,
   And shall avouch God's act, and shall take heed
   Full gravely to his deed.

9 Then in Jehovah shall rejoice the just,
  And place in them their trust;
  And all, that are upright in heart, shall raise
  Their voices to his praise.

Psalm LXV.

1 Thee praise befits in Zion; vows shall be,
  O God, there paid to thee.
2 All flesh before thy aspect shall repair,
  O thou that hearest prayer.
3 Against us our iniquities prevail:
  Atone thou, where we fail.
4 O blest, whom thou dost choose, and put aside!
  Who in thy courts abide,
  Who in thy house, thy temple's sanctitude,
  Like us, are filled with good!
5 O God, our rescue, thou dost answer us
  With judgments marvellous;
  Thou, in whom all the ends of earth confide,
  All on the sea-plains wide;
6 Thou, that the mountains by thy strength dost ground,
  Whom power engirds around;
7 Who still'st the rage of seas, the surges' noise,
  And the roused people's voice;
8 Before whose signs the dwellers of the wide
  Earth's bounds are terrified.
  The outgoings of morn and evening thou
  Makest thy praise avow.

9   Thou visit'st earth and waterest: thou dost dower
  Her with the abounding shower.

The river of God o'erflows with waters then;
Thou orderest corn for men
10 When thou prepar'st the earth; her furrows drink
Full draughts; her ridges sink.
Thou mak'st her soft with raindrops; thou dost bless
Her sprouts with fruitfulness.
11 Thou dost the year's orb with thy goodness crown;
Thy wheels drop foison down;
12 They green the pastures of the waste; they cover
The hills with gladness over.
13 Our meads are clad with flocks; our glens adorn
Their hollow laps with corn.
They shout to one another in their glee,
They utter minstrelsy.

Psalm LXVI.

1 Shout unto God, all earth; with song proclaim
The glory of his name.
2 Exalt his praise; say of the Lord God, how
Dread in thy deeds art thou!
Before the greatness of thy power thy foes
Must yield themselves and glose.
3 All earth shall worship thee, shall thee proclaim
With songs, and hymn thy name.
4 Come you, behold God's works, his dealings scan,
Dread toward the sons of man.
5 He turneth sea to land; the foot hath trod
Where the great rivers flowed.
6 Lo! there in him we joyed! he ruleth by
His strength for ever and aye.

His eyes regard the nations; let none raise
Their heads that hate his ways.
7 Bless God, ye nations; let his praise resound
Upon your voices' sound;
8 Who keeps our soul in life, who will not let
Our feet be overset.
9 Ah God! but thou hast proved us and assayed,
As silver is assayed.
10 Thou to the snare hast brought us; thou hast on
Our loins affliction thrown.
11 Thou hast our heads beneath the rider bent—
Through fire and flood we went;
Yet didst thou bring us out to large content.

12   I will approach with sacrifice thy house,
And pay to thee my vows,
13 Which my lips uttered, which my mouth expressed,
Then when I was distressed.
14 Whole offerings and the fat of rams I'll bear thee,
And goats with kine prepare thee.
15 Come, all who fear the Lord, come hear of me
How for my life wrought he.
16 I called upon him with my mouth; his praise
On my tongue did I raise.
17 If in my heart I found sin, would my word
Have by the Lord been heard?
18 But truly God hath heard me; he gave ear
At the voice of my prayer.
19 Now God be blest, who did not send back my
Prayer, nor did grace deny.

Psalm LXVII.

1 May God be gracious,
   Bless us, and cause his face to shine on us:
2 That all earth may discern
   Thy ways, all tribes thy saving power may learn.
3 Thee let the people praise,
   O God, let every people give thee praise;
   A voice of gladness let all nations raise.
4 For thou the nations well
   Dost rule; thou guidest all on earth who dwell.
5 Thee let the people praise,
   O God, let every people give thee praise.
6 Lo! Earth the fulness of her fruits displays!
   May God, our God us bless.
7 O that God us may bless;
   His fear let all the ends of earth confess.

Psalm LXVIII.

1 Up, God! let scattered be
   Thy foes, let from thy face thy haters flee!
2 As drifteth smoke away,
   As melteth wax before the fire, so may
   The wicked from the Lord God's face decay.
3 And let rejoice the upright;
   Let them exult in sight
   Of God, and utter triumph with delight.

4 Sing, harp ye unto God;
  Build him, that rideth o'er the wastes, a road,
  Whose name's the Lord; exult before his face.
5 A father of the fatherless,
  A judge for widows championless
  Is our God, ruling from his holy place.
6 He makes the outcasts in a home to dwell,
  And frees the prisoners from their bands
  To welfare, whilst in barren lands
  He causes those to inhabit who rebel.

7   When thou led'st forth, O God,
  Thy people, when thy step the waste wilds trod,
8 Earth shook, and down from heaven the rain-drops fell
  Before God's face, yea, yonder
  Mount Sinai quaked thereunder,
  Before God's face, thy God's face, Israel.
9 Thou gav'st thine heritage
  A generous rain, their weary march to suage.
10 Thou mad'st them safely dwell;
  Thy grace, God, for the poor provided well.

11   The Lord God gave the word,
  And female hosts the triumph harbingered.
12 Kings of hosts flee away,
  Flee, and the sitter at home divides the prey.
13 "Sure ye shall rest between
  Your folded flocks, where wings of doves are seen,
  Whom silver plumes enfold,
  And pinions, like the yellowness of gold."
14 When high God put to flight
  Kings in our land, with snow stood Salmon white.

15 Look, what a giant hill
   Is Bashan, Bashan's many crested hill!
16 Why look askance, O hills of many a crest?
   This is the mount of God;
   God here will make abode;
   The Lord hath set here his perpetual rest.

17   Thy cars are thousandfold,
   O God, yea, tens of thousands doubly told.
   They stand around his face,
   As in Mount Sinai, in his holy place.
18 Thou art high overhead
   Gone up, thou hast captivity captive led;
   Hast ransom for men ta'en,
   Yea, Lord, for rebels, midst them to remain.
19 We bless God day by day,
   Our saviour, when men burthens on us lay.
20 The Lord us succoreth,
   The Lord God's are the rescuings from death.
21 Sure God his foes' heads will
   Smite, and their scalps, who go offending still.

22   "I will from Bashan lead," the Lord hath sworn,
   "I'll lead them back, yea, from the deep sea's bourne,
23 That thou may'st dip thy tread
   In foes' blood, and thy dogs' tongue thence be red."
24 They've seen thee, O God, how
   Thou go'st, how tow'rd thy sanctuary go'st thou,
   O God, my God and king.
25 The singers lead the way,
   Around the virgins on the timbrels play:
   The minstrels in the rear come following.

26 Bless you the Lord in throng,
   Bless him, all ye from Israel's fountain sprung.
27 Lo, there the chiefs of Benjamin, youngest one;
   The princes from the land
   Of Judah with their band,
   Princes of Naphthali and Zebulun.
28 Send forth thy strength, God; show
   Thy strength, as thou didst for us long ago;
   For thy Jerusalem temple stand up so.
   The kings of earth shall bring thee tribute then—
29 Rebuke the beast o' th' fen,
   The bull-herds, and the lords o' th' Gentile droves :
   Till humbly at thy foot
   They silver pieces put;
   Break thou the people that contention loves.
31 Then lords shall come of Mizraim ; Cush abroad
   Shall launch her hands to God.

32   Sing, sing to God, ye kingdoms; make accord,
   Whole earth, to God the Lord,
33 Who rides on heaven, the old-world heaven; whose voice
   Goes forth, a lord-like voice.
34 Ascribe ye strength to Israel's God; he rears
   His praise and pomp i' th' spheres.
35 A dread God he, from where he loves to dwell,
   The God of Israel !
   His people he hath strengthened and upraised ;
   Evermore God be praised.

Psalm LXIX.

1 Save me, O God, for on my soul doth press
   The water's heavy stress.
2 I lapse in miry gulf, where is no ground;
   I sink in the profound
   Of waters, and their eddies hem me round.
3 I am weary, having cried
   So long; mine eyes consume, my throat is dried,
   Whilst I for God abide.
4 My foes the hair outnumber on my head;
   Strong are they that would shed
   For causeless hate my blood; whom, lo! I pay
   What I ne'er took away.
5 Thou know'st, O God, my simpleness; in me
   No faults are hid from thee.
6 Let, Lord, thy trusters not in me be shamed,
   Lord, that of hosts art named.
   Abash not by me those that seek thee well,
   Lord God of Israel.
7 Because reproach for thy sake I have borne,
   And clad my face hath scorn.
8 I am estranged and parted from my brothers,
   From children of my mother's;
9 For zeal I bear thy house hath preyed on me,
   And scorners' contumely
10 Oppressed me. They my fasting and my tears
   Make objects of their jeers;
11 And sackcloth for my covering when I take,
   A byword thence they make.

12 My name those bandy, in the gates who sit;
    Drunkards make songs of it.
13 But let to thee, Lord, my petition climb
    In a favorable time.
    Answer me, God, in thy great bounteousness,
    In saving faithfulness.
14 Save me in mire from sinking; me from deep
    Floods and my foes' hate keep.
15 Let not the eddies whelm, the gulph not draw
    Me downward in its maw,
    Let o'er my head the grave not close his jaw.
16 Answer me, turn thy face,
    Lord, toward me, rich in pity, large in grace.
17 O keep not hid thy face,
    Lord, from thy servant; for I am distressed;
    Make answer, and in haste.
18 Draw near my soul, and ransom her, and me
    Out of my foes' power free.
19 Thou know'st my shame, disgrace and scorn; thine eye
    Doth all my foes descry.
20 Dishonor wounds my heart, and makes disease
    Upon my vigor seize.
    I look in vain for pitiers, and a sweet
    Comforter cannot meet.
21 They give me food of wormwood, gall to drink,
    When under thirst I sink.
22 So let their food betray them, and let snares
    Arrest them unawares.
23 Make their eyes overcast and lightless; make
    Ever their loins to quake.
24 Pour out on them thine ire; let on their path
    Pursue thy burning wrath.

25 Their fastnesses make thou a desolation,
　Their homes no habitation.
26 For whom thou smotest they hunt down, and blows
　Beyond thy plagues impose.
27 Add forfeits on their forfeitures, dissever
　Them from thy peace for ever.
28 Expunge them from thy book of life, and write
　Them never 'mid the upright.
29 But me, the poor, the humble, let with me,
　O God, thy succors be;
30 That I with song may praise God, and proclaim
　With thanksgiving his name.
31 And better such an offering he approves
　Than a bull with horns and hooves.
32 That sight shall glad the humble, and revive
　Hearts, that to-Godward strive.
33 For the Lord hears the lowly; he will not
　Despise his prisoners' lot.

34　Sing praise, O heaven and earth; ye ocean-floods
　And all your gliding broods.
35 For God will Zion save, and rear each town
　In Judah fallen down;
36 That we may dwell there, and possess her; yea
　That there a race may stay
　That serves God; that the adorers of his name
　A sure abode may claim.

Psalm LXX.

1 Up, God, to my deliverance; hasten thee
　O Lord, to rescue me.
2 Let shame together seize them and dismay,
　Who seek my soul to slay.

Driven backward and confounded let them be
Who harm desire for me.
3 Let ruin with their shame upon them fall,
Who triumph o'er me call.
4 Let all be glad who seek thee; let their voice
Be lifted to rejoice.
Let those, who love thy rescue, promulgate
Ever, The Lord is great.
5 And I am poor and lowly; hasten thee,
O Lord, my help to be.
Thou art my saviour and my champion strong;
O God, withhold not long.

Psalm LXXI.

1 In thee, Lord, I have trusted; let not me
For ever ashamèd be;
2 But help and rescue me; for just art thou;
Give ear, and save me now.
3 Be thou my fastness and my stronghold, where
For ever I may repair,
Where thou, my rock and safeguard, wilt ordain
That refuge I may gain.
4 God, save me from the wicked's seizure, and
The violent, wrongful hand.
5 For thou hast been my hope, Lord God; thou dost
From youth compose my trust.
6 For since I left the womb, on thee I lean;
Thou hast my guardian been.
7 To many a fearful portent I am now,
But my strong help art thou.
8 Thy praise shall fill my mouth; from day to day
Thy grandeur I'll display.

9 Cast me not off in age; do thou not, when
   Strength fails, forsake me then.
10 For foes commune against me, and men set
   To take my life have met.
11 God quits him! hunt him down and seize, they cry;
   There is no saviour nigh.
12 But, O my God, be thou not far off hence;
   Haste, God, to my defence.
13 Let them be shamed, let them consume away,
   Who me devise to slay;
14 Let scorn and mockery be their clothing, who
   Would evil to me do.
15 But let me trust thee ever, and add thee more
   Praise on all praise of yore;
   My lips thy righteousness declaring, and
   All day thy rescuing hand.
16 For I can estimate it not; below
   Thy might I'll guarded go,
   O Lord my God, and make remembrance own
   Thy righteousness alone.
17 Thou, God, since youth hast taught me, and till now
   Thy marvels I'll avow.
18 So leave me not, when old and hoary grown,
   O God, to stand alone,
   Till to this race I speak thy arm, thy might
   To every unborn wight;
19 And high set up, O God, thy judgments just,
   And the great works thou dost.
20 God, who is like thee? Thou hast made us go
   Through great and bitter woe,
   Yet wilt thou turn, and living bring us forth
   Yea, from deep under earth,

21 Thou wilt increase my welfare, wilt to me
   Turn, and my guardian be.
22 So I with all string'd instruments will laud
   Thy faithfulness, O God;
   I'll make, O holy One of Israel,
   The harp thy praise to tell.
23 My lips, my soul—whose ransomer thou art—
   Shall in the strain take part.
   My tongue shall likewise utter every day
24 Thy righteousness—when they
   Shall be ashamed, shall be confounded, who
   With injury me pursue.

Psalm LXXII.

1 Give, God, the king thy judgments, the king's heir
  Thy righteousness to share,
2 To judge thy people rightly, and assure
  Of equity the poor,
3 That hills and mountains to thy people may
  Bring welfare 'neath right sway.
4 For justice he shall deal to lowly ones,
  Shall save the poor man's sons,
5 And crush the oppressor. So mankind shall thee
  Fear, while the sun they see,
  And while the moon shall o'er them lift her face.
  Yea, from race unto race.
6 He shall descend as rain on mowed grass, and
  Showers that refresh the land.
7 The just shall flourish in his days, and peace
  Spread, till the moon shall cease.
8 His empire shall from sea to sea extend,

From river to world's end.
9 'Neath him shall bow the dwellers of the waste;
His foes the dust shall taste.
10 The kings of Tarsus and of isles shall bring
Him gifts; yea, Sheba's king
11 And Saba's, tribute pay; all kings the knee
Shall bend, all heathen shall his vassals be.

12 For he'll the poor and mean save, when they cry,
To whom no help is nigh.
13 The lowly and the meek he will befriend,
And the poor's life defend.
14 From guile and force he will their souls redeem;
Their blood to him dear will seem.
15 And he shall live, and offerings shall be told
To him of Saba's gold;
Before him shall men homage ever pay,
And bless him day by day.
16 Earth shall give corn by handfuls; corn shall spread
Over the mountain's head.
Her harvests wide shall wave, like forests on
The flanks of Lebanon.
Her cities like the grasses of the field
Blossoms of men shall yield.
17 His name shall ages live, and stand before
The sun's face evermore.
And therein shall men bless themselves, and high
All heathen speak thereby.

Bless the Lord God, the God of Israel; he
Alone doth wondrously.
O bless his glorious name perpetually,
And let the earth filled with his glory be.

Psalm LXXIII.

1 Ah, God is gracious sure
 To Israel, e'en to those whose hearts are pure.
2 Yet my foot well-nigh hath
 Failed me, my step well-nigh forsook the path;
3 For I with envy viewed
 The wicked, and the welfare of the lewd.
4 For they live on without
 Pangs to the grave; their frames are hale and stout;
5 They share the afflictions not
 Of mortals, nor the plagues of common lot.
6 Therefore their diadem
 Is pride, and violence is a robe to them.
7 From bloated flesh outstart
 Their eyes, and with o'er-weening swells their heart.
8 They sneer, they make their speech
 Of grim oppressions; high-flown is their speech.
9 Their talk ascendeth forth
 To heaven, and with their tongues they range the earth.
10 Therefore to seek them goes
 His people, and their cup thence overflows.
11 And how shall God, they cry,
 Know aught? What knowledge is in the Most High?
12 Lo, evil men are these,
 Who thrive at all times, and their wealth increase.
13 Sure, I did vainly cleanse
 My heart, and wash my hands in innocence.
14 Yea, I have all day borne
 Chast'ning and my rebuke from morn to morn.

15 Yet, were I thus to say,
   Methought, I should thy children's cause betray.
16 I sought to learn aright
   These things; and hard the task was in my sight;
17 Till to God's halidom
   I went, and saw to what end these men come.
18 How them in slippery station
   Thou set'st; and throw'st them down to desolation:
   How in a moment they
   Are desolate, cease and perish in dismay.
20 As a dream when slumber flies,
   Thou, Lord, wilt waking their vain show despise.
21 In all this, when my spleen
   Was roused, and stung my very heart has been.
22 How ignorant and blind
   I was before thee and of brutish mind!
23 Yet thou dost by me stand
   Ever, and upholdest me with thy right hand.
24 Thou wilt with counsel me
   Guide, and receive hereafter gloriously.
25 For whom have I above
   But thee? none else upon the earth I love.
26 When faint my flesh and heart,
   Thou, God, my portion ever and heart's rock art.
27 Lo! they shall die, that loathe
   Thy face, thou smitest all who break thy troth.
28 But unto me God's face
   Is dear, my trust in God the Lord I place.
   So shall I in the gate
   Of Zion's daughter aye thy works narrate.

Psalm LXXIV.

1 Why, God. dost thou abhor us? why incensed
  Is aye thy wrath against
2 The flock out of thy pastures? Think once more
  On whom thou'st bought of yore,
  Thy company, the tribes redeem'd by thee,
  Thine heritage to be.
  Remember yon Mount Zion, where thou hast
  Of yore thy dwelling placed;
3 Set foot on soil for ever and aye laid waste.
  Thy haters with all outrages have come
  Within thy halidom.
4 Thy foes rage in thy precincts, and set high
  Their flags to muster by.
5 They seemed as those that up with axes go
  To lay the thick woods low,
6 When all the carv'd work of the roof by stroke
  Of hammer and wedge they broke.
7 They fired thy sanctuary, they felled with shame
  The residence of thy name.
8 They said within their hearts, "destroy all round;"
  They've burnt unto the ground
9 God's holy places through the land. And we
  No more our tokens see;
  There is no prophet left; there's none with us
  That knoweth, how long thus?
10 How long shall foes blaspheme? shall haters shame
   For ever, O God, thy name?
11 Why draw'st thou back thy hand? nay, draw thy right
   Out from thy breast, and smite?

12 God is my King of old; from him come forth
All succors done on earth.

13 Thou partedst by thy might the sea; thou didst
Break in the waters' midst
14 The dragons' heads; Leviathan's head thou clavest,
And all for meat him gavest
15 To the desert dwellers. Thou didst from the rock
Fountain and flood unlock.
16 Thou driedst up the waterfloods of might.
Day is thine, thine is night;
Thou hast the sun appointed, and the light.
17 The bounds of earth are of thy 'stablishing;
Thou makest Fall and Spring.
18 Remember, Lord, how enemies put to shame,
How fools contemn thy name.
19 O give not of thy turtle-dove the soul
Up to that rout's control;
And let the poor and lowly folk be not
Always by thee forgot.
20 Regard thy covenant, for with grim abodes
Earth her dark places loads.
21 Let not the humble be sent back with shame,
Let rather to thy Name
The poor and lowly glad thanksgivings frame.
22 Up, God, and strive thy strife; recall what scorn
From caitiffs thou hast borne
Each day; forget not of thy foes the cry,
Thy rivals' uproar swelling ever and aye.

Psalm LXXV.

1 We give thee thanks, O God; we glorify
  Thy name, who art so nigh:
2 Thy marvels speak it. When mine hour I take,
  Just judgments I will make.
3 The earth is fall'n to wreck, and all her dwellers;
  'Tis I uphold her pillars.
4 Rave not, I bid the lewd; let not your horn,
  Ye wicked, high be borne.
5 Lift not your horn on high, and speak not ye
  With neck set frowardly.
6 For not from north or south, from west or east,
  Is state to men increased.
7 For God is judge; he maketh one on high
  To rise, one low to lie.
8 For in the Lord God's hand there is a cup,
  With ruby wine filled up.
  He poureth—all the wicked of earth shall quaff
  And drink the dregs thereof.
9 But I for ever will make known and laud
  With music Jacob's God.
10 The horns o' th' wicked I will low down thrust,
  And raise up high the just.

Psalm LXXVI.

1 In Judah God is known, his name is well
  Renowned in Israel.
2 In Salem is the tabernacle of God,
  In Zion his abode.

3 He brake the arrows of the bow, the spear.
 Buckler, and battle there.
4 Glorious and strong! no power, which thine excels,
 On th' hills of rapine dwells.
5 The stout of heart are spoiled; in their deep
 Trance they are laid asleep.
 Of all the men of might not one had still
 To lift his hand the skill.
6 At thy rebuke, O God of Jacob, horse
 And chariot sank perforce.
7 Thou, O 'tis thou art dread; and who the brunt
 Of thy wrath's day shall front?
8 From heav'n thou makest us thy judgment hear,
 And earth is hushed with fear,
9 When God to judgment riseth, and the poor
 On earth to make secure.
10 The wrath of man shall praise thee, when thou hast
 Of wrath assumed thy last.
11 O all ye round him, to your God the Lord
 Vow, and fulfil your word.
12 Bring gifts to the dread One; he of princes brings
 The breath low; he is fearful to the earth her kings.

Psalm LXXVII.

1 I cry, my cry imploreth God, and he
 Will hearken unto me.
2 I seek the Lord, when in distress I stand,
 I stretch by night my hand,
 Which is not wearied out; my soul to look
 On comfort will not brook.

3 I think on God, and am perturbed; I muse,
  And all my spirits lose.
4 Thou dost mine eyes hold waking; I am tost
  With pain, and speech have lost.
5 I muse upon the by-gone days, and years
  Of ancient eld rehearse.
6 I call to mind my songs, and by night waking,
  With mine heart counsel taking,
7 I ask myself, Will always God abhor,
  Will he bear us love no more?
8 Doth for aye cease his bounty? fails his word
  From sires to sons averred?
9 Hath God forgotten to show mercy? hath
  He shut pity up in wrath?
10 Nay, I must bear my scourge—but mark the years,
   I think, in which great God's right hand appears!

11   I call to mind the Lord's acts, and from days
   Of yore thy wondrous ways.
12 I muse on all thy works; I fix my thought
   On the deeds thou hast wrought.
13 O God, thy way is holiness! what god
   Is so great as our God?
14 Thou art the God dost wonders, and thy might
   Show'st in all nations' sight.
15 Thou hast by thine own arm thy people freed,
   Jacob and Joseph's seed.
16 Thee, God, the waters saw, the waters saw,
   And fell in throes with awe.
17 The deep flood shook, the clouds their waters poured,
   The welkin's voices roared.
18 Thine arrows flew abroad, thy thunder's peal,

Came on the whirlwind's wheel.
Thy lightnings lit the world; the earth gan shake,
The earth did shudder and quake.
19 Thy ways were on the seas, thy paths upon
The manifold waters, and thy tracks unknown—
20 Thou didst thy people, like a flock of sheep,
By Moses' hand and Aaron's, guide and keep.

Psalm LXXVIII.

1 Attend, O people mine; my precept hear;
To my mouth's words give ear.
2 I will unclose my life to utter lore,
And tales obscure of yore,
3 Which we have heard and learn'd, and which our own
Fathers to us have shown;
4 We will not hide them from their sons, nor from
The races yet to come,
But will Jehovah's praises and his might
And wondrous acts recite.
5 For he his testimony in Jacob raised,
His law in Israel placed,
6 That these in after-time they might declare
To every unborn heir,
That such might rise, and teach their children yet
Their hopes in God to set,
7 And not to let God's works forgotten rest—
But cleave to his behest,
8 Not being, as their fathers were, a froward
Generation, and untoward,
Whose hearts were not establish'd, but unsound
With God their minds were found,

9 Like Ephraim's sons who, arm'd and bearing bows,
  Turned in the battle's close.
10 Lo! they refused to walk by God's behest,
  His covenant they transgressed,
11 His works forgetting and what wonders he
  Had granted them to see.
12 In Mizraim to their sires, in Zoan's field
  What marvels he revealed!
13 He cleft the seas; he reared, that they might pass,
  The waters in a mass.
14 He guided them with cloud by day, with light
  Of fire throughout the night,
15 He clove the rock in desert-land; they quaffed
  As from the floods their draught.
16 He made the hard rock give out streams, and shed
  Water, as a river's head.
17 Yet all the more they sinned, and the most High
  Vexed in that desert dry.
18 They from their hearts God tempted, asking meat
  After their soul's conceit.
19 They spake against him, saying, Can God command
  A table in desert land?
20 In truth he smote the rock, and waters flowed;
  Yea, rivers gushed abroad.
  But can he food bestow? can he provide
  His people flesh beside?
21 This heard the Lord, and was provoked by it;
  Fire in his heart was lit
  Against the sons of Jacob, and against
  Israel he was incensed,
22 Because they had not God believed, nor laid
  Their trust upon his aid—

23 Who his command to the clouds above had given,
   And oped the doors of heaven,
24 And show'red upon them manna down, and wheat
   Of heavenly grain to eat.
25 On bread of princes each had fed, and game
   He sent them at their claim.
26 He stirred in heaven the east-wind, and his force
   Impelled the south wind's course,
27 And flesh like dust, and feathered fowl he rained,
   Thick as the sea-beat sand.
28 Such in the midmost of their camp he sent,
   Round about every tent.
29 Thereof they ate, and were sufficed; and each
   His heart's desire did reach.
30 They failed not of their lusts; and while the food
   Yet in their mouths was chewed,
31 The wrath of God amidst them rose, and slew
   The chiefest of their crew.
32 Yet sinned they all the more, nor him believed
   For marvels they perceived.
33 Therefore their days in weariness, their years
   He brought to an end in fears.
34 What time he slew them, they implored him; they
   Sought God at break of day.
35 They called to mind then God their rock to deem,
   Their rescuer the Supreme.
36 Yet only with false lips they him beguiled;
   Their flattering tongues they filed,
37 And faithless to his covenant and unsound
   At heart with him were found.
38 But he is pitiful, and doth sin remit,
   And not destroy for it.

39 And oft did he withdraw his wrath, not make
His whole displeasure wake;
40 Remembering, that they were but flesh—a blast
That bloweth and is past.
41 How oft i' th' wilderness rebelled they, and
Vexed him in desert land,
And tempted God, and Israel's Holy One
Grieved ever and anon !
42 They minded not his hand, that day, when he
From their foe set them free,
43 What time his signs in Mizraim he revealed,
Portents in Zoan's field.
44 He changed their waters, so that nought but blood
Was drawn from fount or flood.
45 He sent among them flies, a ravaging brood,
And frogs, to taint their food.
46 He gave up unto locusts all their germs,
Their labor's fruits to worms.
47 He killed their vines with hailstones, and with blight
Their fig-trees did he smite.
48 Their cattle over to the hail were given,
Their herds to the burning levin.
49 He sent on them the fierceness of his wrath,
Fury and rage and scath ;
He sent by messengers of bale that message ;
50 He gave his wrath free passage ;
He spared not, but gave up their souls to death,
To plagues their lively breath.
51 He smote in Mizraim the first-born, inside
Ham's tents their flower and pride.
52 His people he led forth like a flock, and through
The wastes like sheep them drew.

53 He brought them safe and fearless, and bade close
    The sea above their foes.
54 To the limits of his holy soil he brought them,
    To the hill his right hand bought them.
55 He drove the Gentiles out before their face,
    He portioned them their place
    With measuring lines, and gave to Israel
    In heathen tents to dwell.
56 Still they the high God tempted, and rebelled,
    Nor by his covenant held.
57 They fell back as their fathers that had lied,
    As a false bow springs aside.
58 They grieved him with high places, and against
    Their idols him incensed.
59 God heard, and was displeasured, and a sore
    Anger toward Israel bore.
60 He left his tent at Shiloh and the abode
    Where among men dwelt God.
61 He gave their strength up unto thraldom, and
    Power to the enemy's hand.
62 He gave his people to the sword, and rage
    Loosed on his heritage.
63 In fires their young men fainted; they led forth
    No maid with bridal mirth.
64 Their priests fell by the sword; their widows keeping
    No rites of solemn weeping.
65 Then from his sleep the Lord woke, as the rousing
    Of strong men from carousing,
66 And smote his enemies in the rear, to shame
    For ever and aye their name.
67 Then shunned he Joseph's tent, and Ephraïm
    Found grace no more with him;

68 But Judah's tribe he chose, and Zion's height
  Found favour in his sight.
69 He built his sanctuary, like heav'n on high,
  Like earth set fast for aye.
70 He chose his servant David from among
  Sheepcotes, by ewes with young,
71 E'en that his people Jacob he might feed,
  His heirs of Israel's seed.
72 So them with faithful heart he shepherded,
  And with discreet hands led.

Psalm LXXIX.

1 O God, on thine inheritance have come
  The hosts of heathendom;
  Thy holy fane's profaned; Jerusalem
  In ruins laid by them.
2 The corpses of thy servants they have given
  To feed the fowls of heaven;
  The flesh of thy believers is thrown forth
  To all the beasts on earth.
3 Their blood like water is all round about
  Jerusalem poured out,
4 And no man buries them. We have the scorn
  Of all our neighbours borne,
  From all men round reproach and contumely.
5 Lord God, how long wilt be
  So wroth against us? Shall thy jealous ire
  Burn like perpetual fire?
6 Rather, on each Thee not-confessing nation
  Pour forth thine indignation,

And on those kingdoms, that would heretofore
Never thy name adore;
7 For Jacob they've devoured, and desolation
Made of his habitation.
8 Remember not our olden sins; but speed,
Prevent with pity our need.
9 Lord God, our safeguard, for thy name's renown
Help us, low sinking down;
Deliver us, our transgressions expiate,
And thy name vindicate!
10 Why should the Gentiles say, Where is their God?
Send in our sight abroad
Thy vengeance upon all the heathens' guilt,
Thy servants' blood who spilt.
11 Let to thy presence come the prisoner's sigh,
Save the condemn'd to die
12 Through thy great power, and cause our neighbors' scorn,
Whereby they did thee scorn,
Sevenfold unto themselves to be restored,
Back in their bosoms poured.
13 So we, thy people, and thy pasture's sheep,
Thee worshipping will keep
World without end, and make thy praises known
From father down to son.

Psalm LXXX.

1 Give ear, who Israel feedest!
Thou shepherd, who the sons of Joseph leadest.
2 Come radiant, thou that sit'st
The wings of throning cherubim amidst.

3 Arouse for us thy might
  In Ephraim, Benjamin, Manasseh's sight;
  Draw near and save. Restore us, God, and give
  Light from thy face, that rescued we may live.

4   Lord God of hosts, against
  Thy people's prayer how long wilt be incensed?
5 Thou makest them on tears
  To feed, and largely drink from cups of tears.
6 Thou mak'st us a division
  Amongst our neighbors, and our foes' derision.
7 Restore us, God of hosts; let thy face give
  Light back to us, that rescued we may live.

8   Thou didst from Mizraim bring
  A vine: thou didst aloof the Gentiles fling.
9 Thou'st planted her and till'd
  All round, that striking root the land she filled.
10 Her shade enwrapped the broad
  Hillsides, her shoots the cedar-groves of God.
11 Her branches to the sea,
  Her boughs to the great river extended she.
12 Why didst thou break her fence,
  That all way-wandering wights might pilfer thence?
13 The wildwood boar his feast
  There makes; there browses every moorland beast.
14 Turn, God of hosts, we pray,
  Look, gaze from heaven, and this thy vine survey,
15 Thine hand's own plant, the branch
  That thou mad'st whilom for thyself so stanch.
16 Laid waste with fire, hewn down,
  Her scions perish in thy aspect's frown.

17 Lay help upon thy right
   Hand's child, the child of man, whom thou with might
   Didst for thyself array.
   So will we turn from thee no more away.
18 O quicken us once more,
   And we for ever will thy name adore.
19 Restore us, God of hosts; let thy face give
   Light back to us, and rescued we shall live.

Psalm LXXXI.

1 Lift unto God our strength, lift to rejoice
   In Jacob's God your voice.
2 Awake the psalm, bring lute and tabret hither,
   And pleasant harp together.
3 Blow at new moon the trumpet, when our great
   Feast-day we celebrate.
4 For this to Israel is a statute, and
   To Jacob God's command.
5 This testimony in Joseph he commenc'd,
   When God the land of Mizraim went against.

   I hear the voice of one unknown. Saith God—
6 I eased his hands from bearing of the hod,
   His shoulders from the load.
7 Thou hast my help in hour of trouble craved,
   And I have heard and saved;
   To thee from bower of thunders I replied,
   Thee at the waters of debate I tried—
8 Hear, O my people; I will plead with thee;
   Israel, give ear to me.

9 No alien god must bide with thee, nor thou
   To unknown idols bow.
10 I am the Lord thy God, by whom thou hast
   The bounds of Mizraim passed.
   Spare not to open wide thy mouth; for I
   Will freely satisfy.

11   Yet did my tribes to hear my voice not choose,
   Israel did me refuse.
12 So to their hearts' lusts I resigned them; they
   Walked their own evil way.
13 If but my tribes obeyed, if Israel could
   Unto my paths be wooed,
14 I soon would quell their tyrants, and oppose
   My hand against their foes.
15 Then the Lord's haters should feigned homage give,
   But these for aye should live;
16 And I would feed them with fine flour, and fill
   With honey, that the flinty rocks distill.

Psalm LXXXII.

1 God standeth in the council of the strong,
   Judge o'er the godlike throng!
2 How long unjustly will ye judge, and grace
   Yield to the wicked's face?
3 Judge ye the orphans and the weak; assure
   Of right the friendless poor.
4 Save ye the weak and helpless, and withstand
   For them the oppressor's hand—
5 They know not, they regard him not, they will
   In darkness walk on still.

The mainprops of the world are all infirm.
6 I called them by the term
Of gods. Ye are the sons of God most High,
E'en all of you, said I ;
7 Yet shall ye perish now like men, and fall
Like the world's princes all.—
8 Rise, God, and judge the earth ; for unto thee
Must the inheritance o'er the nations be.

Psalm LXXXIII.

1 Hold not, O God, thy peace : thyself restrain
No more, nor mute remain.
2 For lo! thy enemies murmur; they lift high
Their heads, who thee defy.
3 They take hid counsel 'gainst thy people, they
Plots for thy prized ones lay.
4 They cry. Come let us rase them from the score
Of nations evermore ;
That in remembrance may no longer dwell
The name of Israel.
5 They counsel with one heart, and to unite
Against thee pledge their plight—
6 The tents of Edom with the Ishmaelites,
Hagarenes, Moabites,
7 Burghers of Tyre, Ammonites, Philistim,
Gebal, Amalekim.|
8 With them is Asshur, and his arm is not
Withheld the sons of Lot.
9 Do unto them, as thou hast done amidst
Midian ; yea, that thou didst

      To Sisera and to Jabin in the slaughters
      By Kishon's running waters.
10 (They sank at Endor, and became as dung
      Which o'er the ground is flung.)
11 As Oreb and as Zeb, so let them fall,
      They and their princes all.
      Like Zeba, like unto Salmunna, set
      Every their potentate,
12 Who said, Come let us take, to leave our sons,
      God's habitations.
13 Set on them, God, a whirlwind; make them like
      Straws, that the storm shall strike.
14 As when the fire consumes the forest thick,
      As flames the mountains lick,
15 So with thy hurricane persecute them; make
      Them in thy tempest quake.
15 Their faces, O Jehovah, fill with shame;
      And let them seek thy name.
17 Make them confounded, and a scorn for aye,
      And abject let them die.
18 That, as Jehovah is thy name alone,
      To be the world's supreme thou may'st be known.

Psalm LXXXIV.

1 How lovely is the place of thine abode,
      O Lord, of Hosts the God.
2 My soul doth long and pine to have resort
      Unto Jehovah's court,
      That there my flesh and heart to the ever-living
      God may return thanksgiving.

3 Lo! the bird finds a home, the swallow a nest,
   In which her brood may rest.
   They to thine altars, Lord of Hosts, take wing,
   E'en thine, my God and King.
4 Blessed who dwell within thy house, who thee
   Shall praise perpetually.
5 Blessed that man, whose strength thou art; whose mind
   Is bent thy roads to find.
6 For such, when through the vale of tears they go,
   Shall founts of waters flow;
   With early rain shall every spring be fed.
7 From strength to strength they'll tread,
   Yea, and in Zion every one shall near
   The God of gods appear.
8 Lord God of hosts, O God of Jacob, lend
   Ear, and my prayer perpend.
9 Look down, O God of hosts, and scan with grace
   Thine own anointed's face—
10 Thou, in whose courts one day is better far
   Than a thousand others are—
   I love less, in the tents of guilt to sleep,
   Than God's house-door to keep.
11 For our Lord God's a sun and shield; the Lord
   Doth honor and grace afford.
   To those that walk uprightly on their way
   No good will he gainsay.
12 O Lord of hosts, blessed that man shall be
   Who sets his trust in thee.

Psalm LXXXV.

1 Lord, mercy toward thy land
  Thou'st showed; thou'st led back Israel's captive band.
2 Thy people's guilt thou didst
  Forgive, and all their trespass from thee hid'st.
3 Thou didst upgather all
  Thine anger, and thy burning wrath recall.
4 Turn, God of our salvation,
  Withdraw from us again thine indignation.
5 Shall ne'er against us end
  Thine ire? shall wrath from sires to sons extend?
6 Wilt thou us not restore
  To life, and glad thy people in thee once more?
7 Show us thy mercy, Lord,
  And unto us thy saving health accord.
8 Hark! I the word will seek
  Of the Lord God, for peace he will forespeak
  His people and saints, that they
  May never swerve again toward folly's way.
9 O help is near beside
  His fearers; glory upon our land shall bide.
10 Truth meeteth face to face
  With mercy; peace and righteousness embrace.
11 Truth blossoms out of earth,
  And from the heavens doth righteousness look forth.
12 Welfare to us the Lord
  Grants, and her fulness shall the land accord.
  Lo! righteousness precedes
  His face, and forward on his pathway leads.

Psalm LXXXVI.

1 Incline thine ear, Lord, and to me give heed,
Who stand in straits and need.
2 Preserve my soul, which is thy worshipper,
And save thy servitor,
3 Who trust in thee, my God. Vouchsafe me, Lord,
Thy grace, all day implored.
4 Make glad, (for unto thee I lift my soul,)
O God, thy servant's soul.
5 For thou'rt good, Lord, and placable—full of grace
To all who seek thy face.
6 Lord, hearken to mine orison; give ear
At the voice of my prayer.
7 'Tis in my day of need to thee I cry,
For thou wilt sure reply.
8 There is none like thee 'mid the gods; not one,
Lord, who such works hath done.
9 All nations—for thou madest them—to thee
Shall come, Lord, and their knee
Shall bend before thy countenance, and proclaim
The glory of thy name.
10 For thou art great, and thou dost wondrously;
There is no God save thee.
11 Lord, show to me thy path, and I will lay
My steps upon thy way.
Make firm my heart, that I may persevere
To walk in thy name's fear.
12 I'll praise thee, Lord my God, with all my soul,
And aye thy name extol.

13 For toward me great thy mercy was, to save
　　My soul from lowlaid grave.
14 O God, the proud have arms against me reared;
　　The throng of men much feared
　　Are bent upon my life: thine awe do they
　　Before their eyes not lay.
15 But thou, Lord, art a God of pity and ruth,
　　Plenteous in grace and truth,
　　And slow to anger. Turn on me thy face,
　　And show again thy grace.
16 Unto thy slave, the child of thy bondmaid,
　　Grant of thy strength and aid.
17 Some gracious signal let me meet from thee,
　　Whereby my foes may see,
　　Lord, that thou wilt support and comfort me.

Psalm LXXXVII.

1 Her foundations
2 Are on the sacred hills; the Lord above
　　All Jacob's habitations
　　Doth the gates of Zion love.
3 Many, many a weighty word,
　　City of our God, to thy renown is heard.
4 I have noted
　　Rahab and Babylon to compeers of mine;
　　Tyre and Cush I have quoted,
　　And the land of Palestine.
　　Lo! there were such born there.
5 And men shall say of Zion, such was born in her.

> The most High will defend us,
> The Lord, i' th' count of nations, will commend us,
> For who was born in her.
> 6 The singers and the minstrels answering, We
> Have all our founts in thee.

Psalm LXXXVIII.

> 1 O Lord God of my weal, to thee do I
> By day and night-time cry.
> 2 Let come to thee my prayer, let to my plea
> Thine ear inclinèd be.
> 3 For sorrows fill my soul, my life doth sink
> To the grave's edge and brink.
> 4 As one laid in the pit I am esteemed,
> Devoid of force I'm deemed,
> 5 Strown mid the dead, like men with mortal wound
> Fall'n, slumbering under ground,
> Who dwell no more in thy remembrance, and
> Are sundered from thy hand.
> 6 Thou'st laid me in the pit, the gulf beneath,
> Darkness, the shadow of death.
> 7 Thy wrath against me presseth; heavily all
> Thy breakers on me fall.
> 8 Thou keep'st aloof all my familiars; thou
> Mak'st them abhor me now.
> I am shut fast, I cannot abroad make way,
> 9 Mine eyes through grief decay.
> Yet daily unto thee, O Lord, I cry,
> Lifting mine hands on high.

10 Wilt thou show wonders to the dead? wilt raise
   The extinct, uttering praise?
11 Shall the pit bruit thy mercy, or nothingness
   Divulge thy faithfulness?
12 Shall night thy marvels, or the lackthought land
   Thy justice understand?
13 Nay, now I call thee, Lord; my voice makes way
   Toward thee at dawn of day.
14 Why, Lord, hast thou forsaken me, and why
   Turnest away thine eye?
15 I'm feeble and outspent; I bear thy fears,
   Trembling, since childish years.
16 Thy wrath has o'er me swept, thy terrors me
   Have urged incessantly.
17 They have encompassed me like water, they
   Close round me every day.
18 Thou'st hid my kith and kindred from me quite—
   My friends, as with deep night.

Psalm LXXXIX.

1 Aye will I sing the mercies of the Lord;
   His truth I will record
2 From age to age: saying, Beyond all term
   Thy grace is planted firm.
   Thou 'stablishest the heavens, thou dost like these
   Maintain thy promises.
3 "I to my chosen servant gave my troth,
   To David swore this oath;
4 His seed for ever I will uphold, his throne
   From father unto son."

5 Let now the heavens the Lord's achievements boast,
  His truth their hallowed host.
6 For what mate hath the Lord in heaven? what peers
  In the sons of the spheres?
7 God is in the holy ones' great host revered,
  By all those round him feared.
8 Lord God of Hosts, in strength what peer is found thee,
  In truth tow'rd all around thee?
9 Thou rulest in the raging sea; the riot
  Of its waves thou dost quiet.
10 Thou clavest Rahab like a corpse; thy foes
  Thy powerful arm o'erthrows.
11 The heavens are thine, the earth is thine; thou hast
  The world's base founded fast.
12 Thou madest north and south; Tabor thy name
  And Hermon shall proclaim.
13 Thine is the arm of strength, thy hand has might;
  Yea, mastery has thy right.
14 Judgment and justice hold thy throne up; grace
  And truth precede thy face.
15 Blessed the people, who know thy trumpet's signs,
  Whose path thy face beshines.
16 These in thy name, O Lord God, triumph aye;
  Thy justice lifts them high.
17 For sure, the splendor of their might art thou;
  Thy grace uplifts their brow.
18 Sure the Lord is our shield, our King is none
  But Israel's Holy One.
19 Thou hast in visions thy believer told;
  Thou hast declared of old—
20 I've lifted up my chosen from the throng;
  I've laid help on the strong.

David, my servant, I have him appointed,
    With holy oil anointed;
21 Him shall my hand desert not; him will I
    With mine arm fortify.
22 His foes shall not prevail, nor doers of ill
    Exact from him their will.
23 His enemies from his face I will o'erthrow,
    And thrust his haters low.
24 My truth and grace shall keep him; high his horn
    Shall in my name be borne.
25 His hand upon the sea, his right where flows
    The river, I will repose.
26 He shall to me as sire and God appeal,
    As safeguard of his weal.
27 And as my first-born I will set him forth
    High'st 'mid the kings of earth.
28 My mercies I'll reserve him aye, and fast
    My league with him shall last.
29 A seed perpetual I will give him, and
    A throne, like heaven to stand.
30 If then his children from my law shall swerve,
    My judgments not observe,
31 My statutes if they violate, if they will
    Not my behests fulfill,
32 I with a rod their sin, with chastisements
    Will visit their offence;
33 But not yet cast them from my mercy's pale,
    Nor cause my truth to fail.
34 I will not break my covenant, nor undo
    What hath my lips gone through,
35 Once by my holiness have I sworn, and I
    To David will not lie.
36 His seed shall stand for ever, his throne before

The sun's face evermore ;
37 Like as the moon, and as that witness sure
   In heaven it shall endure.
38 But thou'st despised and loathed us : thou'rt against
   Thy 'nointed one incensed.
39 Thou hast thy servant's covenant trodden down,
   Profaned in dust his crown.
40 Thou'st broken all his walls ; thou hast effaced
   And laid his bulwarks waste.
41 All that pass by have robbed him ; he hath borne
   His neighbors' general scorn.
42 Thou'st given triumph to his enemy, and
   Advanced his hater's hand.
43 Thou'st brought his sword's edge back, and made to yield
   His front i' th' battle-field.
44 Thou hast made dim his glory ; thou hast thrust
   His throne down in the dust.
45 His days of youth thou hast cut short, and bound
   With shame his temples round.
46 How long, Lord ? wilt for aye thy face retire,
   Thy wrath burning like fire ?
47 Remember thou my frailness ; hast thou then
   In mockery made all men ?
48 What man shall live, and see not death, and save
   His soul from grasping grave ?
49 Where are thy mercies, Lord, o' th' days outworn,
   Thy truth to David sworn ?
50 Remember, Lord, thy servant's shame—the scorn
   Of many, that I have borne—
51 The contumely, that foes, thy foes, have done
   To thy anointed One.

Blessed be the Lord for evermore.   Amen and amen.

Psalm XC.

1 From race of men to race
   Thou hast, O Lord, been our abiding-place.
2 Before the hills had birth,
   Or ever thou hadst formed the world and earth;
   From all time heretofore,
   Thou art God, and to all time evermore.
3 Thou bring'st mankind to death;
   Thou sayst, Return, children of man, to breath.
4 A thousand years pass by
   As yesterday, as a night-watch in thine eye.
5 Thou causest them to stream
   Onwards—as transient as a sleep they seem,
   Or as the grass's prime,
6 That groweth and is green at morning time,
   And is cut down, and fades,
   And shrivels up before the evening shades.

7   We in thine anger pine,
   We are consumed with parching wrath of thine.
8 Thou keep'st our guilt in sight,
   Our youth's offences in thy aspect's light.
9 Our days come to a close
   In thy displeasure; yea, as breath that goes,
   Do we consume our years.
10 The days we live are ten and threescore years;
   And tho' some men attain
   To fourscore, 't is but weariness and pain:
   For outworn is their might,
   And hast'neth to depart, and we take flight.

11 Who knows of thy displeasure
   The power? who can thy wrath, thy terrors measure?
12 Teach us to count our days,
   So that our hearts to wisdom we may raise.

13   How long? nay! turn thee tow'rd
   Thy servants, and repent thyself, O Lord.
14 Betimes with grace upraise
   Our hearts, and make thou glad and blithe our days.
15 For all our days of tears
   Rejoice us, and for sorrow-visited years.
16 Before thy servants show
   Thy works, and let their sons thy splendor know:
17 Yea, let the Lord God's favor
   Be shown us, and support our hands' endeavor:
   Support our hands' endeavor.

Psalm XCI.

1 He that with God most high
   Takes shelter, in the Almighty's shade shall lie.
2 Thou art, O Lord, I've cried,
   My trust, my fort, my God in whom I confide.
3 Sure he from hunter's snare
   Shall guard thee, and from fell contagious air.
4 He shall his wings wide over
   Thee spread, and with his pinions make thy cover.
   His faithfulness to thee
   A shield and buckler round about shall be.
5 No fear shall thee dismay
   That walks by night, or shaft that flies by day.

6 No plague in the dark hours
   Ranging, nor havoc that by noon devours.
7 When thousands near thee, when
   At thy right hand shall fall ten thousand men,
   Yet shall it reach not thee.
8 Thou shalt but with thine eyes a witness be
   The ungodly's doom to see.

9   "Thou, Lord, art my defence;"
   Thou makest the most High thy confidence.
10 There shall no harm approach
   Thine head, nor plague upon thy tent encroach.
11 For he'll commandment lay
   On his angels, thee to guard in all thy way.
12 They shall beneath thee put
   Their arms, lest with a stone thou strike thy foot.
13 Thou shalt on lion's head,
   On snake, and lion's whelp, and dragon tread.
14 For who hath loved me, I
   Will him deliver; I will raise him high,
   That doth my name revere.
15 He shall implore me, and I will give ear:
   I will in troublous days
   Stand by, and save him, and to sure height raise
16 With length of days shall he
   Be satisfied, and on his enemies see
   His wish fulfilled by me.

Psalm XCII.

1 'Tis good the Lord to praise,
　And melody to thy name, most High, to raise;
2 Thy bounties to recite
　Betimes at morning, and thy truth each night,
3 With lute, with tenfold lyre,
　With harp, and in symphonious sacred choir.
4 For thou, Lord, glad'st me by
　Thy deeds, and in thy hand's work triumph I.
5 What great acts hast thou wrought!
　How deep, exceeding deep, Lord, is thy thought!
6 The churlish will not know,
　The foolish will not understand it so.
7 The wicked, when they spring
　As grass, the doers of wrong when flourishing,
　Shall be for aye o'erthrown,
8 While thou, Lord, keepest thy perpetual throne.
9 For see! thy foes shall die,
　Lord God, the doers of wrong shall scattered fly.
10 But, like the unicorn,
　I'll with fresh oil anointed lift mine horn.
11 Mine eye shall see, mine ear
　Mine adversaries' recompense shall hear.
12 Sure, like a palm shall grow
　The upright, and as Lebanon cedars show.
13 In our God's house their root
　Planted, in our God's court they shall bear fruit :
14 They shall in age be green;
　Vigorous and full of sap they shall be seen,
15 To prove how just thou art,
　O Lord, my strength, in whom wrong hath no part.

Psalm XCIII.

1 The Lord is King, the Lord hath done
His glorious raiment on :
The Lord hath donned his raiment bright,
And girds himself with might.

2   Firm rests, and cannot rock the earth :
Or ever she had birth,
Thou 'stablishedst thy throne on high :
Thou, Lord, art ever and aye.

3   The floods have risen, with all their noise :
The floods have lift their voice.
The springs o' th' deep have burst their caves ;
The floods have lift their waves.

4   The floods, let loud their uproar be :
Let rage the weltering sea :
The Lord is mightier, that on high
Is throned ever and aye.

5   Thy testimonies, Lord, are sure :
Thy temple doth endure,
Adorned ever with her dress,
The beauty of holiness.

Psalm XCIV.

1 Lord God of vengeances,
Be manifest, thou Lord of vengeances.
2 Judge of the world, display
Thyself, and to the proud their meed repay.

3 How long shall wicked men,
 O Lord, how long shall triumph wicked men?
4 Their speech o'erflows with hate,
 The evil doers with proud words debate.
5 Thy people they oppress,
 O Lord, they thine inheritance distress.
6 The widow and orphan they
 Destroy, and of the stranger make their prey.
7 The Lord will not aread,
 They cry, the God of Jacob takes no heed.

8 Consider, men most blind
 And fond, if yet reproof can reach your mind.
9 Shall he not see nor hear,
 Who the eye moulded, and who shaped the ear?
10 Shall he chastise not then,
 Who schools the Gentiles, who gives lore to men?
11 The Lord knows every thought
 Of man, though they with vanity be fraught.

12 Blessed the man, the Lord
 Reproves, and lessons in his law's accord,
13 In troublous times to save
 Him tranquil, till he delve the wicked's grave.
14 Behold, the Lord will ne'er
 His people quit, nor heritage forswear,
15 Till judgment walk again
 With right, and lead up all true-hearted men.

16 Who 'gainst the wicked will
 Stand by me, and confront the doers of ill?
17 Did not the Lord me save,
 My soul were sleeping, silenced in the grave.

18 My feet well-nigh gave way;
 But then, O Lord, thy mercy was my stay.
19 'Mid many griefs that tear
 My heart, thy comforts, Lord, my soul upbear.

20 Hast thou part in the sessions
 Of wrong, that 'gainst the law devise oppressions?
21 The just man's life by them
 Is hunted; they the innocent blood condemn.
22 The Lord my strong tower be,
 And mine own God a rock of trust to me.
23 Let him their guile repay,
 And let him all in their injustice slay;
 The Lord, our God, them slay.

Psalm XCV.

1 Come, let us utter a cry to the Lord, a shout of exultation
 To the rock of our salvation.
2 Let us approach in a grateful acclaim before him, loudly voicing
 A melody of rejoicing.
3 Truly the Lord is a mighty God, and a mighty ruler, far
 Above all the gods that are.
4 All hidden hollows of earth in his hand, and all the mountains' crests,
 Are under his behests.
5 His the sea is, to which he set a bourne; and all the dry main-land
 Was moulded by his hand.
6 Come we, come all to the face of the Lord, who made us, and adore him,
 And bow to kneel before him.
7 Sure God is our God; a people of his we are, the sheep he feedeth,
 Whoever his voice now heedeth.
8 "Harden your hearts not against me, as in the day of provocation,
 The day of my temptation,

K

9 When in the wilderness I was assayed; your fathers tempted me,
　And my great works did see,
10 Forty years long was I grievèd, and said, False-hearted sons are they,
　Who have not known my way.
11 Wherefore in anger an oath to them I recorded, that by none
　Should my repose be won."

Psalm XCVI.

1 Sing to the Lord a new song; let the whole
　Earth's hymn the Lord extol.
2 Sing to him, bless his name; his saving might
　From day to day recite.
3 Tell mid the Gentiles his renown, his grand
　Works in all heathen land.
4 For he is great and much to be revered,
　And above all gods feared.
5 For heathen gods are idols all; but he,
　The Lord, made heaven to be.
6 Worship and glory stand before his face;
　Splendor and might adorn his holy place.

7　Accord, ye nations' kindreds, to the Lord
　Honor and strength accord.
8 Accord him th' honor of his name; resort
　With gifts unto his court,
9 Adore the Lord, in holy pomp adore him;
　Let all earth quake before him.
10 Tell you the nations, the Lord reigns, who cast
　The world's foundations fast,
　That never shall be moved; the peoples he
　Will govern righteously.

11 Let heaven rejoice, let earth exult, let thunder
　　The seas, and their depths under.
12 Let the plains shout, and all that in them be;
　　Roar, every wildwood tree,
13 Before the Lord's face; for he is gone forth,
　　Is gone to judge the earth,
14 To judge the world in justice, and all nations
　　With righteous arbitrations.

Psalm XCVII.

1 The Lord is king; let earth
　　Exult, and let the many isles make mirth.
2 Darkness and cloud enfold
　　His presence; truth and right his throne uphold.
3 Out from before him goes
　　A fire, and round about consumes his foes.
4 His lightnings have revealed
　　The world; the earth beheld them, and she reeled.
5 As wax before the fire
　　Consumeth, so the mountain peaks retire
　　Before the Lord God's face,
　　Before the Lord of all the earth his face.
6 The heavens his equity
　　Proclaim; his glory now all nations see.
7 Now come they all to shame
　　Who idols make, or serve a false god's name.
　　Before him all gods bow.
8 Mount Zion heareth and rejoiceth now,
　　Yea, Judah's daughter raise
　　Their voice, thy judgments, O Lord God, to praise.

9 For thou, Lord, at the head
   Art of the whole world, and thee all gods dread.
10 O you, that love the Lord,
   Amongst you let all evil be abhorred.
   He guardeth of his friends
   The souls, and from the enemy them defends.
11 Now springeth up a light
   Unto the just, and joy to hearts upright.
12 Ye just men, in the Lord
   Joy, and with thanks his holiness record.

Psalm XCVIII.

1 Sing to the Lord a new song, for he has
  Brought wondrous things to pass.
  He hath deliverance wrought him with his right
  And his arm's hallowed might.
2 The Lord shows rescue and his judgments true
  In all the heathens' view.
3 His mercy and truth he has remembered well
  To the house of Israel;
  His saving power God, our God, hath showed forth
  To all the bounds of earth.
4 O all earth, shout you to the Lord; break out
  In concert with your shout.
5 Sound to the Lord your harps, with harps accord
  Your voices to the Lord.
6 Let loud, through peal of trumps, the cymbals ring,
  Before the Lord, the king.
7 Let the sea thunder and his swarms together,
  Earth, and her inmates with her.

8 Let the main rivers yield applause; let sound
  The mountain ridges round
9 Before the Lord's face; for he is gone forth
  To be the judge of earth;
  He'll judge aright the world; all peoples he
  Will judge with equity.

Psalm XCIX.

1 The Lord is king; let nations quake at him.
  Betwixt the cherubim
  He sits enthroned; let earth be awed thereby.
2 The Lord is great in Zion; high is he
  Above all heathenry.
3 Let men his dread and great name glorify:
  For He is holy and high.

4   The king's power loveth right; thou'st founded just
  Observances; thou dost
  In Jacob truth and judgment fortify.
5 Extol the Lord our God; fall down before
  His footstool and adore;
  For he is holy and high.

6   Moses and Aaron of his priesthood were;
  Those that invoked in prayer
  His name, had Samuel in their company.
7 They called on him: his ear to them he bowed;
  He spake in pillar of cloud.
  They kept his statutes, and the laws which he
  Did for their rule decree.

8 Thou heard'st them, Lord our God; thou wast to them
A God slow to condemn;
Yet didst thou their transgressions not pass by.
9 Extol the Lord our God; fall down before
His holy hill, and adore
The Lord our God, for he is holy and high.

Psalm C.

1, 2 Join in acclaim to the Lord, all earth, and joyfully serve ye the Lord;
And come before his face with glad accord.
3 Know of a surety the Lord to be God; he made us his own to be;
His people and his pasture's sheep are we.
4 Enter ye into his gates with a thanksgiving and with praise his court,
Give thanks, and of his name speak good report.
5 For the Lord truly is gracious, and aye are his mercies sure;
His promises from age to age endure.

Psalm CI.

1 Mercy and judgment I will sing;
Thine, Lord, my song shall be;
2 I trace the path of perfectness;
When wilt thou visit me?
Lo! I with perfectness of heart
Will guide me in my home;
3 I will not let before mine eyes
A thought of baseness come.
Deeds of backsliding men I hate;
None such to me shall cleave.

4 With froward hearts I'll make away,
   No guilt will I receive.
5 Whoe'er his neighbor slandereth
   In secret, I will quell;
   I will not suffer lofty eyes,
   Or hearts with pride that swell.
6 Mine eyes the faithful in the land
   Shall mark, to place them by me:
   The man that walks upright his way,
   Shall be my servant nigh me.
7 The worker of deceit within
   Mine house shall never dwell;
   Not one shall stand before mine eyes
   Of those who falsehoods tell.
8 Betimes I will be rooting out
   The guilty from the land,
   That in the city of God there may
   No evil doers stand.

Psalm CII.

1 Hear, Lord, my prayer; let my imploring be
   Admitted before thee.
2 Hide not thy face from me in hour of need;
   When thee I call, give heed.
3 Haste thou to answer me. My days consume
   Like a dissolving fume;
   My bones are parched as with a furnace blast;
4 My heart is sore downcast;
   My heart is dried up like a turf; my meat
   I do forget to eat.

5 My flesh is dried, and cleaveth to my bones,
   Worn out by stress of groans.
6 I am become, as a bittern in the waste,
   An owl, the ruins' guest.
7 I have kept watch, I stand from all aloof,
   Like a bird on the roof.
8 All day the ribalds mocked me; against me swore
   Those who grim hatred bore.
9 My bread hath savored ashes, and my cup
   With tears hath been filled up,
10 All through thy wrath and fury, thou that hast
   Upraised me, and downcast.
11 My days of prime are dwindled like a shade;
   Like parchèd grass I fade.
12 And thou, Lord, sit'st eterne, and thy renown
   Sire to son handeth down.
13 When wilt thou rise, and show to Zion grace?
   Time is come for thy grace;
14 Time is come now. On those her stones that strew
   The ground, thy servants rue:
   They call to mind the remnants of their city:
   And load their hearts with pity.

15   Let, Lord, the Gentiles fear thy name, let all
   Earth's kings thy glory appal,
16 When the Lord builds up Zion, when his splendor
   Apparent he shall render,
17 When toward the prayer of the forlorn he turns,
   And their plaint no more spurns.
18 Let this be writ for sons unborn, that days
   Far off the Lord may praise:
19 " From 's halidom on high the Lord looked forth,

From heaven to scan the earth,
20 To hear the captives' groans, alive to save
Those doomed unto the grave,"
21 That the Lord's name in Zion, and his glory
In Salem men may story,
22 When nations meet together, and in accord
Kingdoms, to serve the Lord.
23 To whom, should he bring down my strength midway—
Cut short my life—I'll say,
24 Take me not, ere my days be half gone by ;
Thy years are ever and aye.
25 Thou foundedst earth aforetime, and to heaven
Thy hands have structure given.
26 They perish ; thou continuest ; they are made
All, like a robe, to fade.
Aside thou dost them, like a vesture, throw,
And changed is all their show.
27 But thou the self-same art, and ne'er shall come
Thy years unto their sum.
28 Thy servants' children shall have welfare, and
Their seed possess the land.

Psalm CIII.

1 Bless, O my soul, the Lord ; let all my frame
Bless his most holy name.
2 Bless, O my soul, the Lord, and let thou not
His bounties be forgot ;
3 Who pardoneth all thy guilt ; whate'er in thee
Is frail, that healeth he ;

4 Who ransoms from the pit thy life; whose grace
   And pity thee embrace;
5 Who fills thy lot with goodness; who renews
   Thy youth like eagles' thewes;
6 The Lord, who justice doth and righteousness
   To them that men oppress;
7 Who showed his ways to Moses, and in sight
   Of Israel works of might.
8 Gracious and pitiful, slow to wrath, and stored
   With bounties is the Lord.
9 He will not alway strive, nor us regard
   Always with aspect hard.
10 He deals not with us after our offences,
   Nor our guilt recompenses.
11 As heaven is high from earth, so high to those
   That fear him, grace he shows.
12 As East is wide from West, he sunders thus
   Our trespasses from us.
13 As sire to son is ruthful, ruthful toward
   His fearers is the Lord.
14 For whence we're made, he knoweth; yea, that we
   Are dust, remembereth he.
15 The days of man are like the grass; he flowers
   As in the field the flowers,
16 Which, when the wind goes by them, are no more,
   Whose places them ignore.
17 But the Lord's mercy is from all time past,
   And through all time shall last
   Toward those that fear him, and from sires to sons
   His righteous dealing runs
18 To those who keep his covenant, and by deed
   His ordinances heed.

19   The Lord hath set his throne in heav'n, and his
   Realm over all that is.

20   Bless ye the Lord, all you his messengers,
   Ye powerful ministers,
   Who execute his word, who ready stand
   In wait for his command.
23 Bless ye the Lord, all you that serve him still,
   Ye hosts that work his will.
24 Bless ye the Lord, all creatures, in the whole
   Empire of his control,
   Bless ye the Lord; bless thou the Lord, my soul.

Psalm CIV.

1 Bless the Lord, O my soul:
   O Lord, my God, how vast is thy control!
   'Tis thou with majesty
2 And splendor art appareled; thou art he
   That is with light arrayed;
   Who like a curtain hath the heavens displayed;
3 Who spreadeth for his high
   Chambers a floor i' th' waters of the sky;
   Who doth of clouds prepare
   His car, and walketh on the wings of air;
4 Who maketh messengers
   Of winds, and flaming fires his ministers;
5 Who built the earth on fast
   Foundations, evermore unmoved to last.
6 Thou clad'st her with the flood
   Like a robe; mountain-high the waters stood.

7 At thy rebuke they fled,
　Before thy thunder's voice they were dismayed.
8 The hills arose, declined
　The dales; they found the place thou hadst assigned.
9 Thou gavest them the bourne
　They shall not pass, nor o'er the earth return.
10 Thou sendest forth in rills
　The water-founts, which gush betwixt the hills.
11 All beasts in field partake
　The runlets, and their thirst wild asses slake.
12 Birds of the welkin house
　Above them, uttering song amidst the boughs.
13 Thou from on high the hills
　Dost water; all the earth thy works' fruit fills.
14 Thou bringest grass up then
　For food of beasts, and corn for tilth of men;
15 That bread may from the earth
　Be raised, and wine, which fills the heart with mirth.
　So wine shall brighten more
　Than oil man's face, and bread his heart restore.
16 The Lord's trees have no scant
　Of sap; the Lebanon cedars thou didst plant.
17 Therein the small birds make
　Their nests, and to the pines the storks betake.
18 Wildgoats the high hill-side
　Inhabit, conies in the cliff confide.
19 Thou bidst the moon dispose
　Her periods, and the sun his rest-hour knows.
20 Thou makest darkness, yea,
　Nightfall, which rouses every beast of prey.
21 Then the whelp-lions roar
　For rapine, and from God their meat implore.
22 The day breaks, and they hie

Together away, and in their dens down lie.
23 Man to his labor goes,
   And to his tasks, until the evening close.
24 Thou, Lord, such works hast done,
   So manifold, and wisely every one.
   Thy riches fill the earth—
25 Yon sea too, great and broad on all sides forth.
   In which are gliding broods,
   Greater and smaller, countless multitudes.
26 There is the ships' resort,
   There thou hast made Leviathan to sport.
27 These all upon thee wait,
   And thou dost them with bread in season sate.
28 They snatch their granted food;
   Thy hand thou op'nest; they are filled with good.
29 Thou thy face hid'st; and they
   Are blasted; thou withdraw'st their breath away;
   And they expire, and must
   Their bodies render to connatural dust.
30 Thy breath thou sendest forth;
   They come to life; thou deck'st afresh the earth.
31 Thy splendor, Lord, shall be
   Perpetual, and thy works aye gladden thee.
32 The earth beneath thy look
   Trembleth; the hills thou touchest, and they smoke.
33 Thee, Lord, my song I'll give,
   Whilst I have breath, and melody whilst I live.
34 He sweetly shall employ
   My musings; in the Lord God I will joy.
35 The ungodly from the land
   Shall be consumed; the sinful shall not stand.
   Praise, O my spirit, praise
   The Lord. Your Hallelujahs to him raise.

Psalm CV.

1 Praise ye the Lord; his name
  Invoke; his deeds in heathendom proclaim.
2 Sing him with minstrelsy,
  Rehearse you all that he doth wondrously.
3 His hallowed name record
  With pride; let joy their hearts, who seek the Lord.
4 O seek the Lord; implore
  His powerful help; seek his face evermore;
5 His mighty works, and all
  His marvels, and his mouth's behests recall,
6 Ye that are Jacob's sons,
  His servant Abraham's seed, his chosen ones.
7 He is the Lord our God,
  His judgments all through earth are showed abroad.
8 His covenant holdeth fast;
  His word is for a thousand ages passed.
9 Lo! as he gave his troth
  To Abraham, and to Isaac swore an oath,
10 With Jacob he renewed
  His bond; his league eterne with Israel stood.
11 Saying, In Canaan live;
  To you the heritage of the land I give—
12 They being feeble then,
  Sojourners there, and easily numbered men.
13 What time they shifted place
  From land to land, from race to alien race,
14 From men he let them take
  No wrong; nay, kings rebuked he for their sake.

15 Touch not my prophets; do,
   He said, no scath to mine anointed crew.

16   When o'er the land he spread
     A famine, and broke all the staff of bread,
17 A forerunner he gave
   To them in Joseph, sold to be a slave,
18 Whose feet had fetters wrung,
   Whom irons even to the soul had stung,
19 Till for his cause the day
   Was come, when him the Lord's word should assay.
20 The king to loose him sent,
   The nation's lord gave him enfranchisement.
21 He made him ruler o'er
   His house, and steward over all his store,
22 So that his lords he should
   Bind, and his princes check, as seemed him good.

23   When down to Mizraim came
     Israel, when Jacob dwelt the land of Ham,
24 Then God his people so
   Increased, he made them stronger than their foe,
25 Whose hearts were turned to loathe
   His people, and with his chosen break their troth.
26 His servant Moses then
   He sent, and Aaron, his elect of men,
27 Whose words by signs he sealed,
   By portents, in the land of Ham revealed.
28 Darkness he sent, and men
   Went darkling; they his word gainsaid not then.
29 Their waters into blood
   He turned, and slew the fish in every flood.

30 He caused the land to bring
   Frogs forth, yea, in the chambers of their king.
31 He spake, and insect wings
   Thronged all their confines, and foul creeping things.
32 Hailstones to them were given
   For showers, and through their land the scorching levin.
33 He smote their figtrees, and
   Their vines, and all the greenwood in their land.
34 He called for locust broods
   And caterpillers, countless multitudes,
35 To strip of grass their ground,
   And all the fruitage of the trees confound.
36 Their eldest-born at length
   He smote, the flower and firstlings of their strength.
37 His tribes he forth did lead
   With gold and silver, that none suffered need.
38 Egypt, when thence they sped,
   Rejoiced, for on them all their fear was shed.
39 His tent in cloud was pight
   Amongst them, and with fire illumed the night.
40 He sent them, when they sued,
   Quails, and sufficed them with celestial food.
41 He opened them the rock
   In dry land, floods of water to unlock;
42 For he his holy word
   Remembered, which his servant Abraham heard.
43 He led his nation forth
   With gladness, and his chosen ones with mirth.
44 And gave them up the lands
   O' th' nations and the labors of their hands,
45 That they might aye preserve
   His ord'nances, and from his law not swerve.
   Hallelujah!

Psalm CVI.

1 O praise the Lord, for he is good ; for his
    Grace everlasting is.
2 Who shall rehearse his prowess ? who'll record
    All the praise of the Lord?
3 Blessed are they, that aye to judgment cleave.
    That ne'er uprightness leave.
4 Remember, me, Lord, when thy tribes find grace,
    Me let thy succor embrace.
5 The welfare of thy chosen may I see,
    Share thy tribes' jubilee,
    And in the triumph-songs may I engage
    Of thine own heritage.

6   We have sinned like our fathers ; we have run
    Astray, and foully done.
    Our fathers—they in Egypt took no thought
    Of that which thou hadst wrought.
7 They thy great grace forgot; they at the sea
    Fell, scarce at the Red Sea.
8 Yet God delivered them for his name' sake,
    And his power known to make.
9 He smote the Red Sea for them, that dry-shod
    Across the deep they trod.
10 Out of their haters' and their foes' hands he
    Saved, and redeemed them free,
11 And on their enemies closed the waves again :
    There did not one remain.
12 Ah ! then did they believe his works, and raise
    To him their songs of praise.

L

13 Yet they made haste, and all his works forgot;
   To God's way cleaved they not.
14 They fell a-lusting in the wildwaste, and
   Proved him in desert strand.
15 He gave them their desire, and gaunt disease
   He caused their souls to seize.
16 They railed at Moses and the Lord God's saint,
   Aaron, from tent to tent.
17 Then earth on Dathan gaped, and living swallowed
   Those that Abiram followed.
18 Fire blazed out on their levies, and a fierce
   Flame snatched up the perverse.
19 They made a calf in Horeb, and besought
   That which their hands had wrought.
20 To the likeness of an ox that eateth hay,
   Their glory changèd they.
21 But God their saviour, and his great works wrought
   In Mizraim they forgot;
22 (For wonders in the land of Ham wrought he,
   Dread works by the Red Sea).
23 Then thought he to destroy them, but there rose
   Moses, the man God chose,
   And in the breach stood up, to turn away
   His wrath, lest he might slay.
24 They scorned his land of pleasantness; they heard
   Incredulous his word;
25 They murmured in their tents, they would not heed
   That the Lord's voice decreed.
26 Therefore he raised his hand, to make them fall
   In the desert one and all,
27 Their race to winnow through the nations, and
   Disperse in every land.

28 They clove to Baal-peor next; they fed
    On offerings of the dead.
29 They vexed him by the evil that they wrought,
    Till plagues on them he brought.
30 Thereat arose up Phineas, and prayed,
    By whom the plague was stayed.
31 A title thence of good deserts he bore
    To all age evermore.
32 At Meribah's waters they did anger wake;
    And God chode for their sake
33 Moses, whose spirit grievously they stirred,
    Till with his lips he erred.
34 They rooted not the nations out, of whom
    He charged them with the doom:
35 But mingled with the heathen, and did learn
    To their ill ways to turn,
36 And service to their idols paid, which were
    Unto their souls a snare.
37 They sacrificed to evil powers, with slaughters
    Of their own sons and daughters,
38 And stained the land with blood of guiltless ones,
    Their daughters and their sons,
39 Whom they to Canaan's idols offered, and
    Defiled with blood the land.
40 Corrupt were all their ways. Then 'gainst his nation
    Burned the Lord's indignation.
41 He loathed his heritage, and to heathens gave them,
    Their haters, to enslave them.
42 Thenceforth their enemies oppressed and broke
    Them down with grievous yoke.
43 And yet did he them many a time deliver;
    But they revolted ever

Against his mandates, and to dire distress
Sank for their guiltiness.
44 Yet always looked he down on their sore need,
And at their cries gave heed.
45 He called to mind his covenant, and repented,
And rich in grace relented,
46 And made them find compassion in the eyes
Of all their enemies.

47 Save us now, Lord our God, and gather us home
Out of all heathendom,
That we thy holy name abroad may blaze,
And celebrate thy praise.

48 The Lord, the God of Israel, from all age
Be blessed to all age,
And let the people say with one accord
Amen, bless ye the Lord.

Psalm CVII.

1 O praise the Lord, for he is good, for he
Shows mercy constantly.

2 Let speak the ransom'd of the Lord, whom he
From foes' hands hath set free,
3 Whom from all countries he hath gathered forth,
From south, east, west, and north—
4 Those that in wilds and desert ways did roam,
And found no city or home;
5 Whose spirit, hard by thirst and hunger pressed,
Was ebbing from their breast.

6 Them, crying to the Lord in their sore need,
  He from their straits hath freed.
7 Yea, forth he brought them, by a speedy road,
  To a town where men abode.
8 Let them the Lord praise for his goodness then,
  Who doth such marvels for the sons of men;
9 For he contents the hungry soul with food,
  The fainting soul with good.

10   Those that in darkness and death's shade have lain,
  Ironed with misery's chain.
11 Because the Lord's word they have disobeyed,
  And small regard have paid
12 To high God's mandates; those of whom with woe
  He made the heart sink low,
  Who stumbled in their course, and looked around,
  And no deliverer found;
13 Them, crying to the Lord in their sore need,
  He from their straits hath freed.
14 He them from darkness and death's shade delivered,
  And their chains' links dissevered.
15 Let them the Lord praise for his goodness then,
  Who doth such marvels for the sons of men;
16 For he hath burst the brazen gates, and broken
  The chains of iron open.

17   The foolish must their sinful courses rue,
  And all the wrongs they do.
18 Their soul abhors all meat, and near the brink
  And porch of death they sink.
19 Them, crying to the Lord in their sore need,
  He from their straits hath freed.
20 He sends his word to heal them, and to save

From sinking to the grave.
21 Let them the Lord praise for his goodness then,
Who doth such marvels for the sons of men.
22 Let them do sacrifice of praise, and noise
His deeds with thankful voice.

23   Those that in ships go seawards, and on wide
Waters whose trade is plied—
24 To them God's works and wonders are revealed
On the deep Ocean's field.
25 For at his word the stormy wind outflies,
And the broad waves uprise.
26 They mount up high as heaven, they launch down low
Their souls dissolve with woe.
27 They reel and stagger like the drunk; their art
And wit they let depart.
28 Them, crying to the Lord in their sore need,
He from their straits hath freed.
29 He makes the storm to cease; the waves' uproar
He sheddeth stillness o'er.
30 Then they rejoice, and rest, and he doth speed
Them towards the port they need.
31 Let them the Lord praise for his goodness then,
Who doth such marvels for the sons of men.
32 Let them extol him in the elders' sessions,
And people's congregations.

33   He turneth the main rivers to dry land,
The watersprings to sand.
34 He makes the good soil waste, to recompense
Its dwellers their offence.

35 He bringeth pools of water in dry lands,
   And fountains from the sands;
36 And he the hungry setteth there, to plant
   Cities that men may haunt.
37 They sow the field, they plant the vine, they bring
   Their fruits and harvest in.
38 He blesses them, and largely multiplies;
   And makes their herds suffice.

39 Again when they are 'minisht, and brought low
   By misrule, plague, and woe,
40 He pours contempt on princes, who exiled
   Must tread the pathless wild.
41 But he from trouble saves the poor, and makes
   Like sheep their households wax.
42 The upright see this, and rejoice; and wrong
   Must hush thereat her tongue.
43 Whoe'er is wise will these things ponder, and
   The Lord's grace understand.

Psalm CVIII.

1 My heart is ready with praise,
   My heart is ready, O God: I will song with harmony
      raise.
2 Awake up, O my delight,
   Psaltery, wake up and harp: I will up with the
      morning's light.
3 I will utter, Jehovah, thy praise
   To the nations, I will to the heathen my harmony
      raise;

4 For thy mercy beyond heav'n rears
 Her stature; thy truth is exalted above the spheres.
5 Set thyself, O God, forth
 Beyond the heav'n, thy glory above all earth.

6   Come to thy lov'd ones' rescue; save us, and
 Answer by thy right hand.
7 O joy! God hath by his holy word replied!
 Now Shechem I'll divide,
8 And share the glebe of Succoth; Gilead's mine,
 Manasseh's land is mine.
9 Ephraim be my stronghold; Judah be
 Lawgiver under me.
 Shout for me, Philistines; let the Edomite
 Serve me, and Moabite.
10 Who'll lead me toward the city fortified?
 Who'll me to Edom guide?
11 Thou, Lord, who didst reject us? thou that go'st
 No more out with our host?
12 O grant us help in trouble, for to gain
 The help of man is vain.
13 Through God we shall do mighty deeds; our foe
 He for us treads down low.

Psalm CIX.

1 Hold not thy peace, God of my praiseful song!
 Because the mouth of wrong,
2 Against me, and the mouth of guile hath spoken,
 And lying lips are open.

3 With words of hate they compass me, and for
   No cause against me war.
4 For all my love they bear me hate; but I
   Do ever on prayer rely.
5 They quite my good with evil; they repay
   With hate my love's outlay.
6 Set over each a tyrant, and let stand
   The fiend at his right hand.
7 Send him, when judged, the guilty man's award:
   His prayers as sin record.
8 Make his days few, and in his functions let
   Another man be set.
9 Make of his children orphans, and his bride
   Let widowhood betide.
10 Abroad like beggars let his children roam,
   Out from their ruin'd home.
11 Give usurers his goods; his labors put
   Under the stranger's foot.
12 Let no man show him kindness; let no grace
   Betide his orphan'd race.
13 Destroy his remnant; let them have no station
   In the next generation.
14 Let all his father's guilt be held before
   The Lord's face evermore,
   And let his mother's sins be not erased.
15 Always let them be placed
   Before the Lord, that he his memory may
   Clear from the earth away.
16 For mercy he remembered not to do,
   But sternly would pursue
   The poor and weak; the hopeless overthrown
   To the death he followed on.

17 As he loved cursing, let that be his lot;
   As blessing pleased him not,
18 So keep it from him far. Let malison
   Be the robe he puts on,
19 And sink like water through him, and about
   His bones, like oil poured out.
20 This the Lord yield to them, who peace refuse me,
   Who lyingly accuse me.
21 But with thy name deal by me in accord,
   And save me, God, my lord,
22 Through thy dear mercy. Lo, I am weak and frail;
   Mine heart disasters quail.
23 I fade like shadows lengthening; I go to
   And fro as locusts do.
24 My knees are weak through fasting; and through want
   Of sap my flesh is scant.
25 I am become the scorn of men; they see,
   And shake their heads at me.
26 Send help, O Lord my God, and me deliver,
   As thou art gracious ever.
27 And let men recognize thine hand, and read,
   Lord, that this is thy deed.
28 Bless thou, when they do curse; cast thou dismay
   Amidst their war-array.
29 Let them with shame and scorn be robed and clad;
   And make thy servant glad.
30 And thee, Lord, loudly I will boast, and raise
   In the great throngs thy praise;
31 Who sav'st my soul from tyrants; who dost stand
   Fast by the poor's right hand.

Psalm CX.

1 Jehovah to my lord hath said,
 Have at my right thy seat,
 Until thy enemies I shall make
 The footstool of thy feet.

2   Jehovah will from Zion send
 The sceptre of thy sway,
 That thou may'st rule amidst thy foes;
3 That in thy empire's day,
 Thy people may with holy pomp
 Large offerings bear to thee:
 Thy young men's mustering as the dews
 That dawn brings forth, shall be.
4 Hereunto hath Jehovah sworn:
 (It shall repent him never)
 Of the order of Melchizedek
 Thou art a priest for ever.
5 The high Lord at thy right shall wound
 Kings in his day of wrath.
6 Amongst the heathen he shall judge;
 The dead shall strew his path.
7 He shall the heads in sunder cleave
 O'er countries far and near.
 Since of the wayside brook he drank,
 His crest he high shall rear.

Psalm CXI.

1 In companies of righteous men, in throngs I will extol
 The Lord with heart and soul.
2 Great are the actions of the Lord, sought into by all those
 Whose pleasure they compose.
3 Grandeur and glory are his ways; his righteous rule is firm
 Beyond all time and term.
4 The Lord hath made his wondrous acts to be well borne in mind:
 He is pitiful and kind.
5 He giveth those who fear him food; his covenant keepeth he
 In mind perpetually.
6 He showed his tribes his deeds of power; he made them of the nations
 To inherit habitations.
7 His hand's effects are truth and right; his ordinances' word
 Is constantly averred.
8 They stand established for all time; in righteousness is done
 And faithfulness each one.
9 He rescue to his people sends; his covenant to remain
 For ever he doth ordain.
10 His name is holy and to be feared; his dread is that wherein
 All wisdom doth begin.

11 To all that his commands observe, they good discernment give;
Their praise doth always live.

Psalm CXII.

1 Blessed, who fears the Lord; the man that takes
Delight in his behest.
2 His seed shall on the earth be strong; the race
Of true men shall be blest.
3 In his house there shall be wealth and state; his merit
Shall everlasting be.
4 From darkness light shall on the just man dawn:
True, tender and kind is he.
5 He prospers well, he gives and lends; his cause
I' th' judgment shall prevail.
6 The righteous never shall be shaken; never
Shall his remembrance fail.
7 He shall not fear for ill reports; his heart
Doth on the Lord repose.
8 His heart is firm and fearless; he shall see
His will wrought on his foes.
9 He casts abroad, he gives unto the poor,
His merit faileth not.
10 His horn shall be exalted: evil men,
When they behold his lot,
11 Shall fret, shall gnash their teeth, and pine away;
That which the wicked coveteth shall decay.

Psalm CXIII.

1 O all ye servants of the Lord,
Praise ye the Lord God's name.
2 From henceforth and for evermore
Blest be the Lord God's name.
3 From rising sun to sinking be
, Extolled the Lord God's name.

4 The Lord above all heathen rules,
Above all heaven sits high.
5 Who is there like the Lord our God,
That hath his throne so high,
6 And yet upon the things of earth
And heav'n casts down his eye?

7 He from the dust and dung-hill rears
The child of tribulation,
8 That with the princes he may sit,
The princes of his nation.
9 He makes the barren wife to rule
In a jocund habitation.

Psalm CXIV.

1 When Israel came from Egypt, and the hosts
Of Jacob from strange coasts,
2 God's halidom was Judah; he let dwell
His power in Israel.

3 The sea beheld, and fled; and Jordan's course
  Was turned back to his source.
4 The mountains leapt, as though they had been rams:
  The little hills like lambs.

5   What ailèd thee, O sea, that thus thou fleddest?
    Jordan, that back thou speddest?
6 What ail'd the mountains, that they leapt like rams?
  The little hills, like lambs?
7 Tremble, thou earth, before Jehovah's face,
  The God of Jacob's face,
8 Who turns the rock to waterponds; who rills
  Draws from the flintstone hills.

Psalm CXV.

1 Not, Lord, for us; not, Lord, for us, but claim
  The glory for thy name,
2 Being true and kind. Why should the Gentiles say,
  "Where is your God, we pray?"
3 Our God is in the heavens; all that which he
  Finds fit, he brings to be.
4 Their gods are gold and silver; they are nought
  But what men's hands have wrought.
5 They have eyes, and they see not; mouths have they
  And not a word can say;
6 Ears, and they hear not; nostrils, and of scent
  Have no distinguishment;
7 Hands, and they touch not; feet, and cannot walk;
  Throats, and they cannot talk.

8 Their makers are like unto them, and those
  Who faith in them repose.
9 Let your trust in the Lord, O Israel, be;
  Their help and shield is he.
10 Your trust i' th' Lord, O house of Aaron, be;
  Their help and shield is he.
11 Your trust i' th' Lord, O you that fear him, be;
  Their help and shield is he.
12 The Lord God heeds us; he will Israel bless,
  And Aaron's household bless.
13 All those who fear him will the Lord God bless,
  The greater and the less.
14 The Lord your God increase you more and more,
  And your sons o'er and o'er.
15 Ye are the blessed of the Lord, who earth
  And heav'n call'd into birth.
16 The heav'ns, the heav'ns are his; but earth he gave
  The sons of men to have.
17 The dead, Lord, praise thee not, nor those that low
  Down to dumb stillness go.
18 But we, O Lord, will blessings render thee,
  Now and perpetually.

Psalm CXVI.

1 I am well pleas'd, the Lord
  Hath heark'ned to my voice when I implored:
2 Since he bowed down to give
  Me ear, I will invoke him whilst I live.
3   The snares of death fell on me,
  The shackles of the grave took hold upon me.

Distress did on me fall,
And pain; then on the Lord's name I 'gan call.
4 I cried, Where art thou, Lord?
Arise, and rescue to my soul afford.
5 The Lord is merciful
And righteous; yea, our God is pitiful.
6 The Lord will save me, when
I have no help; he guardeth guileless men.
7 Turn back unto thy rest,
O soul; for hath not God thy wrong redressed?
8 The Lord my soul from death,
Eyes from tears, feet from falling ransometh,
9 That I may in the land
Of living men before God come to stand.

10   I spake; for I was brought
To such distress; I uttered that I thought.
11 I said (for my soul then
Was struck with fear), deceivers are all men.
12 What shall I render thee,
Lord God, for all thou hast awarded me?
13 I will the cup fill high
Of thankfulness, and on the Lord's name cry.
14 Yea, to the Lord I will
In all his people's sight my vows fulfil.
15 Sure a thing dear to prize
Is his believer's life in the Lord's eyes.
16 Behold, O Lord, and see
Thy servant, and thy handmaid's child in me.
17 To thee that hast unsealed
My bonds, the sacrifice of praise I'll yield.

18 Yea, the Lord's name I will
   Invoke, and in thy people's sight fulfil.
19 In courts of the Lord's house,
   In midst of thee, Jerusalem, my vows.

Psalm CXVII.

1 O praise the Lord,
   All people, and extol him every nation!
2 For great his loving-kindnesses
   Are toward us, and confirmed his promises,
   From generation unto generation.

Psalm CXVIII.

I.

1 Praise the Lord, for he is gracious,
   For his mercy is everlasting;
2 Speak, O Israel, and aver it,
   That his mercy is everlasting;
3 And aver it, house of Aaron,
   That his mercy is everlasting:
4 Fearers of the Lord, aver it,
   That his mercy is everlasting.

II.

5 On the Lord I called in trouble.
   And he heard, and set me free;
6 He is on my side; I will not
   Fear what flesh can do to me.
7 He defends me; my desire on
   Those that hate me I shall see.

8 On the Lord to trust is better
  Than in mortals to confide;
9 On the Lord to trust is better
  Than in princes to confide.

10   Though all nations me encompassed,
  In the Lord's name I destroyed them;
11 Though they compassed and beset me,
  In the Lord's name I destroyed them;
12 They have come like bees about me;
  But like fire in thorns are sunken;
  In the Lord's name I destroyed them.

13   They thrust hard to overthrow me,
  But the Lord hath rescued me,
14 Him I made my song: my fortress,
  My deliverer is he.

III.

15   Through the encampment of the righteous
  Triumph with thanksgiving rings;
16 For the Lord's right hand is lifted,
  The Lord's right doth mighty things.
17 I shall live, I shall not perish;
  I shall voice those marvels ever,
18 For the Lord hath me corrected,
  But to death will not deliver.

19   Open me the righteous portals;
  I will pass, to praise the Lord.
20 Yonder, open to the righteous,
  Are the portals of the Lord.
21 Thee I'll praise, who didst rebuke me,
  But salvation dost award.

22 That is chiefstone in the corner,
   Which the builders did despise;
23 From the Lord God this proceedeth,
   And is wondrous in our eyes.

24 This day hath the Lord appointed,
   We will blithe and jocund be;
25 Up, O Lord God, and deliver,
   Up, O Lord, and set us free.
26 Blessed in his name who cometh:
   From the Lord's house bless we thee.

27 He is God the Lord, who lights us;
   Bind the sacrifice with cord,
   Bind it on the altar's corners.
28 Thou art my God; I will praise thee,
   Thee I will exalt, my Lord.

29 Praise the Lord, for he is gracious,
   For his mercy is everlasting.

Psalm CXIX.

ALEPH.

1 Blessed, whose way is guileless; they whose walk
   By the Lord's law is guided.
2 Blessed, who keep his testimony, who God
   Seek with hearts undivided.
3 Those that do no iniquities, whose feet
   Do from his paths not swerve.
4 Thou hast on us thy ordinances laid,
   Right worthy to observe.

5 Would that my ways were so disposed, that I
  Thy statutes kept aright!
6 Then should I not be shamed, when I should keep
  All thy commands in sight.
7 With upright heart I'll praise thee, when thy just
  Judgments thou teachest me.
8 Thy statutes I will keep; do thou me not
  Forsake perpetually.

BETH.

9 How shall a young man keep unstained his way?
  Let him thy word observe.
10 With all my heart I've sought thee; let me not
  From thy commandments swerve.
11 I've hid thy promise in my heart, that so
  I may not sin toward thee.
12 Blessed thou art, O Lord; I pray thee, teach
  Thy statutes unto me.
13 My lips do all the judgments, that have passed
  Out of thy mouth, display.
14 I have enjoyed beyond all gold and store
  Thy testimonies' way.
15 My thoughts upon thy ordinance, my hopes
  Upon thy paths are set.
16 Upon thy statutes I lean fast; no word
  Of thine will I forget.

GIMEL.

17 Deal with thy servant bounteously, O Lord,
  While to thy word I cleave.
18 Purge thou mine eyes, that I may wondrous things
  Out of thy law perceive.

19 I am on earth a pilgrim; thy commands
  Keep thou not hid from me.
20 My spirit faints, pursuing with much zeal,
  Thy judgments constantly.
21 I hate the overweening, who are cursed,
  From thy commands who swerve.
22 Remove from me contempt and shame, while I
  Thy testimony observe.
23 Though princes 'gainst thy servant sit and speak,
  Thy statutes I rehearse.
24 My trust upon thy testimonies leans;
  They are my counsellors.

DALETH.

25 My soul in dust hath sunken: quicken me
  According to thy word.
26 Teach me thy statutes; I have owned my ways
  To thee, and thou hast heard,
27 Teach me thy ways and ordinance; I do muse
  Upon thy works of might.
28 My soul for grief hath melted; make me stand
  For thy word's sake upright.
29 Remove from me false ways, and graciously
  Thy law to me impart.
30 I have preferred the way of truth; I lay
  Thy judgments to my heart.
31 I cleave unto thy testimonies, Lord;
  O let not shame o'ertake me.
32 I will the way of thy commandments run,
  If thou a large heart make me.

HE.

33   Show me, O Lord, thy statutes' way, and I
Will follow it for ever.
34 Instruct me, and I will obey thy law
With all my heart's endeavor.
35 Direct me in the path of thy commands,
For I delight therein.
36 My heart unto thy testimony incline,
Rather than gain to win.
37 Withdraw mine eyes from seeing falsities;
Me in thy ways enliven.
38 Make to thy servant good thy promise, which
Is to thy fearers given.
39 Remove from me the shame I fear; for I
Do thy good judgments trust.
40 Behold, thy ordinances I desire;
Enlive me, as thou'rt just.

WAU.

41   Lord, let thy mercies reach me, and thy promise
Fulfil for my defence.
42 My trust is in thy word; I shall reply
To all my mockers thence.
43 Do thou not from my lips the word of truth
Too long a time withdraw;
44 For on thy judgments I depend; I keep
For ever and aye thy law.
45 So I will walk in freedom; for I do
Thine ordinances seek,
46 And of thy testimonies unto kings
Without shame I will speak.

47 I will in thy commandments take delight,
 And lift up for their sake
48 Mine hands, because I love them, and to heart
 Thy statutes I will take.

ZAYIN.

49 Remember for thy servants' sake thy word,
 Which is my confidence.
50 Thy promise gave me comfort in my need;
 Thou didst enlive me thence.
51 The proud have mocked me overmuch, but I
 Depart not from thy law.
52 I call to mind thy judgments from of old;
 My comfort thence I draw.
53 Sore grief hath seized me, to behold the proud;
 Because thy law they break.
54 Thy statutes are my songs, when my sojourn
 In strange abodes I make.
55 I call to mind, O Lord, thy name by night,
 And to thy law I cleave.
56 I say, because thy ordinances I keep,
 This portion I receive.

CHETH.

57 It is my portion, I have said, O Lord,
 After thy word to do.
58 With all mine heart I seek thee; show me grace
 To make thy promise true.
59 I call to mind my ways; thy testimony
 To obey I turn my feet.
60 I make haste and delay not; so that I
 May thy commandment keep.

61 The wicked's snares beset me; but no less
   Heed to thy law I take.
62 I rise at midnight up, to give thee thanks
   For thy just judgments' sake.
63 I cleave to all that fear thee, and that by
   Thine ordinances live.
64 Thy mercy fills the heavens; to me, O Lord,
   To know thy statutes give.

TETH.

65 Thou hast done well unto thy servant, Lord,
   Making thy promise true.
66 Teach me good lore and prudence; thy commands
   Sincerely I pursue.
67 Before I suffered I went wrong, but now
   To seek thy promise turn.
68 Thou art good, and thou dost good; grant me that
   I may thy statutes learn.
69 The proud forge lies against me, but thine ordinance
   I keep with all my might.
70 Their heart is fat as brawn, but in thy law
   'Tis mine to take delight.
71 'Tis good that I have suffered; thence I learn
   Thy statutes fast to hold.
72 The law, thy mouth has uttered, I love more
   Than silver and much gold.

YODH.

73 Thy hands me wrought and made; my mind to learn
   All thy commandments ope.
74 Let those who fear thee, see me and rejoice,
   Since in thy word I hope.

75 Thy judgments, Lord, I know are just; yea, thou
   For truths' sake chast'nest me.
76 Let now thy mercies, as thou promisest,
   Thy servant's comfort be.
77 Let come to me thy pity, and I shall live,
   Who in thy law take pleasure.
78 Abash the proud, who forge against me lies;
   Thy ord'nances I treasure.
79 Thy fearers, who thy testimonies know,
   Let them join cause with me.
80 Let perfect in thy statutes be mine heart,
   That shamed I may not be.

KAPH.

81 My soul for thy salvation longs; mine hopes
   Upon thy word depend.
82 Mine eyes ache for thy promise; when wilt thou
   Thy peace to me extend?
83 I parch like flagons hung in smoke; yet never
   Thy statutes I forget.
84 What day of judgment for the oppressors of
   Thy servant hast thou set?
85 The proud have dug a pit for me; thy law
   In small respect they have.
86 All thy commands are truth; they hunt me down
   With lies; do thou me save.
87 They well-nigh rased me from the land, but I
   Will not thy ordinance leave.
88 Enlive me by thy grace; to the testimony
   Of thy mouth I will cleave.

LAMEDH.

89 Thy mercy is perpetual, Lord : thy word
Firm as the heav'ns doth last.
90 Thy truth endures from age to age; the earth
'Tis thou that groundest fast.
91 After thy judgments they stand firm this day :
For thou dost all control.
92 I should have died in my distress, did not
Thy law delight my soul.
94 Save me, thy servant, for thy ordinances
I seek out constantly.
95 The proud to slay me lurked, but evermore
Thy ordinances I scanned.
96 To all perfection I have seen an end,
But broad is thy command.

MEM.

97 What love I bear unto thy law! therein
I meditate all day.
98 I am wiser than my foes through thy commands,
For these aye with me stay.
99 I have more skill than all my teachers, while
Thy testimony I explore.
100 More prudence than the old ; because I keep
Thy ordinance evermore.
101 I keep my feet from every evil way,
True to thy law to hold.
102 I swerve not from thy judgments ; for 'tis thou
That hast me taught and told.
103 How sweet's thy word of promise to my taste :
No honey-comb is more.

104 Thy ordinances make me wise, all ways
   Of falsehood to abhor.

NUN.

105   A lantern is thy word unto my feet,
   And to my paths a light.
106 This I have sworn; I am resolved to keep
   Thy judgments just and right.
107 I am full sore afflicted; O enlive me
   According to thy word.
108 Accept the free-will offerings of my mouth;
   Teach me thy judgments, Lord.
109 My soul is always in mine hand, yet never
   Do I thy law forget.
110 Snares lay the wicked for me! but I swerve not
   Back from thy ordinance yet.
111 Thy testimonies are mine heirloom ever,
   For they mine heart rejoice.
112 To do thy statutes I have set mine heart,
   For ever is this my choice.

SAMEKH.

113   I hate the double-minded, and thy law
   Is that which I love best.
114 Thou art my shield and shelter, and my hopes
   Upon thy word do rest.
115 Depart, ye wicked, hence; for to my God's
   Commandments I will cleave.
116 Sustain, enlive me by thy promise, lest
   Mine hope should me deceive.
117 Support me, and I shall be safe, and ever
   Thy statutes I'll observe.

118 Thou sham'st them (for their guile is their delusion),
  Who from thy statutes swerve.
119 Thou spurn'st the wicked on the earth like dross:
  I love thy covenant hence.
120 Thy fear afflicts my flesh; I do with awe
  Thy judgments reverence.

AYIN.

121   Judgment I do and right; O give me not
  To mine oppressors' will.
122 In bounty pledge thy servant, that the proud
  May not oppress me still.
123 Mine eye for thy salvation longs; the promise
  Of thy just word to reach.
124 After thy mercies with thy servant deal,
  And me thy statutes teach.
125 I am thy servant; give me wisdom, that
  Thy testimony I may know.
126 'Tis time, O Lord, thou should'st be up, for men
  Thy law do overthrow.
127 Behold, how thy commands, I love, beyond
  Gold and the fine gold ore,
128 And unto all thy ordinances cleave,
  And all false ways abhor.

PE.

129 Thy testimony is wondrous, therefore doth
  My soul to it adhere.
130 Thy word set forth gives light to simple minds
  And understanding clear.
131 I ope my mouth, and gasp; for thy commands
  To reach is all mine aim.

132 Turn toward me, and show grace, as is thy judgment,
　　With those who love thy name.
133 Guide with thy word my steps, that ill desire
　　May o'er me have no sway.
134 From men's oppression rescue me, that I
　　Thy ordinance may obey.
135 Let on thy servant shine thy face, and teach me
　　Thy statutes to observe.
136 Mine eyes drop streams of waters to behold
　　How from thy law men swerve.

SADHE.

137　Thou, Lord, art holy; and uprightness all
　　Thy judgments doth embue.
138 The testimonies thou commandest, are
　　Exceeding right and true.
139 My zeal hath on me preyed, to see my foes
　　How they thy word forget.
140 Thy promise is well tried, and thereupon
　　Thy servant's love is set.
141 I am despised and feeble, but keep ever
　　Thy ordinances in view.
142 Thy righteousness is righteousness eterne;
　　Thy law is just and true.
143 Though grief and trouble seize me, thy commands
　　To me shall comfort give.
144 Thy testimonies are for ever just;
　　Enlive me, and I shall live.

QOPH.

145　With all mine heart I call thee; hear me, Lord;
　　For I thy statutes heed.
146 To thee I cry; O save me; for I keep
　　Thy testimony indeed.

147 I cry to thee, the break of day forestalling,
    And for thy promise wait.
148 Mine eyes forestall the watches of the night,
    Thy word to meditate.
149 Hear, Lord, my voice in mercy, and enlive me.
    As me thy judgments use.
150 For they are near, that hunt me down with guile,
    They that thy law refuse.
151 Thou art full near me, Lord, and thy commands
    Are faithful altogether.
152 I know long since thy testimonies, which
    Thou'st grounded fast for ever.

RESH.

153   Look on my need, and save me; for my mind
    Hath from thy law not erred.
154 Strive thou my strife, redeem and quicken me
    According to thy word.
155 Far is salvation from the wicked, since
    Thy statutes they neglect.
156 Thy mercies, Lord, are boundless; quicken me:
    Thy judgments recollect.
157 Many are my foes, who seek my life; yet from
    Thy testimony I swerve not.
158 I gaze on the dissemblers, and am wroth,
    For they thy word observe not.
159 Look how I love thy ordinances, Lord;
    Enlive me in thy grace.
160 Thy word is perfect truth; thy judgments after
    Pure justice aye take place.

SHIN.

161 Princes with wrongs pursue me, but mine heart
Fears thy word evermore.
162 Over thy word rejoice I more than one
That findeth spoil good store.
163 Falsehood I hate and loathe, but mine affections
Are set upon thy law.
164 Seven times a day I praise thee; whereto me
Thy righteous judgments draw.
165 Great peace is for the lovers of thy law;
They no mishap shall prove.
166 For thy salvation I do watch, O Lord,
And thy commands I love.
167 My soul observes thy testimonies, yea,
Great love I bear thereto.
168 I keep thy testimony and ordinance;
My ways all bide thy view.

TAU.

169 Let to thy face approach my prayer, and after
Thy promise rescue me.
170 Let my petition come before thee, Lord;
Me may thy word set free.
171 My lips shall utter praises, when thy judgments
Thou'st made me understand.
172 My tongue shall sound thy promise, for upright
Is every thy command.
173 Let thy hand be my helper; for to do
Thine ordinance is my choice.
174 For thy salvation I do watch, O Lord,
And in thy law rejoice.

175 Let live my soul to praise thee ; let thy judgments
    Me in safe shelter set.
176 Bring home thy servant, a lost sheep, and thy
    Commands I'll ne'er forget.

Psalm CXX.

1 In hour of woe
  Unto the Lord I cried, and he gave ear.
2 I said, Lord, set me free
  From lying lips, and from the traitorous tongue.
3 What shall God give to thee,
  Or make thy portion, O thou traitorous tongue?
4 Sharp-pointed arrows from the strong man's bow,
  And fire from fuel sere.

5   Ah, wretched me,
  To dwell with Meshech, and so long to make
  In Kedar's tent my stay!
6 My soul amongst the haters of all peace
  Doth overlong delay.
7 For I on my part proffer only peace,
  But when thereof I speak, immediately
  They to their weapons take.

Psalm CXXI.

1 I lift mine eyes up toward the hills,
  For thence proceeds mine aid.
2 Mine aid is even from the Lord,
  Who heaven and earth has made.

3 He shall not let thy foot be warped;
   Thy guardian will not sleep.
4 Lo, he that guardeth Israel,
   Will slumber not, nor sleep.
5 The Lord thy guardian be, the Lord
   Thy shadow at thy right,
6 That neither sun may hurt by day
   Thy head, nor moon by night.
7 The Lord protect thee from all harm;
   May he thy soul defend,
   Thy going out and coming home,
   Henceforth and without end.

Psalm CXXII.

1 I have heard with joyous heart
   Those saying, To the Lord's house let us go.
2 Our feet stand in thy gates, Jerusalem!
3 Jerusalem, O thou that builded art
   As a city, where in good accord men dwell!
4 For the tribes thither flow,
   The own tribes of the Lord God flow to thee,
   To bear to Israel
5 Their witness, and the Lord's name praise to them.
   For there are set the thrones of equity,
   The thrones of David's seed.

6   O pray for peace upon Jerusalem!
   God those that love thee, speed.
7 Peace be within thy walls, and plenteousness
   Among thy palaces.

8 For my companions' and my brethren's sake,
   I will thy peace implore;
9 For the abode's sake of the Lord our God,
   I will thy peace implore.

Psalm CXXIII.

1 To thee, O dweller in the heavens, mine eyes
   I raise, as servants' eyes
2 Wait on their masters, as the bondmaid stands
   And views her mistress' hands;
   So wait our souls on the Lord God, till he
   Deal with us graciously.

3   Deal with us, Lord, deal with us graciously:
   For filled of scorn are we—
   Soul-sick with taunts of those who live at ease,
   And proud men's contumelies.

Psalm CXXIV.

1 Had not the Lord been for us,
2 (Let Israel say,) had not the Lord been for us,
   When men against us rose,
3 We had been swallowed living by our foes,
   When they with furious wrath against us glowed.
4 The waters had closed o'er us,
   The floods had to the pitch of death gone o'er us,
5 The high-proud waters had us overflowed.

6   But blessed be the Lord,
   Who to their teeth would not our spoils accord.

7 We have escaped them free;
　As birds escaped the fowler's nets are we;
　The nets are broken, and we are set free!
8 Our rescue has gone forth
　From the Lord's name, who made the heavens and earth.

Psalm CXXV.

1 Who on the Lord rely,
　Are like mount Zion, which maintains for aye
　Through every shock her station.
2 Look, as the hills surround
　Jerusalem, the Lord keeps watch around
　His nation,
　From this time, and henceforth perpetually.

3 　For o'er the just man's lot
　The scourge of the ungodly cometh not,
　Lest haply even they
　Their hands upon unrighteous works should lay.
4 Lord, toward the good and true
　Of heart according to thy mercies do;
5 But all such as confide
　In crooked ways, to the end of wrong-doers guide.
　Let peace on Israel be.

Psalm CXXVI.

1 Zion, when home the Lord thy captives brought,
　We were as those who dream;
2 Our mouths were filled with triumph, and a hymn
　Of praise our lips out-poured.

Then said the Gentiles, Wondrous things the Lord
3 Hath done. Yea, marvels for us he hath wrought;
And this let our exulting voice record.

4   O Lord, do thou the captive tribes restore,
Like southern floods in flow.
5 There are, that in distress and sorrow sow,
But shall with gladness reap;
6 Behold, the man that goeth forth to weep,
Bearing good seed, he'll come in joy once more,
And strainèd sheaves against his bosom heap.

Psalm CXXVII.

1 If the Lord do not build
The house, their labour is but lost, that build.
If the Lord do not guard
The city, vainly keeps the watchman guard.
2 'Tis all in vain ye haste
To rise up early, and so late take rest,
And eat the bread of cares; while sleep he sheds
On his beloved their heads.

3   Lo! children and the flower
Of births are from the Lord a gift and dower.
4 Like arrows in the hands
Of giants are the growing children's bands.
5 Blessed the men, whose quiver
Is filled with such; for shamed they shall be never,
When with their enemies in the city's gate
They come to hold debate.

Psalm CXXVIII.

1 How blessed are all they
  Who fear the Lord God, and who walk his way,
2 Sure thou shalt eat the increase
  Of thy hand's labor, shalt have weal and peace.
3 Like on thy house's side
  The vine, thou shalt beclustered see thy bride.
4 Thy children like the green
  Olive-shoots round thy table shall be seen.

5   Thus blest the fearers of the Lord shall be!
  The Lord from Zion thee
  Shall prosper; thou shalt in Jerusalem view
  Welfare, thy lifetime through;
6 Yea, with thy sons, and sons born unto them,
  Peace on Jerusalem.

Psalm CXXIX.

1 Up from my youth have they
  Warred on me oft, may Israel now say;
2 They have made war on me
  Up from my youth, but not had mastery.
3 The ploughers on my back
  Have ploughed; they have prolonged the ploughshare's track.
4 But the Lord God is true,
  Who has the ungodly's trammels broken through.

5   Let them be put to shame,
  And flee, O Zion, that abhor thy name.

6 Like grass on housetops let
　Them fade, before a hand on them be set.
7 That grass no arm receives
　Of mower, nor his breast who binds up sheaves.
8 Not one doth o'er it say,
　" God bless you," or, " the Lord you speed, we pray,"
　Of all who pass the way.

Psalm CXXX.

1 Out of the depths have I
2 Called unto thee ; O Lord God, hear my cry.
　O Lord God, to mine orison give ear.
3 What man, if thou inquire for trespasses,
4 Shall bear thy face ? but thine forgiveness is ;
　Therefore shall men thee fear.

5 　I wait upon the Lord ;
　My soul doth wait ; my trust is on his word.
6 To the Lord my soul before the morn takes flight,
7 Before the morning watch. O Israel, place
　In him your trust ; for with the Lord is grace
　And succors infinite.

Psalm CXXXI.

1 Lord, I have no proud looks nor lofty eyes ;
　I do not exercise
　Myself in things too high and hard for me ;
2 But with humility
　And quietness I have myself demeaned,

Like a child newly from his mother weaned;
Yea, like a weanling is my soul in me.
3 O Israel, on the Lord your God rely
Henceforward and for aye.

Psalm CXXXII.

1 O Lord, remember thou
2 David and all his trouble; how a vow
Before the Lord vowed he,
And pledged an oath to Jacob's Majesty.
3 "From shelter and from roof,
From couch and pillow I will stand aloof;
4 Mine eyes I will not close
In sleep, nor to mine eyelids give repose,
5 Till for the Lord I find
A home, till Jacob's Majesty I've shrined."
6 Thereof we heard a sound
In Ephrath, and the place in Jaar we found.
7 We'll toward his dwelling go,
And at the footstool of his feet bend low.
8 Come up to thine abode,
Thou and thine ark of Majesty, O God!
9 Let thy believers glad
Shouts raise, thy priests with righteousness be clad.
10 From thine anointed take
Thy face not, for thy servant David's sake.

11   The Lord hath ta'en an oath
To David; he will swerve not from his troth;
12 "From offspring of thine own
Blood, I will set thine heir upon thy throne.

And if thy children will
My covenant keep, and those behests fulfil,
Which I to them make known,
Their children too shall sit upon thy throne."

13   Mount Zion surely God
Hath chos'n and set apart for his abode.
14 "Here will I take my rest
World without end; for this delights me best.
15 With blessing I will bless
Her vi'tual, and her poor shall bread possess.
16 Her priests I will deck out
With saviourship, and cause her saints to shout.
17 There David's horn shall flourish;
The lamp of mine anointed I will nourish.
18 His foes will I with scorn
Clothe, but the crown his temples shall adorn."

Psalm CXXXIII.

1 Behold, how fair and well
It shows, for brethren in accord to dwell!
2 Like precious oils outpoured
Upon the head, which down the beard distil,
The beard of Aaron, and his skirts o'errun;
Like Hermon's dew, like dew down Sion's hill;
3 For there his benison
And life perpetual promiseth the Lord.

Psalm CXXXIV.

1 Bless now the Lord, ye servants of the Lord!
All ye to whom 'tis given
By night-time in the house of God to stand.
2 Let each his hand
Uplift before the inmost holiness,
And bless the Lord.
3   Thee also may the Lord from Zion bless,
Maker of earth and heaven.

Psalm CXXXV.

1 O praise the Lord, ye servants of the Lord,
Praise the name of the Lord;
2 Ye, that are standers in the Lord's abode,
In the courts of our God,
3 Praise him, for he is good; let praisèd be
His name; for kind is he;
4 Who chose out Jacob, who made Israel's sons
To be his treasured ones.
5 For sure, the Lord is great; a lord, I deem,
Above all gods supreme.
6 Whate'er the Lord sees good, that fashions he
In heaven and earth and sea,
7 And in all deeps. The clouds he marshals forth
From the ends of the earth;
He brings the winds out of his stores; the rains
And lightnings he ordains;

8 He that in Mizraim did the first-born strike,
   Mankind and beast alike;
9 Who wrought dread signs, O Mizraim, through thy
      coasts
   On Pharaoh and his hosts;
10 Who smote on our behalf great nations, who
   Kings dread and powerful slew.
11 He slew us Sihon, king of Amorites,
   Og, king of Bashanites,
12 And Canaan's kings, and gave to Israel
   Their lands, therein to dwell.
13 O Lord, from age to age endures thy name;
   Perpetual is thy fame.
14 Thou dost thy people judge, and vengeance take
   For thy own servants' sake.
15 The heathen gods are gold and silver, nought
   But what men's hands have wrought.
16 They have eyes, and they see not; mouths have they,
   And not a word can say;
17 Ears, and they hear not; nostrils, and of scent
   Have no distinguishment.
18 Their makers are like unto them, and those
   Who faith in them repose.
19 But do ye bless, O Israel, the Lord;
   Bless, Aaron's house, the Lord.
20 Bless him, O house of Levi; bless the Lord,
   Ye fearers of the Lord.
21 Blest be the Lord from Zion, and the God
   Who in Salem makes abode.

Psalm CXXXVI.

1 O thank the Lord, for good is he,
For his mercy is everlasting;
2 The God of gods acknowledge ye,
For his mercy is everlasting;
3 The Lord of lords acknowledge ye,
For his mercy is everlasting;

4 Who only granteth wondrous aid,
For his mercy is everlasting;
6 Who heaven in passing wisdom made,
For his mercy is everlasting;
5 Who earth above the seas fast laid,
For his mercy is everlasting;

7 Who with great lights did heaven array,
For his mercy is everlasting;
8 Who made the sun to rule the day,
For his mercy is everlasting;
9 The moon and stars the night to sway,
For his mercy is everlasting;

10 Who the first-born in Mizraim slew,
For his mercy is everlasting;
11 And with a strong hand Israel drew,
(For his mercy is everlasting,)
12 And with a stretcht-out arm therethrough,
For his mercy is everlasting;

13 Who the Red Sea in sunder clave,
   For his mercy is everlasting;
14 And passage unto Israel gave,
   For his mercy is everlasting;
15 And shut on Pharoah's hosts the wave,
   For his mercy is everlasting;

16 Who through the wastes his people led,
   For his mercy is everlasting;
17 And great kings for them visited,
   For his mercy is everlasting;
18 Yea! blood of mighty kings he shed,
   For his mercy is everlasting;

19 Of Sihon, king of Amorites,
   For his mercy is everlasting;
20 And of Og, king of Bashanites,
   For his mercy is everlasting:
21 Their lands he gave the Israelites,
   For his mercy is everlasting;

22 To his people to possess for ever,
   For his mercy is everlasting.
23 He our low state forgetteth never,
   For his mercy is everlasting;
24 But from all foes doth us deliver,
   For his mercy is everlasting;

25 By whom is food to all flesh given,
   For his mercy is everlasting;
26 O give thanks to the Lord of heaven,
   For his mercy is everlasting.

Psalm CXXXVII.

1 By Babel's waters we sat down and wept,
 Zion, to think of thee;
2 Our harps we hung on each near willow tree;
3 For they required our song,
 Who captive led us to far lands along—
 A melody, whilst our hearts dull sorrow kept;
 "Sing, sing to us," they cried, "a Zion song."
4 The Lord our God, how shall his song be sung
 By us in strangers' land?
5 If I forget thee, so let my right hand
 Forget her wonted skill!
6 Jerusalem, when thee I shall not still
 Prefer mid all my gladness, let this tongue
 Cleave to my palate, and for aye be still.
7 O Lord, our God, remember Edom's sons
 In Zion's evil day.
 "Down, down, yea, bring her to the ground," said they.
8 Right blessed shall he be,
 O dolorous daughter of the stern Chaldee,
9 Who dashes on the walls thy sucking ones,
 Who that which thou hast wrought us, wreaks on thee.

Psalm CXXXVIII.

1 With all my heart to thee
 In the gods' sight I will make harmony;
2 I will kneel down before
 Thy hallowed temple, and thy name adore,
 O true and kind to crown

Thy promise, yea beyond thy own renown.
3 For when I called on thee
 Thou heard'st, and did'st with might my soul set free.
4 All kings of earth, O Lord,
 Shall praise thee, hearing that my lips record.
5 Yea, they shall sing thy ways,
 O Lord, and thy exceeding glory praise;
6 Saying, The Lord on high
 Casts on the poor and o'er the proud his eye.
7 In midst of trouble when
 I walk, thou dost with life enforce me then.
 Against my foes thou sendest
 Thy hand, and with thy right hand me defendest.
8 Withdraw not, Lord, thy hands from that they do:
 Thy mercy is perpetual: bear me through.

Psalm CXXXIX.

1 Thou hast me sought and known:
 Thou know'st my rising, Lord, and sitting-down.
2 Thou readest far away
3 My thoughts; thou dost my path, my couch survey.
4 Thou seest where'er I go;
 No word is on my tongue, but thou dost know.
5 Thou dost before me stand,
 And by me, and enfold'st me with thy hand.
6 Too wondrous is this lore
 For me, and higher than I can explore.

7 How, therefore, shall I hie
 Beyond thy spirit, or thy presence fly?
8 If up to heaven I flew,

Thou art there; if I sought the grave, there too.
9 If I the wings of morn
Should lift, and light beyond the Ocean's bourne,
10 Lo! there thine hand would hold
And lead me, yea, thy right would me enfold.
11 In darkness should I say
That I would cower, my night would be as day.
12 No darkness dark would be;
For dark is clear, and midnight day with thee.

13   Sure! thou hast wrought my frame;
Hast tissued me, ere from the womb I came.
14 I will give praise to thee,
Fearfully being made and wondrously.
For surely are thy deeds
Right wondrous, and that well my soul areads.
15 From thee were hidden not
My bones, although in secret I was wrought,
Pattern'd in earth full deep—
16 Thine eyes beheld my embryon, thou did'st keep
My limbs in thy book set,
While day by day they grew, while none was yet,
17 O God, how fathomless
I find thy thoughts, how vast their ampleness.
18 For if to tell them o'er
I strove, they pass the sands upon the shore.
I waken out of sleep,
To stand afresh in thy perpetual keep.

19   Ye men of blood, away
From me! wilt thou not, God, the wicked slay?
20 Who speak against thee lies,
Who to do guile, as foes of thine, devise.

21 Have I not hated, Lord,
  Thy haters, thine antagonists abhorred?
22 As foes of mine I rate them,
  Yea, with the utmost of all hate I hate them.
23 Search me, O God, survey
  Mine heart, and prove me, and my thoughts assay.
24 And see if guile sojourn
  In me, and lead me in the paths eterne.

Psalm CXL.

1 Save me from evil men, Lord; rescue me,
  From sons of cruelty,
2 Whose heart deviseth wrongs, who war array
  Against me day by day;
3 Who whet their tongues like serpents; 'neath whose lips
  The adder's poison drips.

4 Keep me from evil hands, Lord; rescue me
  From sons of cruelty.
5 They plot to overthrow my feet; their snare
  The proud for me prepare.
  They spread a net with cords across the way;
  Their traps for me they lay.

6 To the Lord I cry, Thou art my God; give ear
  At the voice of my prayer.
7 O Lord, my strong help, thou hast covered
  In battle-hour mine head.

o

8 Fulfil not, Lord, the ungodly's wish, nor grant
   Their lusts, that they may vaunt.
9 Let on their heads, who have beset me, all
   Their own lips' malice fall.
10 Throw brands amongst them; let them sink in fire
   And flood, beyond retire.
11 No reinless tongue shall thrive upon the earth;
   Disaster shall hunt forth
   And overtake the injurious, and full fast
   Shall to the ground him cast.
12 I know the Lord, that he will judge the poor.
   And weak men's rights assure.
13 Therefore the just shall praise thy name, the upright
   Dwell in thy aspect's light.

Psalm CXLI.

1 I cry, O Lord, to thee;
   Hear mine imploring cry; haste unto me.
2 O that before thine eyes
   My supplication may like incense rise;
   And as the offering's savor
   At evening, may my lifted hands find favor.
3 Set, Lord, a watch before
   My mouth, and of my lips guard thou the door.
4 Let to nought evil stray
   Mine heart, lest I should walk the ungodly's way,
   Or share the bad men's deed;
   Nor on their dainty morsels would I feed.

5   If me the righteous strook,
    I would esteem it grace, and their rebuke
    Mine head like oil should bear,
    And flinch not, though to twice descend it were.
    Nay, but my prayer shall be
    For those that now are suffering wrongfully.

6   When down the rocks were thrown
    Our country's judges, these men heard the tone
    Of patient words from me.
7   As when on ground one cleaves and fells a tree,
    Our people's bones thus have
    Been scattered, ev'n upon thy jaws, O grave.

8   Mine eyes are set on thee;
    Thou, Lord God, art my trust; forsake not me.
9   Guard me from their hid snare,
    From nets that men of guilt for me prepare.
10 Let in the toils they shape
    Sink all the wicked; let me ever escape.

Psalm CXLII.

1 My voice before the Lord
   Hath cried; my voice the Lord God hath implored.
2 I have unlocked my thought
   Before him, and my grief unto him brought.'
3 My spirit hath sunk low
   Within me; thou dost my wayfaring know!
   Thou know'st how they prepare
   Against me, on the path I walk, a snare.

4 I look upon the right,
And watch, and none that know me are in sight.
Mine hope of help is perished;
There lives not one, by whom my soul is cherished.
5 I cry, O Lord, to thee;
I cry, Thou art a tower of strength to me,
6 Mine heirloom in the nation
Of living men; hear thou my supplication;
For in sore need I stand.
My foes prevail: O save me from their hand.
7 Out of the snares they frame
Save thou my soul, that I may praise thy name,
That righteous men may see,
And may exult, when thou rememberest me.

Psalm CXLIII.

1 Hear thou, when I entreat; thine ear accord
Unto my prayer. O Lord.
Answer me, as thou righteous art and true.
2 Come not to strictly sue,
Lord, with thy servant; for before thy sight
Who shall be found upright?
3 Behold, mine enemies chase my soul; they'd put
My life down underfoot;
In darkness, with the dead of ages past,
They would my dwelling cast.
4 My spirit is in me faint, and sore oppressed
Is my heart in my breast.
5 I think upon the ancient days, and all
Thy dealings I recall;

I muse on all the wonders of thine hand.
6 I stretch to thee mine hand;
My soul for thee pines like a thirsting land.

7   Haste, Lord, and answer; my soul pines for thee;
Hide not thy face from me,
Lest I be like them, who to the pit are borne.
8 Cause me to hear at morn
Thy bounty; for on thee my trust I throw.
Do thou the pathway show
That I may walk on; for to thee is it
That I my soul commit.
9 O set me from mine adversaries free,
Lord, for I fly to thee.
10 Teach me to do thy pleasure, and impart,
Since mine own God thou art,
To me thy gracious spirit, that it may
Guide me in a perfect way.
11 Quicken me, Lord, for thy name's sake; and lead
My soul out of sore need;
12 And scatter thou my foes, and in thy grace
Slay them my soul who chase;
For I am one thy service who embrace.

Psalm CXLIV.

1 Blest be the Lord, my might,
Who teacheth mine hands war, mine arms to fight.
2 Mine hope, my fort, my tower,
My shield, my buckler under whom I cower.

3 Lord, what hast thou in man
  To care for, and in woman's child to scan?
4 Man is like nothingness;
  His days go by, like shadows remnantless.
5 Come down, and lower the skies;
  Touch, Lord, the mountains, and their smoke shall rise.
6 Lighten thy lightnings round;
  Shoot out thy shafts, and scatter, and confound.
7 From height superne extend me
  Thy hand, and save me, and protection send me,
8 Against the mighty swarms
  Of waters, and against the heathens' arms,
  Whose mouth 's with guile replete,
  Whose right-hand is a right-hand of deceit.

9   O God, to thee I'll sing
  A new song; I will strike the tenfold string.
10 'Tis thou that giv'st, O Lord,
  Victory to kings; that didst from baleful sword
  Thy servant David save.
11 Save, snatch us from the aliens' hands, we crave;
  Whose mouth 's with guile replete,
  Whose right-hand is a right-hand of deceit:
12 That our sons, bravely growing
  In their youth, may like sapling trees be showing;
  Our daughters may with fair
  Smooth pillars in the temple's coigns compare;
13 That our barns eke with store
  Of all sorts may be full and running o'er;
  Our sheep may in the mead
  By thousands and by tens of thousands breed.
14 That strong our oxen may

To labor grow; that there be no decay,
No leading into thrall,
No voice of murmuring in our streets at all.
15 Blest is the people, who
Fare thus, the tribes the Lord is God unto.

Psalm CXLV.

1 Thee, God, my king, I will exalt, and bless
Thy name for ever and aye.
2 Thee I will bless from day to day, and laud
Thy name for ever and aye.
3 Great is the Lord, and highly to be praised;
His greatness hath no bound;
4 Age unto age shall glorify thy deeds,
And thy great power shall sound.
5 Of thy majestic grandeur, and thy works
Of wonders I'll converse,
6 That men the might of thy dread acts may voice;
Thy greatness I'll rehearse;
7 That thy large mercy's memory they may cherish,
Thy righteousness may praise.
8 The Lord is ruthful, tender, slow to wrath,
And plentiful in grace.
9 The Lord is good to each; his mercies flow
On all he makes to live.
10 Let all thy creatures praise thee, Lord, and blessing
Let all thy saints thee give.
11 Let them the glory of thy kingdom speak,
And thy power celebrate,

12 To show the sons of men thy power, thy realm's
  Bright glories celebrate.
13 Thy kingdom is the kingdom through all time;
  From age to age thy reign.
14 The Lord uplifteth them who fall, and those
  That sink doth he sustain.
15 On thee, Lord, wait the eyes of all; their meat
  Thou dost in season give.
16 Thou openest thy hand, thou satisfi'st
  The wants of all that live.
17 The Lord is true and just in all his ways,
  To all his works right kind.
18 The Lord is near to all who call on him,
  Who call with upright mind.
19 The wants of those that fear him he supplies,
  He listens to their cry,
20 And saves them; yea, on all that love the Lord
  He keepeth fixed his eye;
  And all the ungodly will the Lord destroy.
21 Thus shall my mouth proclaim
  The praises of the Lord, and let all flesh
  Bless ever and aye his name.

Psalm CXLVI.

1 Praise the Lord, O my soul!
2 Whilst I have life I will the Lord extol.
  Whilst aught remains of me,
  Unto the Lord I will make harmony.
3 Trust not in woman's son,
  In princes not, for help in them is none.

4 Their breath goes forth ; they hie
   To their dust back ; their thoughts that day all die.
5 Blessed, whose help 's the God
   Of Jacob, whose trust is the Lord our God !
6 Who made the heavens, the earth,
   The sea, and all whereunto they give birth,
   Whose truth abides for ever,
7 Who doth by judgment the oppressed deliver.
   The Lord with bread sustains
   The perishing, and unlocks the prisoner's chains.
8 The Lord the blind man's sight
   Restores, the Lord upholds the staggering wight.
   The Lord the upright defends,
9 The Lord the homeless wanderer befriends.
   The widow and fatherless
   He guards, and thwarts the works of wickedness.
10 The Lord for ever reigns—
   Thy God, O Zion, whilst the world remains.

Psalm CXLVII.

1 Extol the Lord !
   For this is good, to psalm our God, yea, sweet ;
   For to give praise is meet.
2 The Lord doth Zion build ; the scattered race
   Of Israel doth replace.
3 He heals the broken-hearted, and by him
   Is bound the wounded limb.
4 He tells the number of the stars ; he all
   Their host by name doth call.

5 Great is the Lord, and of surpassing might,
   And wisdom infinite.
6 The Lord upholds the needy; he doth thrust
   The ungodly down to dust.
7 O thank the Lord in responses; applaud
   With sound of harp our God:
8 Who covers heaven with clouds, who rain distils
   O'er earth, who greens the hills;
9 Who giveth food to beasts; the raven's brood
   Caw to him for their food.
10 He doth not in the strength of steed or might
   Of manly thewes delight,
11 But in his fearers he delights, in those
   Whose hopes on him repose.
12 Praise, O Jerusalem, the Lord; do thou
   Zion, thy God avow,
13 Who makes thy gate-bars fast; who benisons
   Sheds in thee o'er thy sons;
14 Who gives thy borders peace; with finest wheat
   Who maketh thee replete;
15 Who sendeth out his mandate, who on earth
   Biddeth his word run forth;
16 Who scatters frost like ashes, and who makes
   His snows like woollen flakes;
17 Who casts his ice in morsels forth; his cold
   Who is there can outhold?
18 Who sends his word and melts them, who lets blow
   His wind, and the waters flow.
19 He shows his word to Israel, manifests
   To Jacob his behests.
20 He hath not dealt with other nations so;
   His law they do not know.

Psalm CXLVIII.

1 Praise from out of heaven the Lord God,
 Praise him on supremest height,
2 All his angels, all his armies,
3 Sun with moon and stars of light.
4 Praise him, heav'n of heav'ns, and water
 Which art over heav'n expanded.
5 Let the name by all be praised
 Of the Lord God; for commanded
 By his word they had their being.
6 He appointed them for ever,
 And his ordinance laid upon them:
 They shall overpass it never.

7 Praise from out of earth the Lord God,
 Dragons and abysmal deeps,
8 Snows and vapors, hail and lightning,
 Storm-wind, that his mandate keeps,
9 Hills and every mountain, cedars,
 And all trees that fruitage yield;
10 Fowls that wing the air and reptiles,
 Beasts of forest and of field;
11 Kings of earth and every nation,
 Lords and all who earth control,
12 Youths and maidens, children, elders,
13 Let them all the name extol
 Of the Lord, for high and hallowed
 Is no name beside the Lord;

From the earth and from the heav'n your
  Praises render to the Lord;
14 Who his people's horn exalteth,
  Whom the praise befitteth well,
  Of the nation he is near to,
  Of his chosen Israel.

Psalm CXLIX.

1 Sing before the Lord a new song,
  Praise him 'mid his faithful ones ;
2 Glory, Israel, in thy Maker,
  In your king, O Zion's sons.
3 Let them to his name in dances,
  Touching lyre and drum, give praise ;
4 For the Lord his people loveth,
  And the meek with help arrays.
5 Let his leal exult and glory,
  From their couches uttering joy ;
6 Let his praise their lips, and double
  Edged swords their hands employ ;
7 To do vengeance on the nations,
  And to teach the heathen pains,
8 Binding fast their kings with fetters,
  And their lords in iron chains,
9 Thus to exercise upon them
  Every judgment that is writ!
10 Lo! such honors to his faithful
  Servants doth the Lord commit.

Psalm CL.

1 Praise God, praise him amongst his saints, in th' heav'n of his empire ;
2 Praise him in his prowess, in his might's infinitude praise him.
3 Praise him on harp and fife, to the sound of clarions praise him.
4 Praise him upon timbrels, to the lute and psaltery dancing.
5 Praise him upon resonant cymbals, with clashing of cymbals.
6 Praise ye him, all that breathe ; O praise ye, praise ye the Lord God.

NOTES ON THE PSALMS.

THE psalms in the Hebrew Bible are called the book of T-hillīm, a word etymologically denoting "praises," (as of a superior being). The title psalms, psalmoi', comes from the Greek of the Septuagint, and signifies hymns or poems to be recited with the accompaniment of musical instruments. Such a word is more appropriately used for the Hebrew "Mizmōr," in the titles of several special psalms. It is evident, in fact, that the collection is not wholly, though it is for the most part, composed of lyrical poems; it includes several which are mere collections of aphorisms or religious formulas, like Psalm xxxiv. and Psalm cxix., of which the construction is even regulated by alphabetic sequence; besides others of intermediate character and poetic rank, and many obviously of the elegiac class; to all which the translator owes different styles of verse and diction; to make hymns or odes of all were an irrelevant affectation.

The psalms appear to have been written at various periods, extending from the reign of David, to the time of Haggai, and Zachariah. Some, indeed, according to several commentators, were composed under the Maccabees, but it is generally thought that the canon of the Hebrew Scriptures was completed before that æra. The collection is divided into five books, according to which we may distinguish to some extent, though by no means positively, the relative antiquity of the poems contained in it; as indeed the style of the last books is generally more fluent and polished, and sometimes more artificial. These books were arranged one after another, but even the first two, De Wette thinks, not till soon after the Captivity, to which we find allusions in Psalms xiv. and li., supposing them to have suffered no interpolations. The close of each book, except the last, is marked by a doxology, which must not be mistaken for an integral part of the preceding psalm; see in the authorized version the last verse of Psalm xli., the last three of Psalm lxxii., and the last of Psalm lxxxix., and of Psalm cvi. The psalms in the first book, if we might judge by the titles, are all Davidical, except two or three, and even before these the omission of the name might in part seem casual; other authors appear occasionally in the second book, and in the third book begin to predominate; so that here we manifestly arrive among the interesting lays of the Captivity and the Repatriation, and meet with the broader religious views of a cultured epoch. But these titles often express a date to which the contents of the psalm do not allow us to attach any credit; see Psalms xxxiv., li., liv., etc., nor have those terms in the titles which relate to the music or rhythm been consistently explained, or in a manner to involve interesting discussions. Indeed, if we criticize the psalms by the rigor of De Wette's method, and refuse to David the authorship of all those in which we find allusions to the temple and its site, the works of the royal poet will be reduced within a very narrow compass. It may be preferable to suppose that some such poems involve interpolations or modernizations of ancient themes; but to distinguish these in detail would be a hazardous and fruitless speculation. At best, the title of a psalm may give us some general clue to the period during which it was composed, or, in some cases, to the date of an earlier composition on which it was founded; *see* notes on Psalm cxliv. and others.*

---

* The title of a Psalm in the Masoretic or recognized Hebrew text, is often counted for the first verse. I have, however, both in my version and my references, followed the modern arrangement; I may sometimes, through inadvertence, have confounded the numbers. In rendering the various tenses of the Hebrew verb, I may appear to have taken too much liberty with the text; but the vagueness of the received rules and the discrepancies of all the translators, will justify my abstaining, in general, from the discussion of such points, on which I am content to appeal to the context. In quoting Hebrew words I have adopted the following equivalents in the Roman alphabet for each letter: 1, for Aleph (with its vowel) a or 'a, and so on; 2, for Beth, according to the points b, (bb) or bh; and for the rest, 3, g or gh; 4, d, or dh; 5, h; 6, w (where the character is not to be inferred from the long vowel); 7, z; 8, ch; 9, t italic (as recommended by Professor Max Müller); 10, y, under the same conditions that w is used; 11, k, or kh; 12, l; 13, m; 14, n; 15, s'; 16 with its vowel, "a, and so on, (see Lepsius, Allgemeines alphabet; the sign of the aspirate in Greek ['a] is objectionable, because it expresses a surd and not a sonant element); 17, p, or ph; 18, s italic (see 9); 19, q; 20, r; 21, sh or s; 22, t or th. The vowels are written thus " a " short, ā long; e, ē; i, ī; o, ō or ōw; u, ū; the *shwa* being omitted or indicated by a hyphen. Proper names are left as in the authorized version.

PSALM I.—This psalm is anonymous, but treated as Davidical in some copies of the Septuagint; in some Hebrew manuscripts it bears no number. It was perhaps prefixed to the collection on account of its general moral import. It asserts, in terms that seem very unqualified, the justice of Providence in the distribution of worldly felicity, a point more anxiously discussed in Psalm lxxiii. and elsewhere, in which we are reminded of the reasonings of Job and his three friends.

1. *Of wicked men.*—The first of the three designations implies the gravest charge, viz., of positive injustice by force or fraud; the two others are more general.

2. *But who doth in the Lord's law.*—That is to say, Jehovah's law, this name being always replaced in the authorized version by "the LORD" in capitals.

3. *Like by the waters of the rills.*—The gardens of the East were usually irrigated by artificial channels, which may here be meant; (see with Rosenmüller Isaiah lviii. 11); the present verse is referred to in Jeremiah xvii. 8.

Ibidem. That man shall be—That is to say, *is generally*, can be always predicated about to be. This idiomatic use of the Hebrew future can be imitated, within certain limits, with the corresponding tense in English; but the reader should be careful, in passages less plain, not to think of any remote epoch.

PSALM II.—This psalm promises victory to the anointed of the Lord, that is, a certain king of Judah, against a league of heathen nations that have rebelled against him. It does not seem to refer to David, who was not crowned on Mount Zion, nor yet to Solomon, whose reign was in general so peaceful, but to one of their successors. The boldness of the language has led many to give it a purely Messianic interpretation. But the psalm, observes De Wette, accords neither with Jewish nor with Christian representations of the Messiah. According to the former, he should initially have to conquer and subjugate the peoples; but here would peoples already subjugated rise up against him and emancipate themselves; according to the latter, the Messiah is no subduer of peoples, wielding the iron sceptre of force; "his kingdom is not of this world."

P

This psalm being anonymous, it seems not necessary to ascribe it, on the authority of Acts iv. 25, to the pen of David; for we have in this verse no direct Scriptural assertion that it is Davidical, but only the citation of an opinion which made it so—the assembly of Christian converts saying, " Who said'st by the mouth of thy servant [or son] David, Why have the nations, &c." Another verse is referred to in Acts xiii. 33, from the different readings of which passage " in the second," and " in the first Psalm," as also from Origen's comment quoted by Rosenmüller, it would appear that this psalm was by many accounted a portion or continuation of that which precedes it. And it seems, indeed, placed here as a kind of sequel thereto; Psalm i. introducing to us the ethic principles of the Hebrews, Psalm ii. the foundations of that faith and hope by which they were and are connected as a people.

4. *Shall contemn.*—That is to say, contemneth, or is just about to contemn, at the point of time into which the writer transports us, the tense being used poetically.

7. *My son thou art, &c.*—In similar language the relations of Jehovah to his anointed are described in Psalm lxxxix. 26, 27.

11. *And joy before him.*—Rejoice with trembling, authorized version. Most likely this rendering has not been fully explained; but there is a platitude, to which I cannot reconcile myself, in De Wette's " quake with trembling"—erbebet mit *Zittern.*

12. *Lest Him you move to wrath.*—That is Jehovah, not the "Son" or king.

PSALM III.—In the title the word psalm is used for Mizmōr (see introductory note), as it will be found elsewhere hereafter: but on these terms I shall not detain my readers. The title continues, " of David when he fled before the face of his son Absalom ;" see ii. Sam. 17; for Paulus [Clavis Psalmorum] supposes the psalm to refer to the night which David passed in the camp at Mahanaim, beyond Jordan. But neither to this occasion, nor to any part of the narrative of Absalom's rebellion, does the psalm contain any circumstantial allusions that can fairly satisfy us as to the authenticity of the heading.

2. *Of my soul that have said.*—Of course " the soul" is throughout the Psalms the vital principle, not the rational or moral, and we might often substitute " life " or " self;" but I have preserved a poetic usage, to which the reader, I suppose, will have opportunity enough to familiarize himself.

Ibm. There is for it no aid.—Our translators give " no help for him," under the persuasion, I suppose, that the Hebrew *Nephesh*, soul, is a noun feminine, and not referred to by the masculine pronoun in the word " lō." But see Gesenius in his Lexicon.

Ibm. Selah.—This word seems always to denote a pause, and most generally a logical one, as at the conclusion of a paragraph; but sometimes, only a pause of emphasis. It appears also, here and elsewhere, to mark a rhythmical pause, dividing stanzas or strophes, which are frequently composed of the same, or nearly the same number of verses. It will be omitted henceforth, since it was not intended to be read.

4. *From his holy hill.*—Mount Zion, near which the Ark of the Covenant had been already placed, *i.e.*, in the City of David, ii. Sam. 6, but not under Saul's reign. This expression goes against the view of some writers, that the psalm refers to David's persecution under the reign of Saul.

8. *Have the jaws of the wicked been broke.*—As in an encounter with beasts of prey.

PSALM IV.—This is an elegiac psalm (*Klagdicht*), similar to the preceding, of which the occasion cannot be determined accurately.

1. *Thou'st given me room.*—Perhaps meaning, Thou hast delivered me on former occasions, but the allusion would be remarkably cursory. De Wette takes the perfect of the verb in an imperative sense; and adduces parallel passages, but ignores, in these, the influence of the particle ū.

3. *A votary of his own.*—The word Chāsīdh seems to have both an active and a passive import, including the ideas of a worshipper and a protégé; compare, in secular relations, the word client.

4. *Tremble, do wrong no more.*—Here the Septuagint gives

ὀργίζεσθε καὶ μὴ ἁμαρτάνετε, be ye angry and sin not—which version is referred to in Ephesians iv. 26.

7. *More than in times when corn, &c.*—From this verse it has been conjectured, perhaps plausibly, that the psalm was written in a time of dearth.

Psalm V.—The author of this psalm complains of perfidious and unrelenting enemies, but on what special occasion it seems impossible to conclude with confidence. The mention of the temple in verse 7 seems to show that it is not Davidical.

1. *My fervent utterance hear.*—In the authorized version—" consider my meditation;" as if the word " Hăghīgh" were to be directly derived, neglecting the third radical, from "hăghah," to meditate ; so where it recurs in Psalm xxxix. 3, [in the Masoretic arrangement, verse 4] the Septuagint gives Μελέτη, meditation. However, this etymology does not notice the doubled second radical ; for the root is " hăghagh," not hăghah, and the Septuagint, not consistent with itself, gives in the present verse, Κραυγὴ, clamor. Further we must remark, in deference to the style and composition of the psalmist, that he would not appear, either with elegance or propriety, first to claim the attention of Heaven to distinctly uttered words, then to a cold, silent meditation. For even if we apprehended here a sort of climax, as though God were represented as scrutinizing, not only words but thoughts, the figure would be ill completed by the next clause, " hearken unto the voice of my cry." I have therefore translated the expression in accordance with Gesenius, who derives hăghīgh from an obsolete root, hăghagh, to be explained by the Arabic " hadzha," fervuit.

5. *Presumption bears.*—*i. e.* the presumptuous, as the word is best understood both here and at Psalms lxxiii. 3, and lxxv. 5.

8 *A plain path of thine make me.*—The authorized version rendering, Make thy way straight before my face, is a verbatim one, but does not, I think, allow for the Hebrew idiom ; while the import suggested, The Lord enable me to conduct myself according to his own commandments, has less relevancy than, Show me a path of deliverance.

PSALM VI.—The author complains of a painful and dangerous sickness, aggravated, it would appear, by mental suffering, and by the envy and insolence of adversaries.

5. *For in death none remembers thee.*—This verse, like Psalm xxx. 9, expresses the belief of simple antiquity, that death imports, I will not say positive annihilation, for this notion presents its difficulties to the imagination, but the end of all experiences and emotions that can be anticipated with any human interest. If there are any passages in the psalms, on the contrary, that are rightly judged to refer to a future state, they must represent the philosophy of individual thinkers; the strongest case, I think may be made out for Psalm lxxiii, with especial reference to verses 23 and 24.

PSALM VII.—Respecting Cush, the Benjamite, we have no positive information; though it has been conjectured, with much plausibility, that he was one of the adversaries and maligners of David in the court of King Saul.

2. *Else, lion-like, he'll prey on me.*—The first verse refers generally to David's adversaries; the second, it would appear, to some particular and more formidable persecutor.

3. *O Lord my God, if I have done this,* i.e., if I have incurred any such guilt as I am now about to describe.

4. *Or taken spoil from those.*—To make the second clause antithetical to the first, (as in the authorized version we have, "Yea, I have delivered him that without cause is mine enemy,") involves a harsh construction in the language of the text, and in the speaker an affectation of generosity, which is neither in place where he is vindicating himself from a crime, nor yet in the spirit of ancient morals. The verb means also to strip or plunder, and is so understood here by De Wette.

5. *Mine honor low in dust.*—The word *honor* or glory appears to be used in Hebrew as a synonym of soul; compare Genesis xlix. 6.

7. *That judgment dost decree.*—Literally, Thou hast commanded judgment—as a general observation. (C. B. Michaelis.)

12. *An angered God is he.*—The word God is in the first clause of the text elōhīm, in the second ēl; the former term is more

emphatic, and the latter more vague and general. Hence De Wette, whom I have here followed, to avoid bathos, takes "El" as a predicate, translating, God [*i.e.* Jehovah] is a righteous judge, and a God [that is] angry every day.

14. *Shafts, which as fire he makes.*—Literally, He has made his arrows *to* [or *for*] *burning ones*. The Chaldee paraphrast, who is followed, though equivocally, by the Septuagint, understands "for the persecutors," (see authorized version ;) and the Hebrew word occurs undoubtedly in this meaning, but only, as far as I can judge, in virtue of a particular collocation ; as we read, (Genesis xxxi. 36) Thou hast burnt after me—*i. e.*, hunted me down. But this collocation not obtaining in the present passage, I prefer translating with Rosenm. and De Wette, He has made his arrows to be burning ones—*i. e.*, God has armed himself with lightnings.

PSALM VIII.—In this psalm, as in Psalm xix. and civ., the works of Nature are represented as attesting God's attributes. Man, though so immeasurably inferior to him, is an object of his attention and beneficence. Of many attempts to give a special interpretation to this psalm, the most notable is in the Epistle to the Hebrews, chap. ii., of which I leave the critical value to the reader's judgment.

2. *From lips of babes and sucklings.*—Their inarticulate or broken utterances are signs to us of their dependence on the All-merciful. Compare Psalm civ. 21, cxlvii. 9.

5. *Below what angels are.*—Literally, thou hast made him little short of gods [*i. e.* angels],—or, as some understand, "of God ;" the Hebrew Elohim being virtually either a singular or a plural.

PSALM IX.—This psalm exhibits traces of an "acrostichal" construction, like that of Psalm xxxvii., (see Psalms xxv., cxix., &c.,) so that the initial letters of every alternate verse stood in alphabetical order, the alphabet being completed in Psalm x., which appears therefore to have been a continuation, or rather counterpart, of the preceding, as we might also conclude it to have been from the absence of a distinctive title, and from the arrangement of the Septuagint version. Nevertheless, the contents of the two psalms are so incongruous, that their connexion may well be judged an artificial one. The imperfect observance of the alphabetic law in each, has probably arisen from the omissions and corruptions of the received text; it has been corrected, in some verses, by a variety of conjectural readings, the respective worth of which could only be determined by " grounds more relevant " than I have found insisted on. See Bellermann über die Metrik der Hebräer, Scheid in Eichhorn's Allgemeine Bibliothek II. 944, and other authors quoted by De Wette, who attaches little weight to their conclusions on our present subject. I will venture to remark, that the form of the alphabetic poems was probably suggested by the practice of using the letters as numerals. In this manner they got prefixed to the verses or paragraphs which it was desired to keep separate, and as they were not distinguished in the rude forms of ancient calligraphy from the letters that formed integral parts of adjacent words, it became agreeable to the eye of the reader that they should be *worked* into these words. Hence it should not surprise us that the sequence of the letters is sometimes rather irregular: "nam summa hic," says Hüttinger, " spiritûs sancti libertas;" it will also be strikingly natural that in one early specimen, like that before us, the sequence should terminate with the letter Yōdh (10); the succeeding letters not having been customarily employed to express the succeeding units, but for the tens and hundreds, &c. Nor has any other kind of acrostich been discovered in the Bible. The form of the alphabetic Psalm, as it involved some mechanical difficulty, was found most suitable to compilations of unconnected aphorisms and religious formulas, but was not at first limited to such works. But most of these psalms are of comparatively modern date. The burden of Psalm ix. is a confident anticipation of success in battle by the favor of Jehovah. It seems, from verses 11 to 14, to have been written after the founding of the Temple.

3. *When back my enemies.*—I repeat the word *when* before both clauses, according to the construction advocated by De Wette, literally, in the turning of my foes backward, [in the time when] they stumble and perish, &c.,—so that the indicatives of the second and third verb supply the place of infinitives; compare Psalms xxxi. 14. I consider the verse as referring to time present.

4. *An umpire just.*—I construe, with De Wette, the word shōphēth as a substantive, and ṣaddīq adjectively.

6. *The enemy dies.*—I do not take the word hāōyēbh as a vocative, but as the nominative of a term used collectively, and governing a plural verb. The word *thou* in the subsequent hemistich refers to God. Compare De Wette.

7. *But the Lord sitteth.*—Perhaps the psalmist continues to address Jehovah, though in the indirect manner often suggested by courtesy or reverence.

13. *Have mercy on me, Lord.*—This is the plaint, according to Rosenmüller, of the poor oppressed man who has been referred to.

PSALM X.—v. 2. *He snares them.*—I should construe this passage with De Wette, They [*i. e.* the poor man in a collective sense] shall be [*i. e.* are repeatedly] ensnared in the devices which they [the wicked] have imagined. The authorized version takes the first verb as an imperative:—let them [the wicked] be taken in the devices, &c.,—but this rendering furnishes a more abrupt and hasty transition than is requisite to the purport of the passage. I also follow De Wette in translating the two next verses, the construction of which, however, appears too equivocal to be positively settled. "The wicked plumes himself on [the acquisition of] his desires, and blesses robbers [I have rendered it ' evil gains,' that is, the gains of fraud] and contemns Jehovah. The wicked by dint of his pride—all his thoughts are—he (God) takes no heed; there is (as it were) no God."

5. *Corrupt are all his ways.*—I should, perhaps, have translated " prosperous are all his ways;" literally, *stable* or secure, as De Wette translates in accordance with Jarchi and the Chaldee Targum ; compare on the word yāchīlū, Job xx. xxi.

14. *Treachery, to note it on thy hand.* — Thus De Wette translates after Geier and others, comparing Isaiah xlix. 16.

15. *Lest men should scare them.*—Literally, lest [one] should scare the [weak] man from the land—(see De Wette, who on the meaning of the verb compares Job xiii. 25); the sentence is otherwise construed in the authorized version.

PSALM XI.—v. 1. *How bid you then me?*—The question, it would seem, is not addressed to the adversaries of the speaker, but to his timorous allies and counsellors; he says, Your hill,—not, My hill.

3. *For the pillars of order.*—Literally, For the foundations are destroyed,—a proverbial expression, according to De Wette, importing the overthrow of law and tranquillity.

Ibm. What help has the just?—What else shall the just man, the oppressed Israelite, do, but escape and go into exile? [De Wette.]

PSALM XIII.—v. 3. *With life mine eyes illume.*—The two first words are inserted for the sake of perspicuity; we must not, according to modern usage, consider the "lightening of the eyes" as a metaphor of enlightenment by some kind of doctrine or instruction; it signifies rather, according to Hebrew idiom, the recruiting of the spirits and bodily vigor from a state of languor and exhaustion; compare 1 Samuel, xiv. 27.

PSALM XIV.—Of this psalm we have another version, or perhaps an imitation and new application, in Psalm lii.; the latter, however, is not ascribed to David. Verses 5—7 of the Prayer Book version are found in the Vulgate and Septuagint, and in one of Kennicott's Hebrew manuscripts, but not in the Masoretic text; they are quoted in Rom. iii. 13—18.

4. *With no chastisement meet?*—Literally, *have they not known?* which may mean, in accordance with Hebrew idiom, "Do they experience or feel no punishment?" compare Judges viii. 16; Hos. ix. 7, &c., or, Are they not made aware, by punishment, of the guilt they have incurred? See De Wette.

7. *Out of Zion.*—These words attest the late æra at which the psalm was written.

PSALM XV. — This psalm has a striking resemblance to Psalm xxiv.; it is generally supposed to commemorate the removal of the ark to the City of David, 2 Sam vi. 12, but may very well, as De Wette says, be understood without this special application.

PSALM XVI. — v. 2. *Thou art more dear than all.* — Literally, according to the construction adopted by Rosenmüller, " My welfare is not [in aught] besides thee." So Symmachus, "ἀγαθόν μοι οὐκ ἔστιν ἄνευ σου;" Jerome, Bene mihi non est sine te.

3. *The saints on earth.*—I construe, with De Wette, *In respect to the saints of earth,* [it is] even they [that are] the excellent ones, in whom is my whole delight;—see parallel constructions cited by this commentator.

8. *Who go in haste awry.*—Literally, Who hasten elsewhere, [die anderswohin eilen, says De Wette;] and the meaning of the clause, it must be admitted, is not very explicit; but we cannot, without violence to the original text, find in it the words—after another god.

11. *Thy votary see the Grave.*—Literally, Thou wilt not suffer thy truster to see the grave—not, as we read, in accordance with the Septuagint version, *to see corruption;* for this construction of the word Shăchath, though etymologically admissible, appears unwarranted by Hebrew usage.

De Wette observes:—The apostolic application of this passage does not in any verse, from the historical point of view, render necessary the Messianic exposition. The poet hoped for deliverance from death through Jehovah's protection; a danger of some kind hovered before him, and he hoped for an exemption, not from death absolutely, but only from a premature violent death from hostile persecution; thus his hope of life was a limited earthly one, as in general the hopes of the pious men of the Old Testament were limited to earthly things. In Christianity, on the contrary, all hopes are directed to the eternal, and so, too, is the hope of life. Now all hopes are fulfilled in Christ, and so is also the hope of eternal victory over death. But every hope, even the earthly, includes in itself, as correlative and emblem, the idea of the eternal; so, too, does our poet's hope of life, and so do the apostles understand it. They mean, in the application of the passage before us to Christ's resurrection, that " the full, entire, deep truth of the hope of the psalmist is first fulfilled and evinced in Christ." This was not an accommodation of the text, but an ideal explanation, and the apostles pursue in all cases, in which the Old Testament references to Christ are brought in question, a similar course of explanation.

PSALM XVII.—The author of this psalm, after a protest concerning the integrity of his own life, invokes the protection of Jehovah against the injuries and calumnies of worldly-minded adversaries; he then touches on the prosperity of the latter, and the peculiar blessings reserved for the servants of God. It may be observed, that while the first Psalm seems almost to deny that the wicked can have eminent welfare in this world, and while others, like Psalm lxxiii., seem to intimate that their success cannot be continued to them through lifetime, or, at least, that they cannot (as that is an object men *will* covet) leave behind them a flourishing lineage for several generations, the present writer appears to admit all these apparent contradictions to God's moral government; and yet to promise himself, as one of those who live more conscientiously, the enjoyment of some distinct proofs of the Divine love and favor, whether in the resurrection, as many suppose, or, as I am inclined to think, in the peace and cheerfulness that a pure and pious mind brings with it. Even De Wette considers the last verse to refer distinctly to a future state (while on this ground he denies that the psalm was composed by David). Compare Psalm xxxvii. 16.

13. *From evil men preserve me by thy sword.*—Literally, Preserve my soul from the wicked—thy sword. Here De Wette, who fills up the gap with the preposition, understands the construction to be like that of Psalm iii. 5, My voice, I call to the Lord—*i.e.*, with my voice. The sentiment implied in the authorized version, Deliver my soul from the wicked, which is thy sword—appears too remote and undeveloped. But I have not followed De Wette in extending the construction I have explained into the next verse so as to put, Deliver me from the man, by thy hand,—for we should then have two parallel clauses, such that the second would fall short of the first in force and vividness.

15. *Thy likeness, when I wake.*—That is, I think, The sense of Thy presence when I wake daily, or take in hand the duties of life; but perhaps the Resurrection is referred to, as I have above intimated.

PSALM XVIII.—This psalm is cited as David's in 2 Sam. xxii., so that less doubt can attach to its authorship than to that of many others which bear his name. The style is most antique and characteristic, and should be borne in mind to assist us in distinguishing the compositions which have a common origin. The citation above referred to exhibits important variations; to some of which, but a few only, I have paid attention in the present version. The events to which it bears reference, include, to all appearance, nearly all the contests which David was engaged in with foreign and domestic enemies, both before and after his accession to the throne of Israel.

6. *My voice he did out of his temple hear*—i.e., from his heavenly temple, as in Psalm xxix. 9.

7. *Earth quaked and trembled.*—Compare the figurative descriptions of Jehovah's interposition in Zec. ix. 14, &c.

11. *The dark vapors round him went.*—I think it evident that the phrase, Dark waters, will bear this acceptation, which may also attach everywhere to "the waters above the firmament."

PSALM XIX.—v. 3. *There is no speech among them.*—There is a well-known ambiguity in the Hebrew expression, of which this exposition is supported by early Jewish commentators.

7. *The soul thereby is rendered whole.*—That is, properly speaking, refreshed and invigorated; compare the parallel expressions in Lam. i. 16; Ruth iv. 15. The *judgments* are not what God commands, but the *customs* he acts on.

13. *Guard thou thy servant from the* proud.—I understand the last word of *persons* in accordance with its usual acceptation; see parallel passages cited by De Wette.

PSALM XXII.—A portion of this psalm having been repeated by our Saviour on the Cross, [Matthew xxvii. 46, &c., where compare the Chaldee paraphrase,] while verse 18, " They parted my garments," &c., is referred to by the Evangelists, [Matthew xxvii. 35, and John xix. 24], as typifying a circumstance that accompanied the Crucifixion, and some other verses [7, 8, 15, 16] admit of an application to the same event ; it has become, perhaps, a prevalent opinion that the whole poem was written for the purpose of prefiguring this important scene. Many features, on the other hand, have been observed in it, which have no consonance with the situation of the suffering Messiah; these De Wette sums up as follows:—" 1. The sufferer in the psalm is not yet in his enemies' power, but only in imminent peril from them, [verses 11, 12, 20]; 2. His suffering is one of long duration, for he prays several nights and days, [verse 2]; 3. He complains and supplicates for the preservation of his life in a way too abject and unworthy of Jesus, [verses 11, 21]; 4. The sufferer speaks of his deliverance from his enemies and the preservation of his life, [verses 20, 21,] as incentives, for foreign nations even, to praise and honor Jehovah . . . so that not his sufferings, but his deliverance from suffering, is looked upon as a means of furthering the true service of God. Now Christ founded the kingdom of God by his Passion, which he underwent of his free-will; so that this, his most peculiar and decisive work of redemption would be in this psalm rather belied than indicated. But of what value for Christians can be the Messianic exposition of a psalm, in which the Christian idea of the Messiah does not come forward?" The above arguments, it is evident, may be evaded by supposing that the psalm has a double intention, historical and prophetical, that the author, according to his own design, was writing of one event while the inspiration that mysteriously controlled his pen was guiding him to the description of another; but the very nature of this view must preclude one from developing it in a literary and critical comment.

8. *They say, Trust God, let God him save.*—The Hebrew verb is in the imperative, and may be taken to represent an ironical reflection of the crowds.

16. *They pierced my hands and feet.*—The recognized Hebrew text, according to the most obvious construction, gives, As a lion—my hands and my feet—which may be the fragment of a true reading, but is not sufficiently complete to be here translated, nor am I willing to piece it out with mere conjectures. The same word [kâ'ari,] allowing some irregularity in the orthography, may give "piercing my hands," &c.; and it gives by a slight modifi-

cation, "they pierced," [kā'arū], sanctioned by the marginal reading, as well as by many manuscripts and the old translations. But the form of the word is quite unusual, and we may not be justified in affixing a precise conception to it. Hitzig, cited by De Wette, thinks it refers to the effect of chains.

29. *Who in the dust were sinking.*—In De Wette, Alle zum Grabe gebeugten—men almost dying with misery—who are contrasted with the rich of the preceding clause.

PSALM XXIV.—This psalm, in spite of the title, seems to have been written when the Temple was already an ancient structure.

6. *These after Jacob's God enquire.*—Here the text is probably corrupt, and would certainly appear too obscure in a verbatim rendering; but the Septuagint version seems to represent the sense fairly. Αὕτη ἡ γενεὰ ζητούντων αὐτὸν, ζητούντων τὸ πρόςωπον τοῦ θεοῦ Ιακώβ.

PSALM XXV.—This is the first of the undoubted "acrostich" psalms, or of those so constructed, that the initial letters of the separate verses, taken in order, compose a Hebrew alphabet. I have thought it advisable, in the present translation, to copy one of these in its pristine form.

It must be observed that the sixth letter, Wau, not commencing any Hebrew word except the particle ū (and), cannot conveniently commence an independent proposition. Hence this letter has no verse to itself here, but only, perhaps, an hemistich, and the number of the letters, twenty-two, is made up with an extra--alphabetic verse, whether by the original author or by a later hand.

The difficulty with the letter Wau may have suggested the form of Psalms cxi., cxii., in which only a half-verse is allowed to each letter. In Psalm cxix., the difficulty is braved by forced constructions, eight successive verses beginning with the same conjunction.

PSALM XXVI.—v. 1. *And falter not.*—Literally, I shall not totter or tread amiss—which we might doubtless understand, with the authorized version, relatively to material prosperity. I prefer, however, with De Wette, to take the expression in a moral sense, and have similarly rendered that in Psalm xxxvii., 31 ; for by this rendering the import of the psalm will appear to be developed more gradually, and without unnecessary anticipation.

3. *Thy paths of truth I trace,*—*i. e.* I walk in the truth thou lovest.

12. *My foot stands fast i' th' right.*—Compare note on verse 1.

PSALM XXVII.—v. 8. *My heart has told me of the Lord.*—Literally, My heart has said in respect to thee, Seek ye my face—*i. e.*, " that thou commandest us, seek ye," &c. So De Wette explains, Seek ye my face, is the command of Jehovah, which the heart of the poet calls before his recollection.—To seek Jehovah's face may mean, to pray to him, or ask help of him, as the expression To seek God, in 2 Samuel, xii. 16, or indeed to visit his temple as in Psalm xxiv. 6 ; in which latter case we may here have an allusion to the commandment in Exodus xxiii, 17.

PSALM XXVIII.—v. 2. *Toward thy most holy place.*—In the authorized version, Toward thy holy oracle,—the word D-bhir being translated Oracle in accordance with the supposed derivation from Dābhar, to speak.   In most of the old versions, it is explained as the temple or structure containing the ark ; but the literal signification, as illustrated by modern critics from similar Arabic words, appears to be the back or west end of the tabernacle or temple ; thence the most holy place ; see Exodus xxvi. 33. See Iken, Dissert. Phil. Theol., referred to by Rosenmüller and De Wette.

8. *Strength to his people.*—Literally, to them—the pronoun being explained by the word people in the following verse.

PSALM XXIX.—v. 1. *O sons of light.*—Literally, O sons of gods, which expression De Wette, after the Chaldee Targum, understands in reference to the angels ; compare Psalm lxxxix. 7.

2. *In solemn pomp with holiness.*—The original expression appears to signify in sacred apparel—as we may also understand it in 2 Chronicles, xx. 21 ; the poet describing the angelic worship under a figure drawn from human festivals ; compare Psalm xcvi., 9.

6. *And like a roebuck Sirion.*—Another name for Hermon or Antilibanus; see Deuteronomy iii. 9.

9. *The Lord's voice the tall fir trees.*—Reading ēylōth, pines, for ayyālōth, hinds, and understanding the verb metaphorically; see Lowth's Sacred Poetry of the Hebrews.

10. *All in his Temple.*—*i. e.*, in his heavenly temple; see verse 1.

Ibm. The Lord o'er the Flood sat high.—These words are best understood of the Deluge.

PSALM XXXI.—This psalm, from the mixture it contains of prayer, complaint, and thanksgiving, appears to represent the emotions of a believer at different times and under different circumstances, and to form rather an imitative than an occasional poem.

13 *And terrors are all round.*—Hence Jeremiah, The Lord hath not called thy name Pashur, but Magor Missabib.—[xx. 3.]

PSALM XXXIII.—This psalm appears to be of artificial *formulary* construction; the word Jehovah being repeated in every group of two verses, except that which is composed of the fifteenth and the sixteenth; while the number of verses equals that of the letters in the Hebrew alphabet. The parts, though often highly beautiful, are but irregularly connected together.

PSALM XXXIV.—This psalm is alphabetic with two partial irregularities; the sixth letter being represented by an hemistich instead of a complete verse; and the last verse being supernumerary or interpolated; it closely resembles the last verse of Psalm xxii., and begins with the same letter P, which reminds some of the place of Phi in the Greek alphabet. The word Jehovah is mostly repeated in each verse. It is a didactic, aphoristic composition, and bears no reference whatever to the subject mentioned in the title.

PSALM XXXVI.—v. 2. *That his wrongful bent, &c.*—Literally, To find his iniquity, to hate—by which I understand, with De Wette, "to fulfil—or attain the objects of—his misdeeds, to gratify thereby his hatred of God and man." The authorized version gives somewhat obscurely, Until his iniquity be found to be hateful—by which we may understand, in accordance with Rosenmüller's explanation of the passage, He flatters himself, lest he should confess to himself his iniquity, so as to hate it—which involves, I think, a harder construction of the Hebrew; but the passage is anyhow a very difficult one.

8. *Out of thy mansion they partake.*—The verb may be construed, as in the preceding verse, in the present tense—and the word "house" referred to the *world*, in which the Universal Father brings up his creatures. The authorized version gives, They shall be satisfied with the pleasures of thy house—understanding, perhaps, There shall be a time when all men shall serve thee, and, as it were, offer sacrifices in thy Temple—but such a rendering would not suit the simplicity of the context.

PSALM XXXVII.—The following is one of the acrostich psalms, in which every *other* verse, for the most part, begins with a prescribed letter. The tenor of the composition, as might hence be expected, is very desultory. To make the rule of the initial letters general, it would be necessary to divide some of the verses and introduce some trivial emendations, as has been attempted by Bellermann [Versuch über die Metrik der Hebräer;] to such conjectures, which, where they affect the meaning, cannot be implicitly trusted, I do not in most places think it necessary to refer more particularly.

3 *And live secure.*—Literally the passage is, Dwell in the land, and feed [in] truth—which is open to several interpretations.

23. *'Tis of the Lord.*—In the authorized version, The steps of a [good] man are ordered by the Lord, and he delighteth in his way—the word *good* being supplied as a gloss, or from a vague notion of excellence inhering in the term "Gebher" *vir*, man, or from the context; but perhaps we may understand the passage, in accordance with Hebrew idiom, The steps of such a man, as in whose way he delighteth, are ordered by Jehovah.

35. *Like trees in native earth.*—"Ezrach," according to De Wette, signifies in other places an indigenous resident; here a tree standing where it sprang up, not transplanted, and so well rooted in the soil.

PSALM XXXIX.—v. 13. *Hold and grant me peace*—Literally, Look away from me and let me have comfort—or, Make [my face] to shine—according to the Arabic derivation of the word "ābhlīghāh," proposed by Schultens, [Origg. Hebraicæ i. 1, quoted by Rosenmüller.] The same expression occurs in Job ix. 27 and x. 20. The authorized version gives, That I may recover my strength—compare the Rabbinical interpreters. The Septuagint and Vulgate, " that I may be refreshed."

PSALM XL.—v. 2. *When in blusterous gulf*—Literally, gulf or well of noise, according to the usual interpretation of the word shā'ōn, as in Psalm lxv. 7 [verse 8 in the Hebrew text,] Isaiah xvii. 12, &c. I understand the expression in reference to that ringing in the ears which might be experienced by a person overwhelmed with water.

6. *Mine ear thou'st opened.*—Literally,—Thou piercest—which is understood, according to the analogy of similar Hebrew phrases, to mean,—Thou revealest to me—namely, according to De Wette, the things above signified, that thou regardest not sacrifice, &c.—*i.e.*, in comparison with the heart's devotion. This passage is quoted in the Epistle to the Hebrews, as if bearing reference to our Saviour ; see x. 5 ; which appears rather an application of the text, than an exposition of the author's direct meaning,—as must appear, I think, from the general tenor of the psalm.

7. *Then said I, Lo, I come.*—That is, as I understand the passage with Rosenmüller, Behold, I am ready, I am utterly desirous to live according to thy will ; even as in the volume [or scroll] of the book [of the law] it is written, that is, prescribed for me—the words kāthūbh "ālāi, being understood as in 2nd Kings xxii. 13. For these, however, the Septuagint, again quoted in Hebrews x., has ὡς περὶ ἐμοῦ γέγραπται—as is written concerning me—as if the Psalmist referred to some ancient prophecy concerning the life which he, or the personage he represents, was actually to lead, an exposition which has not been circumstantially justified.

11. *Do thou thy love, Lord.*—Here begins a new prayer for help and deliverance from trouble, after the author has already, at the

commencement of the psalm, commemorated some similar mercies previously afforded him. The vicissitudes, here implied, of welfare and of affliction, are judged to relate, not to the life of an individual, but to the fortunes of the nation he represents; so that the psalm, as Jarchi says, appears " to be uttered in respect of all Israel."

PSALM XLI.—v. 14. This verse marks the conclusion of the first book of psalms; see preliminary note.

PSALM XLII.—This psalm is the first that bears the name of the 'sons of Korah," a Levitical family, on one of those whom "David set over the service of song in the house of the Lord." [1st Chronicles, vi., 22—31;] compare 2nd Chronicles xx. 19. They were descended from Korah, who rebelled against Moses, [Numbers xvi.]; compare Numbers xxvi. 11, and the passages above referred to]. Their name is repeated in the titles of the following psalms to psalm xlix. inclusively, and in those of psalms lxxxiv., lxxxv., lxxxvii., lxxxviii. It has been doubted whether they were the authors of these poems, or had only the charge of setting them to music; some of these psalms have been attributed to David, but in all of them some peculiarities of style have been observed, which point to different authors from David; [Eichhorn, Einleitung, part iii.] and the greater number seem to have been written during or after the Captivity.

The present psalm is closely connected in style and import with Psalm xliii., in which verses 6, 10, and 12, are repeated in the manner of a refrain. The two psalms are united in the Septuagint version, and in 46 of Kennicott and De Rossi's manuscripts. Their common argument is stated as follows by De Wette:—A pious Israelite, living far from Jerusalem on the banks of the Jordan, in adversity, and suffering from the contumelies of his enemies, expresses a vehement desire to see God's Temple and to assist at his public service. He compares his present affliction and past happiness, and prays [Psalm xliii.,] for help against his enemies, and for the privilege of revisiting the Temple. The idea of Rosenmüller, that the psalm was composed by David when he fled beyond Jordan before the face of his son Absalom, appears, as De Wette has stated, not to agree exactly with the scene of the poem, [*vide* note on verse 6,] nor with the circumstances pointed out in verses 3 and 10—viz., that the writer was alone in the midst of enemies, who turned to ridicule his confidence in Jehovah. I am inclined to consider Psalm xlii. as a beautiful variation or expansion of Psalm xlii.

6. *From Mizar and Hermon hill.*—This chain of mountains, called Hermon, [or in the plural, as here, Hermōnīm,] and otherwise Sirion, Sion, or Shenir, [see Deuteronomy iii. 9 and iv. 48,] formed the northern and eastern boundary of the territory of Manasseh, and of the whole inheritance of Israel beyond Jordan, and contained the sources of that river. Of Mount Mizar, probably a branch of the same ridge, we have no accurate information. The scene of the poem appears hence to have lain at a considerable distance from Mahanaim, in the land of Gilead, the furthest point reached by David, in his flight before Absalom, 2nd Samuel xvii. 24—26.

7. *One deep unto another shouts.*—A metaphorical expression, denoting an unbroken succession of calamities, which followed one another like rolling waters. For the word waterspouts—*sinnōrīm*, in the next line, [used elsewhere for conduits or gutters,] [2nd Samuel v. 8,] J. D. Michaelis would understand cataracts or waterfalls, [Supplementa ad Lexica Hebraica,] but the effect will be the same. It is superfluous to imagine, with this commentator, any reference to the peculiar scenery of the region, as if abounding in waterfalls.

PSALM XLIV.—This psalm is explained by Calvin as referring to the oppressions of the Jews under Antiochus Epiphanes, who twice seized, without resistance, and plundered Jerusalem, grievously persecuting the adherents of the Mosaic law ; [see 1 Maccabees i. 20 and 29, et seq., and Josephus, Antiq. lib. 12, c. 5,] and by Venema of a somewhat later period, when the Jews, having enjoyed some comparative successes during the time of Judas Maccabees, were again, after his defeat and death, harassed by the generals of Demetrius Soter. [1 Maccabees ix.]

To all views of this kind De Wette objects, that the sacred

canon of the Hebrews was completed at an earlier period than they would require; he further points out some passages in this psalm, which could hardly be explained of the time of Antiochus, as verse 10, (because the Jews had then no army,) and verse 18, because there were many apostates among them; and he notes further the inadequate manner in which some events of the period would be characterized. These last arguments have less cogency, perhaps, in regard to Venema's hypothesis, provided we allow the author some latitude in glancing back beyond the history of his times. De Wette himself would consider the psalm as belonging to the days of Jehoiakim, when the Chaldeans assailed Jerusalem. [2 Kings, xxiv. 2,] or of Jehoiachin, who was carried away captive with a part of the people, ibm., verse 10.

2. *And threwest out.*—Otherwise translated, Thou didst afflict the heathen, and enlarge them—*i.e.*, the Hebrews; the verb being used of a tree spreading out her branches, as in Psalm lxxx. 11, Ezekiel xvii. 7.

5. *Our enemies we thrust back by thee.*—I translate this verse, with De Wette, in the present tense, as referring to the general tenor of the history of God's people, rather than in the future, as expressing a hope that they should again be made a victorious nation; for this idea would seem too hastily introduced in the discourse. On the contrary view see Geier, who is seconded by the authorized version. Rosenmüller uses the past tense, with which I think the passage, in the absence of a suitable conjunction, reads less fluently than might be expected.

19. *Though us thou drive to jackals' haunts.*—That the plural noun Tannim means jackals, and is not to be confounded with Tannin or Tannim, a "dragon" or large serpent or reptile, has been shown in E. Pococke's Dissertation on Micah, quoted by Rosenmüller and De Wette.

PSALM XLV.—This psalm is generally regarded as an allegory, signifying the union to be established between God and his people, or between the Messiah and the Church triumphant; and this interpretation is suggested by the *prima facie* construction of verse 6, though by no means, I think, thereby necessitated [see the note]; it is recommended also to common opinion by the desire of finding a theological, or at least a grave moral meaning in every poem that is embodied in the sacred Canon, even where such a poem might appear partially to have a secular import. [On the abuse of this feeling, in regard to the Song of Solomon, some excellent hints have been published in the Rev. C. Kingsley's novel of "Hypatia."] The allegory would be more veiled, indeed, than is usual in the sacred writings. Rosenmüller compares it gravely with the praises of love and wine in the Persian poet Hafiz, to which it has been attempted to attach a spiritual significance; but it is allowed by most critics that the psalm, in its first acceptation, has an historical import. It is doubted whether it can refer to Solomon's marriage with an Egyptian princess, for Solomon, unlike the personage depicted in verse 3, 4, 5, was a man of peace; we find not, however, any later Hebrew king to whom the context would seem appropriate: hence Rosenmüller, in the first edition of his scholia, conjectured that the warrior referred to was a king of Persia; which view I should not find necessary.

1. *My tongue is a ready writer's quill*—*i.e.*, the pen serves me for a tongue—or, I compose and dictate, (not merely recite,) as the scribe follows me.

2. *And shows thou wearest aye.*—This must be substantially the meaning, if we understand "al-kēn as *therefore;* it may also be translated by *because.*

4. *And thy right hand.*—Meaning in substance, Thou shalt terribly by thy deeds prove to thyself thy own power.

6. *Thy throne, &c.*—This verse, according to its *primâ facie* construction, means, Thy throne, O God, is for ever and ever [authorized version], and is quoted in Hebrews i. 9, as if the warrior referred to in the preceding verses were now addressed as God, *i.e.*, as an embodiment of the supreme Deity. But it would be more natural, if we allowed this construction, to suppose the clause parenthetical, and as intimating that because God reigns for ever, and his sceptre is a right sceptre [sceptre of justice], therefore the king who loveth righteousness, &c., is made to prosper, [see the following verse], and thus the import of the

passage is handled in Donaldson's Book of Jashar. Or we might say, with Rosenmüller, "the poet confers on the king the title Elōhīm, God, by which name magistrates and rulers of states are elsewhere designated, either metaphorically, because they appear even so to be the lords and governors of other men, as the supreme God is above all, or because God seemed to have imparted to them his functions and dignity." Compare Psalm lxxxii. 6.—"I have said ye are gods, and all of you are children of the most High," Exodus xxi. 6, "Then his master shall bring him unto the Elōhīm, literally, God or the gods" by which we understand, as in the authorized version, the judges; and to the same effect Exodus xxii. 8 and 9. I will not dwell upon the opinion that the poet imitates the custom of heathen nations in the East, who saluted their kings as gods; for the high moral tone of the psalm would not allow us to put such a construction upon the author's language. [See Drusius, Obs. Sacræ xii. 11 in the Critici Sacri, vol. 9.] But I must also mention Gesenius and De Wette's mode of handling the passage, who translate, Thy throne of God—or thy divinely appointed throne—is for ever and ever—tracing in the words before us the very same construction which is allowed in Ezekiel xvi. 27, where we have, Thy way of lewdness, for thy lewd way—the substantive in the state of construction governing a double genitive, in the affixed personal pronoun and the noun that follows, as would here be the case with the words Kis'akhā Elōhīm. See also Lamentations iv. 17. To a similar purport Aben Ezra translates, Thy throne is a throne of God—and Saadias, whom he quotes on the verse, God establishes thy throne for ever.

8. *Thine ear shall harps from halls of ivory please.*—Of this verse, not a comparatively important one, the meaning is disputed on account of the ambiguity of the word Minnī. [1.] The authorized version taking this, as in other places, for the preposition "Min," *from,* and supplying the word *which* (though this involves a harsh ellipsis) gives "out of the ivory palaces, whereby [wherefrom] they have made thee glad"—the word palaces being taken, perhaps, for wardrobes or cabinets, in which the robes [and the spices] had been laid up. So Vatablus, Palatia vocat magnas arcas, in quibus reponuntur vestimenta. [2.] Minnī is taken for

the name of a country; and according to the Chaldee Targum for Armenia, as in Jer. li. 27, so that we should have "out of ivory palaces of Armenia they make thee glad," *i.e.*, the Armenian princes from their palaces adorned with ivory [see 1 Kings xxii. 39 on the palace of Ahab], gladden thee by sending gifts. Minnī, as a noun proper, has been also understood of the Minæi, a nation dwelling in Arabia Felix, who are not, however, elsewhere mentioned in Scripture. These interpretations are unsatisfactory from our ignorance of the condition and political relations of the peoples referred to. They are also incongruous with the punctuation of the received Hebrew text, which separates the word Minnī from the preceding words—"ivory temples," and joins it with the following words, "they glad thee." For which reasons [3] Gesenius and De Wette take Minnī for Minnīm, "stringed instruments" [see Psalm cl. 4], supposing the final *m* omitted, whether idiomatically or by a corruption of the text, as in the word "sholshī," 2 Sam. xxiii. 8, and in other examples less unequivocal, to which view I have referred in the present version.

9. *Kings' daughters are thy pensioners.*—In the authorized version, Honorable women—which, as the pronoun *thy* is in the masculine, and refers to the king, seems to be a euphemism for "odalisks" or concubines, being daughters of conquered kings, among whom the "queen" is the favorite Sultana.

11. *For thy lord is he.*—The authorized version gives Lord with a capital letter, and the Prayer Book "thy Lord God," but without necessity, for Sara calls Abraham her Adhōnīm, or lord, in Gen. xviii. 12.

Ibm. Shouldest bend the knee.—In the authorized version, Worship thou him—which does not necessarily signify adore him as God—for the same word is used of the homage that Mephibosheth renders to David, 2 Sam. ix. 8; see other examples in Gesenius.

13. *That quite within.*—"The king's daughter is all glorious *within*"—that is, in the interior apartment of the palace; for so the passage is understood, and with most simplicity, by Rosenmüller and De Wette.

PSALM XLVI.—v. 4. *But the Lord's city*—Literally, A river—the streams [branchings] thereof shall glad the city of God—which we can only understand in a metaphorical sense, as signifying a continuous flow of peace or blessing.

PSALM XLVII.—This psalm, it is observed, may very well have commemorated the return of the ark to its place, after it had been borne, in a successful expedition, against the enemies of Israel, as appears to have been the custom from well-known passages in the history of Eli.

7. *Awake your hymn, and music make.*—The authorized version gives, in accordance with the Septuagint, Sing ye [praises] with understanding. But the word maskhīl appears only to denote a particular species of hymn or tune, as in the titles of Psalms xxxii., xliv., &c. [De Wette.]

9. *The princes of the nations.*—Probably, as De Wette remarks, the rulers of conquered or confederated nations, now acknowledging the supremacy of Israel and his God.

Ibm. Of those who shield the earth.—Literally, "For his are the shields of earth"—a phrase which I have expanded for the sake of clearness.

PSALM XLVIII.—This psalm has been considered as referring to the victory achieved by Jehoshaphat, [2 Chronicles, c. xx.,] over the combined arms of Moab, Ammon, and their confederates. In which case the allusion to the ships of Tarsus, [verse 7,] would appear irrelevant and infelicitous; inasmuch as the trading expedition, which, at about the time in question, was sent in this direction by the kings of Judah and of Israel, is recorded, in the chapter just cited, to have been frustrated by Providence. Besides, as De Wette remarks, the allies above mentioned were defeated in the desert of Tekoa, and never advanced so far as to threaten the Holy City. De Wette mentions, as a more probable hypothesis, that the enemies here referred to were the confederates of king Sennacherib, when he laid siege to Jerusalem, in the days of Hezekiah; for which view, however, we again lack positive criteria.

1. *In his holy hill.*—The mountain of the Temple, Moriah, which, however, is considered as a part of Sion.

2. *Full fair in seat and place.*—Or as Rosenmüller explains after Reland, [Palestine, page 848,] fair in elevation or uprising [schön erhebet sich der Berg Zion,] the rare word nōph being taken in the same sense as its Arabic root.

Ibm. Whence runneth to the north.—I translate this clause according to the common interpretation, "on the north side is the city of the great king." To this De Wette objects that "if we understand by Zion the two hills, on which, according to Josephus, lay the city of Jerusalem proper, then the upper city occupied the western, and the lower city the eastern side thereof. It is true that the upper city stretched out from south to northwards, but if the author had specified this situation by the phrase —'the sides of the north,' he would have left out of the picture the lower city, which extended towards the south-east." This consideration, it appears to me, would involve a prosaic accuracy. De Wette himself construes, Beautifully riseth the joy of all earth, mount Zion, [even the joy] of the furthest north, *i.e.*, in the world. He compares Isaiah xiv., 13 ; but this passage labors under an equal obscurity.

7. *Like ships of Tarsus.*—We may translate, with grammatical propriety, either, In the east wind thou shatterest the ships of Tarsus—or, In the east wind, [which] shatters, &c. Either way we must supply the particle of comparison, or else the verse will have no significance. In the first case, the subject of the pronoun is to be found in verse 8, or might be inferred, as the reader will feel, without any express mention. I have intimated my adherence to this view in writing "by thy Levantine blast." The ships of Tarsus were large vessels, adapted for a long and difficult voyage, perhaps for the circumnavigation of Africa.

PSALM XLIX.—This psalm vindicates the moral government of the world, asserting that God will award a recompense, however late and apparently precarious, to the righteous and to the wicked in accordance with their conduct ; on the question, whether this doctrine is supported by a reference to a future state, see note on verse 15.

4. *I'll give ear to dark lessons.*—This obscure clause has been variously understood by commentators. "I hearken," De Wette paraphrases, "to the song that is shaping itself within me,—so men hearken (in poetic language,) to the Muse's inspiration." Perhaps the meaning is rather, I will diligently myself study the discourses of wise men, and *then* explain my conclusions to the multitudes.

5. *When steals encroachment round my heels.*—The word "aqēbhī is to be taken, according to Rosenmüller, as a participle, signifying "my supplanters," or the envious men, who would, as it were, trip me by the heels, and encroach on me for their own emolument; compare the use of the cognate verb in Genesis xxvii. 36, Hosea xii. 3, &c.

9. *That he may live for ever.*—These words seem to be united in construction with verse 7; the eighth verse being inserted parenthetically.

11. *To give the lands their name.*—Literally, "they call [in] their names on the lands," whence the authorized version, after Symmachus and the Vulgate, "they call the lands after their own names." But Rosenmüller and De Wette consider this construction as un-Hebrew, and explain, "people call upon [or glorify] their names in the lands (in various countries.)"

13. *They trust in this their way.*—Literally, as I translate, after Rosenmüller and De Wette, This their way is their confidence,—taking the word "kesel" as in Psalm lxxviii. 6; it may also be translated "folly," as in the authorized version, but with what significance?

17. *But God my soul.*—These words seem to imply the hope of a resurrection, or of an eternal life ordained for the servants of God. They may also, however, be understood, and more in conformity with ancient Hebrew notions, to signify that they will be preserved by Providence from a violent and premature end; compose the blessing in the fifth commandment. From our interpretation of this verse the rest of the psalm must receive a coloring.

PSALM L.—v. 1. *The Lord, yea God, high God.*—Literally, God, God, Jehovah, the second word for God being a more emphatic term ; so I translate El, Elōhīm, in accordance with the punctuation of the Hebrew, not, as in the authorized version, the God of Gods. It is, however, a favorite conjecture of mine, that the very word Elōhīm, when construed with the verb singular, is a contraction for ēl Elōhīm, god of gods, and so B-bēmōth for beast of beasts, and so on.

2. *From Zion, beauty's consummation.*—I take the second of these clauses in apposition with the first, not with the Divine name ; compare Psalm xlviii. 2.

20 *Charge and convict thee still.*—Literally, I will rebuke thee, and lay in order before thee, *i. e.*, the particulars of thy guilt.

PSALM LI.—This is entitled, a psalm of David, when Nathan the prophet came to him, after he had gone in unto Bathsheba. But De Wette objects to this supposition as incompatible with verse 18, (where see the note,) and refers the Psalm to the days of the Captivity.

4. *Before thee, thee alone.*—Or, Against thee, thee only, have I sinned—which is the more obvious interpretation ; the words, however, would hardly be applicable to the affair of Bathsheba, for therein David sinned against man also ; and if even we explain, as De Wette thinks admissible, that "it is in relation to God, the Holy One, that the poet especially considers the offence he has committed to be abominable—' when he thinks of God under the consciousness of his guilt, then first it becomes truly oppressive to him,' " the sentiment is yet unnatural and objectionable. Rosenmüller mentions, as a probable exposition, that the psalmist is said to have sinned unto God alone because his crime was disguised and hidden before the eyes of men, and by God alone known and witnessed; and in accordance with this view I have translated, Before thee, &c.,—which rendering also is confirmed by the parallel clause, "I have done this evil in thy sight." I remark, in conclusion, that, even if the title of the psalm were rejected as irrelevant, still the action referred to in it must have included bloodguiltiness, [Hebrew, blood], as appears from verse 14 ; and any

notion of an offence against human life or rights would leave unaltered the difficulty under consideration.

18. *Build thou the walls anew.*—Or "build thou the walls of Jerusalem," an expression which, as De Wette and Rosenmüller most naturally consider, must have been uttered after the overthrow of Jerusalem by Nebuchadnezzar, and before the re-establishment of the Jewish nation under the kings of Persia. It has been, indeed, attempted, as Rosenmüller tells us, to find in these words only a prayer for the completion and perfection of the Temple and the city under David; but we can hardly suppose these not comparatively indispensable objects would be alluded to, in an hour of spiritual anguish, with so much earnestness. Rosenmüller would consider the last two verses of the Psalm as an interpolation, and so justify the received title at the sacrifice of a portion of the text—a process which we should be cautious of imitating, especially as the poem would conclude but abruptly at verse 17. He justifies this attempt by the apparent inconsistency of verses 16 and 19—for God is said not to desire sacrifices; why should they then be promised him? De Wette, after Paulus, reconciles the two verses by the hypothesis, that the ritual services of the Jews being suspended by the destruction of the Temple—God is said, for the time only, not to desire sacrifices, but it was hoped that, when the temple should be restored, he would accept from his votaries, as formerly, the celebration of the Mosaic ritual. "But there is nothing in the words cited" [verse 16,] says Rosenmüller, "to suggest that any such idea had entered the poet's mind; nay, the following verse would militate against this supposition." In my own notion the two verses are not incongruous; the author of the psalm, laboring under a sense of moral guilt, is ashamed of offering to God those external rites, which should be the ornaments and adjuncts of a conscientious moral service; he would not therefore, however, have them neglected by other and comparatively blameless worshippers; nay, he would himself resume, at a future time, the performance of them, could he first remove the burthen from his conscience by giving proofs of an amended disposition, and by a revived faith in God's reconciling mercy—"bestow therefore," he says, "thy blessings upon my nation, which I am unworthy to solicit on my own behalf, so

that *they* may offer thee the *sacrifice of righteousness,* or perform, in an acceptable spirit, the rites which to me would be unprofitable." Compare the sentiment of the exhortation to the Communion Service.

PSALM LII.—Of the title of this psalm, bearing reference to the affair of Doeg the Edomite, (see 1 Samuel, xxi. xxii,) the propriety has been questioned by De Wette, chiefly because reference is made, in verse 7, to a rich or powerful oppressor, which Doeg was not.

2. *Wounding as whetted blade.*—In the authorized version, Thy tongue deviseth mischiefs; like a sharp razor, working deceitfully. But as there is a difficulty in connecting the last words, "working deceitfully" with the razor ; De Wette understands in the vocative, Thou worker of deceit, " du Trug uebender."

PSALM LIII.—This psalm is copied, with a few verbal alterations, from Psalm xiv., on which see the notes.

PSALM LIV.—On the title, see 1 Samuel, xxiii. 19 &c., and xxvi. 1 ; for David was twice betrayed by the Ziphites. The occasion referred to seems not to accord with verse 3, in which " strangers," *i.e.,* heathen enemies, are complained of. For the word Zārim, however, we have zaddīm—proud men—in some Hebrew copies, which are supported by the Chaldee version, and by a similar passage in Psalm lxxxvi. 14: but the emendation was perhaps conjectural. It is probable, however, that zaddīm, as a comparatively rare word, was sometimes changed to zārim by the Masoretic copyists, as in Isaiah xxiii. 2 and 5, where see Lowth. The Syriac version gives, When David sent Joab and his army to fight against Absalom. See De Wette and Rosenmüller.

PSALM LV.—To this psalm an historical occasion has been assigned by the Chaldee paraphrast, whose view, though accepted with some modification by Rosenmüller, has little apparent appositeness —see 2 Samuel xv. 31.

2. *For to and fro.*—For the Hebrew ārīdh I understand—I go to and fro—*i.e.,* in mental perturbation ; literally, I wander like a

sheep in the desert, as Michaelis explains the word from the Arabic, and in conformity with the most probable exposition of Jeremiah ii. 31, (where the authorized version gives, We are lords, as from the root yāradh,) and Genesis xxvii. 40, where read, When thou [the Edomite] shalt be a wandering man, [as it were a Bedouin,] thou shalt break his yoke from off thy neck.

13. *Or if so much mine adversaries did.*—Literally, Nor did any hater do great (bold or heinous) things against me—rather than " magnify *himself* against me," as in the authorized version, if this be taken to mean—" gave himself airs" or defied me.

PSALM LVI.—On the title, which is not satisfactorily confirmed by internal evidence, see Rosenmüller.

PSALM LVII.—On the title, which has no striking congruity with the contents of the psalm, see 1 Samuel xx. 1, or xxiv. 1.

PSALM LVIII.—9. *Let strong and fierce.*—Literally, As living, so wrath or, as we may idiomatically understand, with Jarchi, "alike strong and [in] wrath." These words I refer to the subject of the sentence—whether we translate yis"ārēh, Let a storm carry away" —or, Let God with a storm carry away ; and they may also relate to the object of the verb, viz., the wicked, or, as some think, the contents of the pots—see next note. We can hardly, however, divide the terms, as in the authorized version, "He shall carry them away as with a whirlwind, both living [them living, or in their strength], and [he] in his wrath ;" or, as in the Prayer Book, " So [*i.e.*, in so short a time] let indignation vex him [*i.e.*, each one of the wicked], even as a thing that is raw." Where the word chāi, living, is taken, not very plausibly, in the sense of *raw*. Rosenmüller translates, "The fresh alike and the burning," that is to say, the thorns, as yet not wholly kindled—giving to the word chārōn a signification of physical heat, which is not justified, etymology apart, by the usage of the Hebrew writers.

Ibm. God's tempest them disperse.—For the word "them" the Hebrew gives the affix equivalent to *him* or *it*, by which we may understand, agreeably to well-known usage, each one, viz., of the wicked; unless with Rosenmüller, we make the pronoun refer to the *rhamni* or burning thorns; or, with our Prayer Book, to the meat in the pots, but the latter notion seems too homely to have suited an Oriental mind. I do not consider the metaphor with which the verse begins to be carried on through the whole, as if, indeed, with a commentator whom R. has quoted, we should imagine a description of travellers cooking their meat in the desert, and having their apparatus overturned by an unexpected tempest. I would simply explain the words as follows—" In less time than a caldron can be heated with thorns, let God, as with a strong, fierce tempest, confound the machinations of His enemies."

PSALM LIX.—On the title of this psalm see 1 Sam. xix. 11. Its authenticity is impugned by De Wette, on account of the allusions to Gentile or foreign enemies in verses 5 and 11.

6. *Let them return at evening.*—The verb, as in verse 14, may be considered an imperative.

9. *Thou art my strength.*—For these words the Masoretic Bible gives "uzzō—his strength—by which Rosenmüller understands, "As concerning the strength of each of the enemies (or of their king)." So the authorized version, Because of his strength I will wait upon thee. But I would rather read in accordance with some of the Kennicott manuscripts, "uzzī, my strength, which supplies an easier construction, and suits better with the parallel clause in verse 17.

12. *Let their lips' words, their sinning mouth.*—So the authorized version, "For the sin of their mouth and the words of their lips,—wherein we are told, by a bold figure, that the sinfulness of these men is co-extensive with all their words and conversation.

PSALM LX.—On the events referred to in the title, see 2 Samuel viii., and 1 Chronicles, viii. As the wars there recorded appear to have furnished Israel a series of unbroken triumphs, De Wette asks how they could have given occasion to the present psalm, in which the most grievous checks and calamities are looked back upon? and on this ground he denies the authenticity of the inscription. But we may allow, I think, with Rosenmüller and others, that the view of the poet should go back from the victories of David over the surrounding heathen, to the period of civil war and disorder which had preceded the establishment of his kingdom, and to the disasters which attended the defeat of Saul at Gilboa, when the Israelites, even beyond Jordan, had abandoned their cities before the Philistines, 2 Samuel, xxxi. 7.

4. *Thou show'st an ensign to thy fearers.*—*i. e.*, thou givest to Israel, divided by faction, and oppressed by foreign enemies, a leader, [even David, thy own anointed], under whom they may rally and recover strength.

Ibm. For truth's sake.—Literally, To rally to on account of truth,—*i. e.*, of the cause of true religion. The Septuagint and Vulgate give, To fly-to from before the bow, *à facie arcûs*,—reading, in all probability, qesheth for the rarer word qōshe*t*.

6. *And Shechem portion out.*—This verse and the next two appear to signify, first, the reunion of the ten tribes with the kingdom of Judah, which David had effected after the assassination of Ishbosheth, [2 Samuel, iv.,] and secondly the subjugation of the Philistines, and other adjacent nations, which he achieved soon after.

8, 9. *Shout for me, Philistim.*—That is to say, Do homage, and learn to serve me with alacrity—but the expression does not appear quite adequate to signify so much, nor indeed appropriate to the internecine enmity that subsisted between Philistim and Israel, and which resulted in the extermination, not the amalgamation of the former nation, wherefore we may, perhaps, better read, as in the parallel passage, Psalm cviii. 10,—"I will shout or triumph over Philistim,"—or with a slight variation of the vowels, My shouting [shall be] over Philistim—"alēy P'blesheth hithrō"ā"ī, [Rosenmüller.]

Ibm. Let the Edomite, &c.—This verse is fully rendered by Professor Keble,

"I wash my feet in Moab ; o'er
Proud Edom cast my shoe."

i. e., I will employ Moab for the vilest uses, [like a footbath, says the Syriac version], and make Edom a slave to remove my shoes. But the precise meaning of the Hebrew being hard to ascertain, I have thought it allowable to employ more general terms.

PSALM LXI.—This psalm is inscribed with the name of David, who would hardly, however, appear to speak in his own person in verses 6 and 7, [De Wette]. We may fairly conceive that the psalmist speaks of himself in verses 1 to 5 inclusive, and in the rest of the poem of his king and nation. Our translators have not, like the Chaldee paraphrast, explained this poem as a prediction of the Messiah: they probably judged, and with good reason, that the strong expressions of verses 6 and 7 might be understood hyperbolically, and considered as applicable to an historic sovereign.

5. *For thou, God, hear'st my vows.*—With these lines, as being preceded by the word Selah, I have commenced a new paragraph; De Wette, however, would annex them to the preceding.

6. *Thy king may'st thou.*—The authorized version gives in the indicative mood, Thou wilt prolong the king's life—but the sentence may fairly be construed as a mere prayer.

PSALM LXII.—v. 4. *How long will you infest a man.*—In the authorized version, supported by Kimchi and Aben Ezra, How long will you imagine mischief—but the meaning and etymology of the Hebrew verb t-hōththu cannot be considered as ascertained. Rosenm., in accordance with the Chaldee version, and comparing the Arabic root "h't," gives How long will ye clamor? The Septuagint and Vulgate, How long will ye attack?—which De Wette also vindicates by the analogy of the Arabic "h'sh." It is not in perfect reliance on this rendering, but to express an idea which underlies the three translations, that I have employed the word *infest.* The next verb, according to an accredited reading, may be taken actively,—How long will you all strike at him, as at a broken fence, &c.

12. *And thine, O Lord, is't mercy to display.*—Query, in forgiving the sinner, or in delivering the faithful from his oppressions? The context and the tone that pervades the Hebrew poem, seem to decide for the latter interpretation.

PSALM LXIII.—The inscription—a psalm of David, when he was in the wilderness of Judah—see the narrative in 2 Samuel xxii. to xxiv.—was probably suggested to the compiler by verse 2, where we may understand, In a dry and thirsty land—for which I have given, with De Wette, Like a land, &c.

2. *To view thee in thy holy place.*—From various expositions of this verse I select De Wette's, who understands the psalmist to say, My soul thirsts for thee—*i.e.*, to be near the place where thou art worshipped, and accounted to inhabit ; for [were I] so, I should view thee in thy sanctuary—to see thy power, &c.— "Alsdann sehau' ich dich im Heiligthum, um deine u. s. w. zu sehen." The rendering in the authorized version, To see thy power, &c., so as I have seen thee in the sanctuary,—is more obvious, but satisfies less fully the laws of parallelism, and makes no convenient addition to the meaning.

3. *Now will my lips.*—We might understand, My lips *would* praise thee—*i.e.*, if I obtained the privilege of approaching thee, as above referred to—and in the same manner take the following verses in a conditional sense, and by this method give the psalm more appearance of continuity ; for, as Rosenm. says, " omnia referenda videntur ad istam beatitudinem, si conventibus sacris frui ei concedatur iterum."

6. *For taking rest I mind thee.*—Similarly De Wette ; for it does not seem convenient to annex this verse to the preceding sentence, and to make both clauses governed by the conjunction, as in the authorized version.

Psalm LXV.—A psalm of thanksgiving for seasonable weather, (Ewald.)

2. *All flesh before thy aspect.*—See Deuteronomy xvi. 16.

4. *Like us are filled with good.*—The privileges of Israel, in whose name the psalm is uttered, are indirectly stated in the first part of this verse, which is now explained by the substitution of the first person for the third, Blessed whom thou choosest—we shall be satisfied—*i.e.*, blessed whom thou choosest, as thou dost us, that we may satisfied.

5. *With judgments marvellous.*—Literally, Dread works in righteousness—but the word dread may be taken in the sense of

stupendous [compare Psalm cxxxix. 14,] and righteousness in the sense of faithful kindness, for the passage obviously refers to none but merciful visitations.

8. *The outgoings of morn and evening.*—The farthest east and west.

9. *The river of God.*—According to Schultens the rain itself, in accordance with an Arabic proverbial expression.

PSALM LXVI.—This is considered as a national thanksgiving psalm, but the concluding part may, I think, be literally referred to individual experiences.

PSALM LXVIII.—This psalm was formerly supposed to have been written in celebration of the removal of the ark, by David, from the house of Obed-Edom to the place prepared for it in the citadel of Zion, see 2 Samuel, vi. 12, and 1 Chronicles, xv. De Wette explains it, with more probability, of the bringing back of the ark, in triumph, from some scene of warfare to which it had been carried; see note on Psalm' xlvii. "The date of its composition," he observes, "may be thus determined : we cannot place it before the reign of David, because Jerusalem and Sion are mentioned as forming the abode of the King and of the ark ; nor yet after the revolt of the ten tribes, for it speaks of the tribes of Zebulun and Naphthali as united with Judah and Benjamin. Furthermore, the temple is apparently mentioned in verse 29, and in the following Egypt is alluded to as a hostile power, neither of which circumstances would agree well with the reign of David. The above view would compel us to assign the psalm to the reign of Solomon, which we cannot, however, take into consideration without some difficulty, on account of the generally peaceful character of that period ; but see 1 Kings. v. xi." The whole poem is involved in much obscurity, both by occasional verbal difficulties, and by a series of historical allusions, which it is impossible to distinguish and unravel with any confidence.

1. *Up, God, let scattered be.*—These words were sung before the ark in the journeyings of Israel through the wilderness ; see Numbers x. 35.

4. *Build him who rideth.*—I have translated this verse after its most obvious meaning, and in accordance with the expositions of Rosenmüller and De Wette; the rendering of the authorized version, Extol him that rideth on the heavens,—is founded on the Chaldee and Rabbinical comments, [see Aben Ezra], and derives some recommendation from a comparison of verse 33; but has no conformity with the general use of the Hebrew words. On the words " build a road," compare the Septuagint; they must not be understood too literally, but as referring figuratively to the customary preparations which were made for the journeying of a royal personage; compare Isaiah, xl. 3.

6. *To welfare, whilst.*—The word "bakkōshārōth," is understood by J. D. Michaelis, in conformity with the Syriac version and with Arabic etymology, in the sense of multitude or abundance; thus the passage may be read, He brings out [*i.e.*, sets free], those who are bound [to lead them] to abundance [or to opulence]. De Wette compares the use of the cognate verb kāshar in Ecclesiastes, xi. 6. The authorized version gives "Those who are bound with chains;" the Septuagint πεπηδημένους ἐν ἀνδρείᾳ!

7. *When thou led'st forth, O God.*—The two following verses are taken from the song of Deborah, and the second might be rendered more distinct and continuous by supplying from that source a clause which we may imagine to have been accidentally omitted; see Judges c. v., verses 4 to 5; " The earth trembled and the heavens dropped, the clouds also dropped water; *the mountains melted from before the Lord*, even that Sinai," &c.

9. *A generous rain.*—By this expression Schnurrer and Rosenmüller understand the manna supplied to Israel in the wilderness, which is said to have been rained upon them in Exodus xvi. 4, and Psalm lxxviii. 24.

10. *Thou mad'st them safely dwell.*—In the Hebrew, Thy congregation dwelt therein,—which seems to mean, in the land of Canaan, the last word having been understood, I suppose, from the circumstances in which the psalm was recited.

11. *The Lord God gave the word.*—Literally, as in the authorized version,—The Lord gave the word, great was the company

of those that published it ; but those who published, in the last clause, are expressed by a feminine appellative, so that we may understand the passage as follows :—The Lord " commanded victory for Jacob," and numerous, as a great army, were the women, who celebrated the triumph, even as Miriam, " with a timbrel in her hand, and the women after her with timbrels and with dances," had celebrated the first deliverance of the chosen people, [Exodus, xv. 20]. The verses before us seem to allude to the first victories of the Israelites, when they were settling in the land of Canaan and beyond Jordan.

12. *Kings of hosts flee away.*—These words, according to the critics, are introduced as a citation from the song of the female minstrels ; but they may also, if we join them to the first clause of the preceding verse, represent a promise, or oracle imputed to God; the above view, moreover, may help us to account for the enigmatical style of the next verse.

13. *Sure ye shall rest between.*—According to the more obvious translation,—If ye shall rest between,—but the word "im" *if*, serves sometimes to introduce an emphatic affirmation, as in Hosea, xii. 12, [Gesenius]. The correctness of this view must, however, depend upon our rendering of the subsequent word shphattayim, by which our translators, in accordance with the Chaldee paraphrase, understand cooking "pots ;" while before the words—wings of a dove,—they supply the sign of a comparison, —though ye have lien between the pots, yet shall ye be as the wings of a dove, which would mean, Though ye have, under the oppression of your enemies, defiled your garments in mean and servile offices, yet now shall ye, decked with their spoils, triumph over them in glistening apparel. This sentiment, it appears to me, would sound rather meanly in a sacred lyric, and seem expressed in an insufficient manner. Besides, the word tishkbhû, translated ye have lain, should rather intimate a tranquil repose, and in the only other passage where shphattayim occurs, it is rendered "hooks" in the authorized version, [Ezekiel, xl. 43]. The latter word may receive some illustration from the cognate mishpthayim, [Genesis, xlix. 14, and Judges, v. 16] ; but this is also very variously translated. The Septuagint gives in both places, and in

the present verse for shphattayim, "klēroi," lots, by which we may understand portions of land or boundaries, but with no very satisfactory result. The authorized version gives burthens, in the passage from Genesis, and sheepfolds in Judges. This brings us nearer to De Wette's view, who for both words would render— Vieh-hürden, hurdles for cattle. Other commentators understand sheep-troughs, which would have much the same effect. I take the whole passage to mean, Ye shall surely dwell at ease among your cattle-pens, among the wings of doves, (the word yōnāh being used collectively), that is to say, in pastoral wealth and tranquillity, secured by the overthrow of your antagonists.

14. *Kings in our land.*—Literally, In *it*,—but see the next note.

Ibm. With snow stood Salmon white.—I am at a loss to understand this passage, and have merely endeavoured, in translating it, to preserve an imagery, on which the reader may put his own construction. The correctness of the Prayer Book version, Then were they as white as snow in Salmon, must depend on our interpretation of the previous verse; but at all events it would seem strange that Mount Salmon should be represented as having looked like a snow-clad hill, because it was covered with people whose garments glistened with gold and silver. According to some commentators, the mountain was whitened with the bones of slain enemies, left unburied, forsooth, amidst the well-peopled territory of Ephraim; others take the words—it snowed in Salmon, to signify, Salmon and the adjoining country was refreshed with glad news of victory [Schnurrer].

16. *Why look askance?*—That is, why look ye enviously, ye great mountains, on Mount Zion, which Jehovah has chosen? On the translation and etymology of the verb, see Aben Ezra apud Rosenmüller.

17. *As on Mount Sinai, in his holy place.*—That is, over God's sanctuary in Jerusalem, as whilom on Mount Sinai. Or, omitting the first two words, which are not in the Hebrew, Sinai is in the holy place, *i.e.*, the glory, that appeared on Sinai, is transferred to God's sanctuary in the Temple.

18. *Thou hast captivity captive led.*—Many commentators understand simply,—thou hast captived, or led away captives, but this exposition is less poetical, and not, I think, absolutely required by Hebrew idiom.

Ibm. Hast ransom for men ta'en.—This version is, I think, more correct than,—Thou hast received gifts for men—*i.e.*, taken up something to give away to them. The use of the preposition in bā'ādām, in or among men, is certainly somewhat harsh. The passage appears to signify, Thou hast accepted propitiatory offerings from thy people for their transgressions of thy laws.

19. *Our saviour, when men burthens on us lay.*—We cannot well, with the authorized version, understand the verb to mean to load with benefits. The literal translation seems to be—let [any one] lay burthens on us, [so] God [is] our salvation. The word God is preceded by the article, for which reason it cannot be coupled with the following noun, as if this were a genitive, as in the translation referred to.

26. *From Israel's fountain sprung.*—On the construction put on the word fountain, see Proverbs v. 18.

28. *From thy Jerusalem temple.*—Literally, From thy temple, &c., and these words I have ventured to separate from verse 29, to supply an easier construction.

30. *Rebuke the beast of the fen.*—Literally, The beast (or we may understand company) of the reed, which the authorized version takes as equivalent to the company of the spear [men]. The expression, according to some, refers to the crocodile, the emblem of Egypt; according to others, to the lion, as the emblem of Syria or Mesopotamia. The former view would be hard to reconcile with what is said of Egypt in the next verse.

Ibm. The bull-herds, &c.—Other warlike sovereigns with their peoples.

31. *Then lords shall come of Mizraim.*—The meaning of Hashmannīm, translated lords, is rather doubtful, but does not much affect the import of the passage.

33. *Who rides on heaven.*—In De Wette's eloquent German—
Der einherfährt am uralten Himmel.

PSALM LXIX.—This psalm is considered as an elegy on national calamities. Some passages, De Wette observes, are applied in the New Testament ; but the bitter imprecations in the psalm against enemies, could furnish no prediction of the placable, magnanimous character of Jesus.

PSALM LXX.—Is a variation of Psalm xl. from the thirteenth to the last verse, inclusive.

PSALM LXXII.—This psalm is inscribed with the name of Solomon, whether as its author, or its hero, or both ; most likely because the pleonastic mention, in verse 1, of the king and the king's son, was found applicable to a prince invested with the sceptre during his father's lifetime. This construction, however, is not required by the words in question, though there is no positive reason to dispute its authenticity. Many modern writers; in accordance with the Chaldee paraphrast, explain the poem as a prophecy of " the Messiah-king who was to come," a view which is suggested by the statements in verse 17, and perhaps verse 5 (where see my note), respecting the indefinite duration of the king's reign ; but allowing for poetical exaggeration, we may fairly, as De Wette judges, consider the expressions referred to as applicable to an ordinary monarch. Does not even the wicked man in Psalm x. think—"I shall not be removed from generation to generation, [in] which [I shall] not [be] in adversity."

3. *That hills and mountains.*—The word translated "peace" in the authorized version is well known to be frequently used for health or welfare. The import of this verse is, that in the peace and prosperity of the king's reigns, the homes and fields and gardens of men shall spread to such sites as are at first least eligible; the land shall be tilled and peopled even to the wild hill-tops and mountain ridges. Compare verse 16.

5. *So mankind shall thee fear.*—The second personal pronoun has been understood as referring to the King, but if we say that God is addressed, as in verse 1, the construction will be simpler and more natural. The King's just Government, says the psalmist, shall promote the fear of God among his subjects, and lay a foundation of morality among even their remote descendants.

6. *He shall descend as rain on mowed grass.*—As rain to a mowed field, which without it might easily, in a warm climate, have its roots parched up and withered, so shall the King's rule be life-preserving and beneficial to his subjects.

8. *From sea to sea.*—These words do not, De Wette thinks, express a definite boundary on all sides ; the kingdom might extend from the Mediterranean to the next sea, wherever situated, from the great river Euphrates to the world's end. The merely geographical discussions to which the statements respecting Tarsus, Sheba, and Saba have given rise, will not here require to be entered into.

16. *Earth shall give corn by handfuls.*—The word pis s āh is commonly translated Handful in accordance with the Chaldaic, as it may be understood in the paraphrase of 1 Kings xviii. 44. But its meaning in Hebrew is uncertain ; and the context appears to require a word significant of abundance—as the Syriac version gives, " there shall be abundance of corn in the land."

18. and the following form an epilogue to Book iii. of the Psalter.

PSALM LXXIII.—This psalm, and the ten that follow, bear the name of an Asaph, which, however, cannot here indicate the seer contemporary with David, who is mentioned in 1 Chronicles, vi. 29, &c.—because many of his compositions evidently refer to a later period, whether it be that of the first captivity, or of the tyranny of the Syro-Macedonian kings.

4. *For they live on without.*—So De Wette—Denn keine Qualen bis an ihren Tod.

20. *As a dream when slumber flies.*—The conception is rather subtle, but seems to have been shrewdly penetrated by Shakespeare, who makes the Plantagenet prince, (affecting, perhaps, the airs of a ruler in God's stead,) say to his discarded favorite,

> I have long dreamt of such a kind of man,
> So surfeit-swell'd, so old and so profane,
> But being awake, I do despise my dream.
>
> HENRY IV., *sub finem*.

For as it is the inertness of the sleeper's will and intellect that gives reality to the shapes and figments, the very sentiments and purposes which throng his mind, so it seems, as it were, to be the negligence and oversight of the Moral Ruler that makes to prosper the wicked or inane life and influence. So St. Paul says, in reference to the Polytheism of the ancient world, "and the times of this ignorance God winked at." Acts, xvii. 30.

24. *And receive hereafter.*—Probably a reference to the resurrection, as even De Wette admits, while he thence argues that the author of this psalm lived long after King David's time. Nevertheless, this explanation will not be necessary, if we consider the psalm as referring to the destinies of nations rather than of individuals; and it was under this view, perhaps, that the arrangers of the Psalter have made it serve as an introduction to Psalm lxxiv., of which the burden is manifestly the triumph of a heathen nation over the worshippers of Jehovah.

PSALM LXXIV.—It has been much questioned whether this psalm should be explained of the Babylonian Captivity, or of the persecutions of the Jews under Antiochus Epiphanes, the Macedonian King of Syria, after he had the second time captured Jerusalem, A. C. 145, (see 1 Maccabees. i, and 2 Maccabees. v. and vi., and Josephus, xii. 7). Against the first view it is objected, that the synagogues of God in the land, mentioned in verse 8, do not appear, at least from any positive evidence, to have existed before the Captivity, and that in the next verse the words, There is no more any prophet, neither among us any that knoweth how long—cannot apply to the age of Jeremiah, who had distinctly prophecied the deliverance of his nation, (c. l. and li.); and lastly, that the oppression of the Chaldees was not so long and cruel as that which is here referred to. Against the second view it is urged that the canon of the Hebrew Scriptures was probably completed and irrevocably settled before the time of Antiochus; that the position which is occupied in the Psalter by the poems bearing the name of Asaph should forbid our referring them to a later time than that of Ezra; that one of this book (Psalm lxxix.) is quoted in 1 Maccabees, vii. 17, as if it were an old prophecy fulfilled a few years after the time of Antiochus, and lastly that this king, though he plundered the Temple, did not burn it to the ground, like the enemies spoken of in verse 7. The former of these views has been defended by De Wette, the latter by Rosenmüller. I am not tempted to incline to the Maccabean hypothesis. The arguments alleged on both sides will be further brought forward in the notes on individual verses.

3. *Set foot on soil.*—Literally, Lift up thy steps to the perpetual devastations—or as Rosenmüller says, Eleva gressus tuos ad ruinas sæculi—*i.e.*, institute a survey, like a king visiting his citadel overthrown. Nor does he merely say—direct thy footsteps, but lift them up, that he may appear to be demanding a quick and alacritous approaching, as of one who proceeds not slowly, but with extended strides, [?] while the eyes of all men are directed to his rapid advent.

Ibm. Within thy halidom.—Others translate in the plural *thy sanctuaries*—the word miqdōshekha being rather an equivocal form.

Ibm. Their flags to muster by.—Literally, Their signs as signs—by which I would understand with the authorized version—their ensigns [standards]. Others understand—their usages as usages—and this might refer to the idolatrous rites which Antiochus attempted to establish.

5. *They seemed as those.*—Literally, One is known as bringing upwards axes against a thicket of trees—which grammatically speaking may be understood as in the authorized version—a man was famous according as he had lifted, &c. But in what age have men attained to such renown as " hewers of wood ?" or, who has declared to us the generations of the Gibeonites ? It seems preferable to explain the text as follows, Each of them appears as if lifting an axe against a thicket ; and now, &c. See De Wette.

9. *No more our tokens see.*—Literally—our signs—the same word appears as we referred to in verse 5. De Wette again understands, our liturgical usages—others, the tokens of God's care for us—the operations of his Providence in our behalf?

Ibm. There is no prophet left.—These who scruple to interpret the psalm of the Babylonian Captivity may observe, that at the period thereof Jeremiah, at least, had prophecied the Captivity and Repatriation of the Jews; but then it would appear from Jer. li. 63, that he had thrown his prophecy into the Euphrates, to be drawn out in the time of Ezra.

14. *To the desert dwellers.*—Literally, the people of the desert, which may mean, however, the wild beasts; compare Proverbs, xxx. 25. Leviathan evidently represents the hosts of Egypt, whom the Israelites saw dead upon the Red Sea shore. Exodus, xiv. 30.

18. *How fools contemn thy name.*—Properly, a foolish nation. If, however, the poet is speaking of the Chaldees, he can merely intend to call them impious, as the word Nābhāl has been understood in Psalm xiv. 1. If the word signifies ignorance and rudeness, as it seems to, where Abigail says of her husband, that he is a Nabal by name and nature, 1 Samuel, xxv. 25, the description is more likely to apply to the armies of Antiochus, which were probably composed of miscellaneous levies demoralized by anarchy and plunder.

Psalm LXXV. —The argument of this psalm, according to De Wette, is as follows:—" The Israelites give thanks to God for his deeds [v. 1], and he promises, so soon as it is time, to restore order upon the earth [v. 2 and 3]. Then follows a warning to the enemies [the psalmist again speaking in his own person], not to be over-presuming, for God will humble and punish them [v. 4 and 9]. To do this, God himself promises, v. 10." But Geier and others suppose the King of Judah to be speaking in verses 2, 3 as elsewhere. " The psalm," continues De Wette, "affords not a single datum, from which its historical occasion can be conjectured. It is even doubtful whether the Divine help promised in v. 2 and 3 is still anticipated, or has already been afforded. Only from the description of an unquiet period in v. 2, 3, from the arrangement of the psalm, and the author ascribed to it, can we venture to decide that it refers to a comparatively modern time."

2. *Thy marvels speak it.*—Or, according to De Wette, They (*i.e.*, the nation in general) declare thy wonders.

Ibm. When my hour I take.—These words are attributed to

God. On the rendering of mō″ ēdh as an appointed season, see De Wette; the other signification, of an assembly, has been adopted by our translators, who write, When I shall receive the congregation—perhaps meaning, When I shall hold my tribunal.

8. *With ruby wine.*—Some translate, turbid, *i.e.*, seething or effervescing wine—which De Wette explains from the mixture of stimulating condiments. But the word translated "mixture" may merely mean liquor poured out (see Rosenmüller), and the allusion to red wine, by a cognate term to that which occurs in Isaiah xxvii. 2, appears to imply that which is strong and generous. This wine is a symbol of the Divine vengeance, whose terrible suddenness is supposed to confound, bewilder, and as it were, inebriate the mind; compare Isaiah, li. 17; Jer. xxv. 15, &c.

PSALM LXXVI.—This psalm has been supposed to refer to the overthrow of the armies of Sennacherib—the fifth and sixth verses being interpreted of the sudden death that fell upon them.

"When the eyes of the sleepers waxed deadly and chill,
And the hearts but once heaved, and for ever grew still."

But these expressions may evidently be taken, in a wider sense, to apply to the slain of a battle-field.

10. *Of wrath assumed thy last.*—Literally, Thou shalt gird [on thee] the remnant of wrath—for which De Wette, whom I followed, gives—

Wenn mit dem letzten Grimm du dich gürtest.

Others, in accordance with a Rabbinical comment, but unsupported by Hebrew usage, translate, The remainder of wrath shalt thou restrain—which the reader may understand as shall seem good to him.

PSALM LXXVII.—v. 2. *I stretch by night my hand.*—Literally, My hand is poured forth—which modern critics take in the sense that I have indicated. But the Rabbins apparently considered "my hand" as equivalent to—"The hand of God upon me"—*i.e.*, my plague, $\pi\lambda\eta\gamma\grave{\eta}$, or affliction, which they interpret, on account of the following verb, as a sort of purulent ulcer—whence our translators give, My sore runneth in the night season. The exposition is a nauseous one, and appears unsuited to the context. For we should take an ignoble view of the present psalm, if we understood it as a complaint respecting a private affliction by some disease that flesh is heir to ; much rather does the poet present himself as a member of a suffering nation, for whose deliverance he invokes the succors of that Power,—

<blockquote>
Who the Red Sea in sunder clave,
For his mercy is everlasting ;
And passage unto Israel gave,
For his mercy is everlasting ;
And shut on Pharoah's hosts the wave,
For his mercy is everlasting ;
</blockquote>

as appears from the concluding verses.

10. *Nay, I must bear my scourge.*—Literally, This is my disease, —which appears to mean, This is my lot, and I must bear it ; lo! it is a partial evil, for which the equity of God's government should not be questioned. The authorized version, This is my infirmity, —suggests, perhaps advisedly, another signification, viz., These thoughts are but hallucinations of my agony,—but to this gloss I should scruple to commit myself. In the following words the Hebrew text seems to exhibit a harsh ellipsis, which our translators have supplied by the words in italics, But I will remember ; perhaps I may hazard the conjecture that the whole hemistich should be transposed, and made to follow v. 11.

18. *The whirlwind's wheel.*—In the Hebrew, "in the wheel," which idiomatically means the whirlwind (Gesenius), but according to the authorized version the heaven (or sphere).

PSALM LXXVIII.—This psalm is a commentary on the history of Israel, from their deliverance from the tyranny of the Pharaohs to the establishment of the throne of David. The poet appears to charge the Ephraimites—the principal representatives of the Ten Tribes—with a peculiarly heinous participation in the rebellions and the offences of the nation, by which, it is intimated, they deservedly forfeited their original precedence ; hence resulted the appointment of a king over them from the tribe of Judah, and the removal of the Tabernacle from Shiloh to Mount Zion in Jerusalem ; see verses 9, 60, and 67.

9. *Like Ephraim's sons.*—The verse has not been satisfactorily explained of any actual defeat in battle which the Ephraimites ever sustained through their own cowardice or perfidy; it is rather a metaphorical expression (of which v. 10 contains the exposition) of their shortcomings in the service of God which they professed, and in standing forth as champions of his religion.

38. *But he is pitiful.*—I construe this verse, with De Wette, in the present tense, as a general declaration of God's clemency.

60. *He left his tent at Shiloh.*—"That from verse 56 the discourse turns upon the transgressions of the Ephraimites or Ten tribes, and that Israel is to be understood as contradistinguished from Judah is evident," says De Wette, "from what follows, for Shiloh lay in the territory of Ephraim."

PSALM LXXX.—v. 10. *Her shoots the cedar groves of God.*— Literally, By her shoots the cedars of God were covered, the verb and the first preposition being supplied from the first part of the verse; for thus the passage is understood by the ancient translators, and by Jerome and Luther. Modern critics understand, And her shoots were like the cedars of God;—compare the authorized version; but the ellipsis would be harsher, and the image less poetical; for we can more readily imagine a vine spreading from forest-tree to forest-tree than rivalling the stems of such with the solidity of its branches. Besides, the passage, as above rendered, conveys a fine emblem of the extension of Israel's dominion to the sides of Lebanon, which formed its northern boundary. Compare with this verse and the following Deut. xi. 24. For "cedars of God," goodly cedar trees—is a fair idiomatic rendering *in prose*.

15. *The branch.*—Thus the word Ben may be understood as in Gen. xlix. 22. It is also translated Son, *i.e.*, son of man, as the expression is more fully presented in verse 17. But I prefer the former rendering, because the poet has not yet ceased speaking in symbolic language; the ambiguity of the word, however, may be taken to foreshadow the solution of the entire allegory.

17. *Thy right-hand's child.*—This most probably means Israel

collectively, though the words may also refer to the king, or general, by whom they hoped to be delivered from their oppressors.

PSALM LXXXI.—This psalm seems to have been composed for the celebration of some great feast-day, and probably of the new moon preceding the passover, a rite instituted in honor of the events referred to in verses 6 and the following, which are considered as representing a Divine oracle. It was perhaps written at a time when these observances had fallen into temporary desuetude.

3. *Blow at new moon the trumpet.*—The first day of every month was solemnized by the blowing of trumpets. [Num. x. 10.]

5. *When God the land of Mizraim went against.*—In the authorized version, When he [Israel] went out *through* the land of Egypt,—but the preposition "al, as Rosenmüller observes, will not bear this meaning. On the idea of the present rendering, supposing Jehovah to be the person spoken of, compare Exodus xi. 4.

5. *I hear the voice of one unknown.*—Literally, I hear the lip of [one] I have not known; we must supply the word *of*, because "s phath," lip, is in the constructive form; and thus the expression, as Döderlein showed, serves to introduce the Divine oracle.

PSALM LXXXII.—The first verse is variously translated, God standeth in the council of God [see De Wette], or "of the strong," or "of gods," by whom we may understand either angels or earthly rulers. The latter view seems to me best suited to the context.

PSALM LXXXIII.—This psalm describes a contest between the Israelites and a confederacy of foreign nations, the catalogue of whom, as given in verses 6 and 7, cannot be thoroughly explained by any passage in the historical Scriptures. That which comes nearest the mark is found in the annals of the reign of Jehoshaphat, 2 Chron. xx., where we find, however, no mention of the Assyrian [Asshur], nor yet of the Tyrians and Philistines.

6. *Ishmaelites, Hagarenes.*—These words should, properly speaking, refer to the same race, but the Ishmaelites are frequently

s

identified with the Midianites (Gen. xxxvii. 25 and 36), who dwelt to the southward of the Holy Land; the Hagarenes, on the other hand, are represented as inhabiting a territory on the border of Gilead, 1 Chron. v. 10.

7. *Gebal, &c.*—The name Gebal—a hill-country—was applied to a city in Phœnicia, called by the Greeks Bublos, and in Arabic Dzhiblat, but also to a territory to the east of Jordan, adjacent to that of Moab and Ammon. [Michaelis, Supplementa ad Lexica.]

10. *They sank at Endor*—*i.e.*, the Canaanites led by Sisera and Jabin. Endor in the territory of Manasseh, was situated near Taanach and Megiddo [Jos. xvii. 11], which places Deborah mentions as adjacent to the battle-field [Jud. v. 19].

11. *As Oreb and as Zeb.*—The Midianite antagonists of Gideon; Jud. vii. On Zebah and Salmunna, see Jud. viii. 5—10, 18—21.

13. *Set on them, God, a whirlwind.*—Literally, Make them like a whirlwind,—by which we may understand, in accordance with the Hebrew use of the particles of comparison, Let our pursuit of them be like a whirlwind. By this construction we obviate the necessity for translating "gilgal," a wheel, as in the authorized version.

PSALM LXXXIV. v. 5.—*Thy roads to find.*—Literally, In whose heart are the causeways—Msillóth, where the last word, cannot, under any protection from precedent, be allowed the figurative meaning commonly annexed to "the ways of the Lord, and the paths of the Lord," that is, the practice of religion and morality. The psalmist has rather in his view the roads toward Jerusalem, which the hearts of the pious, he intimates, are ever urging them to frequent, by way of pilgrimage, or to appear before the Lord at stated seasons, according to the commandment in Deuteronomy, xvi. 16.

6. *When through the vale of tears.*—The appellative seems derived from Bākhah, to weep, though irregularly written with Aleph for Hē, as is noticed in the Masorah. Some commentators understand by it, the neighbourhood of the mulberry-trees [b-khā'im]

spoken of in 2 Samuel, v. 23, and 1 Chronicles xiv. 14, as if that grove, being situated near Jerusalem, were customarily traversed by the pilgrims. But it has been well remarked, that the city receiving visitors from all the surrounding country, they could not all make use of this road ; there is, therefore, no reason to suppose that the verse refers to a distinct locality.

9. *Thine own anointed's face.*—These words would seem to refer to a king of Israel or Judah ; but we need not, on that account, suppose the psalm to have been written by, or in honor of such a personage. Much more probably is this prayer episodical, as in Psalm xxviii. 8 ; but we may also, I think, apply the expression "thy anointed" to the whole Hebrew people, as in Psalm cv. 15.

PSALM LXXXV. v. 12.—*And forward on his pathway leads.*—And strides, De Wette translates, further on his path—or literally, sets upon the road his feet. The authorized version gives, the road of his feet—which is also grammatical, but makes it necessary to supply arbitrarily the word *us.*

PSALM LXXXVI.—This is a poem of loose and inconsequential structure, similar to that of the alphabetic psalms, and is characterized by an artificial repetition of the words Lord [Adhōnāi,] God and Jehovah. The fourteenth verse is copied, with the alteration of one word, from Psalm liv. 3.

PSALM LXXXVII. v. 4.—*I have noted.*—Literally, I make remembered [record] Rahab and Babylon to [*or* as] those who know me. And these words are commonly supposed to be attributed to Jehovah, as if saying, I will enrol the heathen nations among those who know and serve me ; they shall even be accounted born citizens of Jerusalem, my holy city. But why may we not still suppose that the psalmist is speaking in his own person, to the effect that, having conversed, among his acquaintances and neighbors, on the comparative renown and greatness of the various cities and realms around him, and especially on the eminent men whom they have produced, he has found among his own countrymen the most truly admirable, as among those whom the Lord himself acknowledges to be his saints and servants ?

Ibm. Rahab and Babylon.—Rahab is Egypt, as in Isaiah, xxx. 7, and li. 19, but the etymology and history of the appellation have not been analysed.

5. *For who was born in her.*—This verse may refer to one individual, or be understood in a collective sense; we have no grounds on which the question can be settled.

Psalm LXXXVIII. v. 4.—*I am esteemed.*—I have translated the verb as passive, but have some suspicion from the context that it may be taken in a reflective sense for "I seem to myself."

5. *Strown mid the dead.*—This is generally translated, Free among the dead—as the word chophshī used in Exodus. xxi. 2, and similar passages. This rendering would not be unpoetical, but appears too subtle and indirect for the Hebrew style; whence Michaelis takes the word in a sense derived from the Arabic, khaffasha—to strew on the ground; with which we may compare the Hebrew chōphesh, a carpet or covering, [see Ezekiel, xxvii. 20].

9. *Lifting my hands on high.*—Not in prayer merely, but in sign of protestation; for he goes on to say, Why should'st thou so long keep back justice from the living: the dead cannot acknowledge thee?

Psalm LXXXIX.—This psalm apparently refers to some calamities that befel the kingdom of Judah before the period of its total overthrow, and is explained by Venema of the reign of Josiah, verses 38 to 45 being applied to his defeat and death in the battle with Pharaoh Necho, see 2 Chronicles. xxxv. There is a remarkable element in it of bitter expostulation, showing to what disappointments the Jews had exposed themselves by an unconditional confidence in the protection of Jehovah.

2. *Maintain thy promises.*—Literally, Thy truth,—but the word seems to introduce a citation in the two following verses of the *promises* attributed to the Deity, as if the psalmist had said, "Thy promises, namely, that, as thou hast sworn to David, thou would'st uphold his seed," &c.

10. *Thou clavest Rahab.* — The word Rahab, as I have

already noted, most probably refers to Egypt. Here Jehovah is reminded of some of the first pledges of his favor that he gave to Israel—viz., in the passage of the Red Sea.

12. *Tabor thy name and Hermon shall proclaim.*—Mount Tabor lies toward the western and Hermon toward the eastern side of the land of Israel ; thus the latter part of this verse forms a parallel to the former where we have, Thou mad'st the north and south.

15. *Blessed the people.*—This expression seems to refer to the festivals of the Israelites, among which I have referred to the blowing of the trumpet at the new moon, Leviticus, xxiii. 24. The Rabbins prefer to illustrate this verse by a comparison with Numbers, xxiii. 21, The Lord his God is with him, and the shout of a king amongst them.

19. *Thy believer told.*—Compare 2 Samuel, vii. 4, though it is probable that no special prophecy is referred to. It is doubted whether the noun should be read in the plural form or singular.

25. *The river*, &c.—Euphrates, as in similar passages, Psalm lxxii. 8, &c.

52.—Is left in prose, as forming the compiler's epilogue to the 3rd Book of Psalms.

PSALM XC.—It is a singular circumstance that this psalm should be attributed to Moses, as if forming, as the Targum tells us, "a prayer which he prayed for the people, even the house of Israel, at the time when they had sinned in the wilderness." Verse 10 would be an unnatural expression for a man who himself lived 120 years, and whose brother, father, and all his ancestors since the creation, had attained, as is recorded in the Pentateuch, to a greater age.

3. *Thou say'st, Return, children of man, to breath.*—We may more simply understand, Thou say'st, Return *to dust*—so that the latter part of the verse would be merely an expansion of the former ; but compare Psalm civ. 30. I refer the words not to a resurrection of man as an individual, but to the successive races on the earth.

8. *Our youth's offences.*—Literally, Our youth,—according to the reading and interpretation of the Chaldee paraphrast ; almost similarly the Septuagint gives ὁ αἰὼν ἡμῶν ["ōlām] ; we may also translate our hidden [sin] as the authorized version gives with most commentators. In Jerome and the old Greek versions we find "negligentias nostras," τὰς ἡμῶν ἀμελείας [Symmachus], and παροράσεις [Aquila.]

9. *As breath that goes.*—The word "hegheh" is explained by the Chaldee paraphrast, The breath of the mouth [as seen] on a winter's day. It is elsewhere understood (1) as a thought; which sense De Wette here adopts, comparing a line in Theognis,

Αἶψα γὰρ ὥστε νόημα παρέρχεται ἀγλαὸς ἥβη

"For rapider than a thought, O youth, thy glory departeth."

and, (2), as a breath, sigh, ejaculation, or tale. But the Syriac version, which the Septuagint and Vulgate have confusedly imitated, give "a cobweb."

11. *Who knows of thy displeasure?*—Literally, Who knoweth the power of thy wrath,—and as thy fear [who knoweth] thy indignation ?—*i.e.*, who is there takes due account of thy indignation, in accordance with the terrific judgments thou hast exercised ? [See Agellius, here quoted by Rosenm.]

PSALM XCI.—This psalm has been considered as a dramatic composition, which might be recited by two actors and a chorus, (see Lowth's Hebrew Poetry, Lecture 26); but the structure of verse 9 and others, as Michaelis remarks, appears incompatible with this hypothesis. I prefer treating it as a monody, in which the psalmist, regarding himself as a representative of the believer in God's just providence, speaks of himself alternately in the third, second, and first persons, like a man communing with his own spirit, and at length hearing in it, as in the concluding verses, the inspirations of a Divine monitor.

5. *Or shaft that flies by day.*—The second part of this verse, and the whole of the sixth and seventh, refer probably to the effects of pestilence.

PSALM XCIV.—Here the psalmist speaks in his own person as the representative of a suffering nation, and complains, it would appear, not so much of the oppressions of heathen enemies, as of internal tyrannous and atheistic government.

15. *Till judgment walk again.*—*i.e.*, till a righteous government be re-established, with the approbation and satisfaction of all well-disposed people.

PSALM XCV.—v. 7. *Whoever his voice now heedeth.*—The phrase *his voice* introduces the words attributed to the Deity, as if we had, Hear his voice, which says to you as follows.

8. *The day of provocation.*—For provocation and temptation, the Hebrew gives us the words Massa and Meribah, whence Moses made the historical proper names,—Exodus, xvii. 7, and Numbers, xiv. 22.

PSALM XCVI.—The following psalms up to the hundredth, inclusively, display a remarkable similarity in style and import. The present psalm is quoted in Chron. xvi. 23—26,—with some variations, and as the conclusion of a longer ode, which David is said to have given out when he brought up the ark of the covenant to Mount Sion. In the citation referred to, verse 35 presents a grave difficulty, from its apparently referring to the age of the captivity. The present psalm is entitled in the Septuagint version, On the building of the house [of God] after the captivity, a psalm of David,—as if we had here an ancient poem that had been altered or applied to the events of a much later period.

PSALM XCVII.—This psalm is rather loosely strung together, and betrays numerous imitations of other poems in the psalter.

4. *His lightnings have revealed.*—Compare Psalm lxxvii. 18.

7. *Before him all gods bow.*—*i. e.*, all false religions are confounded. For the word gods is rather a poetical personification of the idols of the nations than a title given to the angels, whose existence was acknowledged by the Hebrews, [De Wette.]

8. *Mount Sion heareth.*—With this verse compare Psalm xlviii., 11.

11. *There springeth up a light.*—Literally, "There is a light

sown," unless the word "sārūach," be a corruption of "sārūa" "arisen," in which case compare Psalm cxii. 4.

PSALM XCIX.—v. 3. *For he is holy and high.*—Or, it is holy, viz., the name of the Lord mentioned in the preceding verse. This phrase is repeated in verses 5 and 9, and may have been assigned to a chorus.

4. *The king's power loveth right.*—A poetical expression for "the king loveth justice, and by his power executes it."

5. *His footstool.*—We are elsewhere told that "Heaven is his throne, earth his footstool;" but here the expression, as in other passages cited by Rosen. seems applied to the holy of holies in the Hebrew Temple, see Psalm cxxxii. 7 ; Lamentations, ii. 1: 1 Chronicles, xxviii., 2.

6. *Moses and Aaron of his priesthood.*—Moses seems to be somewhat loosely called a priest; but we might observe with Rosen. (if indeed the style of the latter part of this psalm required such accuracy), that the Hebrew Qōhēn is in some passages a civic title, applied to the ministers, or servants of a king; see 2 Samuel, viii. 18, in connexion with 1 Chronicles, xviii. 2, and 2 Samuel, xxii. 26 ; 2 Kings, x. 11, and Job, xii. 6.

7. *He spake in pillar of cloud.*—This statement properly refers to Moses only, as its object, as the latter part of verse 8 does to Moses and Aaron, but not Samuel ; for the former were punished, though with clemency, by their exclusion from the land of promise.

PSALM C.—v. 3. *Who made us his own to be.*—In the received Hebrew text, "For he made us, and not we," *i.e.*, we made not ourselves; but we should probably read lōw, "to him," for lō', "not," so as to have, For he made us, and to him [*i.e.*, his] we [are].

PSALM CI.—The title of this psalm refers it to David, who "as a king, avouches and declares to Jehovah, that he will govern honestly and rightfully, removing from before him and extirpating the wicked, and suffering the good only to abide near him." "He must have composed it," De Wette continues, "after he had made Jerusalem his regal residence;" see v. 8.

1. *Mercy and judgment I will sing*—i.e., as the principles which I have set before me in my own conduct; for if we were to understand God's mercy and justice the verse would have no clear connexion with those that follow it.

PSALM CII.—Another elegiac psalm, in which the poet appears to speak as the representative of his nation. Verse 14 has been supposed to refer to the period which was assigned beforehand for the termination of the Babylonian Captivity. The title, A prayer of the afflicted, &c.,—denotes rather the moral use to which the psalm is applicable than the original intention of the composer.

6. *I am become, as a bittern in the waste.*—In our version, Like a pelican in the wilderness. It would be superfluous, in a literary illustration of these lyrical poems, to aim at great accuracy in rendering a term of natural history; but it appears necessary, from the context, that some bird of loud and melancholious cry should here be designated.

7. *Like a bird on the roof.*—The Hebrew *sippōr* may also be translated sparrow, as in the authorized version, but this limitation adds nothing to the force of the expression; for the sparrow is not generally a solitary bird.

10. *Upraised me and downcast.*—The expression perhaps implies—thou hast first uplifted (exalted), and then overthrown me, or made me an example of good and evil fortune; but we may more simply interpret, Thou hast taken me up in thy hand to fling me downwards.

23. *To whom should he bring down.*—Literally, He has brought down my strength on my journey [of life],—whence De Wette remarks, "From the strains of hope the poet here relapses into complaint." But I think this clause may be taken hypothetically, so as to mean, Should death menace me as in this season of calamity, yet will I pray to live, that I may see the deliverance of my people.

PSALM CIV.—v. 2. *Who like a curtain.*—Or awning; such being the literal meaning of the word elsewhere translated firmament.

3. *Who spreadeth for his high chambers.*—The kind of apartment referred to is in eastern houses built over the porch, and forms the only continuation of the first story, from the roof of which it is entered; sometimes, however, the "aliyāh is double. It is used for retirement and devotion, and also for the reception of strangers. So the chambers of Jehovah, in the verse before us, are conceived as built upon the roof of heaven. See Shaw's Travels in Barbary, quoted by Rosenm.

4. *Who maketh messengers.*—The authorized version, contrary to custom, has set aside the most obvious construction of these words, and that which best suits the character of the psalm, in deference to the translation given in Hebrews, i. 7, Ὁ ποιῶν τοὺς ἀγγέλους αὐτοῦ πνεύματα, καὶ τοὺς λειτουργοὺς αὐτοῦ πυρὸς φλόγα; similarly Luther.

Thus the Targum also explains, He makes his messengers rapid as the wind, and his servants strong as the flaming fire.

6. *Thou clad'st her with the flood.*—Not during the deluge of Noah, but in the primeval condition of the earth, according to Genesis, i. 2 and 9. Is this tradition cited to show how the springs were formed?

8. *The hills arose.*—We may grammatically translate with the authorized version, They [the waters] go up [by] the mountains, they go down [by] the valleys; or, They go up as mountains [*i.e.*, the waves], they go down like valleys; and thus the passage may refer to a confused and irregular retreat, which the watery hosts are supposed to make before Jehovah's thunders. But I prefer, with some diffidence, the translation here adopted from Rosenm., intimating that as the waters subsided, the hills appeared to rise above them, and the valleys to sink beneath them; the last clause, however, of this verse must be constructed in reference to the waters.

PSALM CV.—The first fifteen verses of this psalm are found with some variations, in 1 Chronicles, xvi. 8 to 22, as forming part of the poem which was sung when David brought up the ark of the covenant to Mount Zion.

13. *What time they shifted place.* — As when Abraham

sojourned in Egypt, [Genesis, xii.] and in the kingdom of Gerar, [c. xx.], where see the narrative respecting Sarah.

15. *Touch not my prophets.*—It appears difficult to understand literally the titles of prophets and anointed ones in reference to the first progenitors of the Hebrew nation ; but the Jewish commentators take the second of these expressions to signify princes or great men, and compare Genesis, xxiii. 6, where the Hittites say to Abraham, Thou art a prince of God amongst us. So in Genesis, xx. 7, Abraham is spoken of as a prophet ; while Isaac and Jacob were considered as such, in virtue of the benedictions they pronounced upon their children.

19. *Till for his cause the day.*—Compare the Prayer-Book. The authorized version, more literally, but without clearly ascertaining the import of the phrase, gives, until the time that his word came. Which has also been taken, with some probability, in the sense, Till the time that Joseph's word came to pass—*i.e.*, the predictions involved in his interpretation of the dreams of his fellow-prisoners. Compare, on the Hebrew expression, Judges, xiii. 12 and Samuel ix. 9, 6.

28. *They his word gainsaid not then.*—This expression may refer to Pharaoh and the Egyptians, who were ready to yield somewhat to the fear of the ninth plague, [Exodus, xi. 24] or to Moses and Aaron, who literally obeyed at that time the Divine injunctions in all the miracles they executed, not transgressing, as at Meribah, where they smote the rock they should have spoken to ; but the former exposition seems the most plausible.

PSALM CVI.—This psalm, like the preceding, contains a general sketch of the early history of Israel; but the concluding verses, from the forty-fifth, have an especial reference to the days of the Captivity in Babylon, to which, therefore, the composition of the poem must be considered subsequent.

26. *Therefore he raised his hand.*—In token of an oath ; compare Genesis, xiv. 22, Deuteronomy, xxxii. 40, and Ezekiel, xx. 5 and 6.

28. *On the offerings of the dead.*—That is, offerings to the dead, such as may have been used by necromancers.

30. *Arose up Phineas and prayed.*—Aben Ezra and Kimchi translate, And judged or punished—in reference to the massacre of the idolators described in Numbers, xxv.; and this rendering is sanctioned by the use of the Hebrew verb in 1 Samuel; ii. 25, and the corresponding substantive in Exodus, xxi. 22, and Job, xxxi. 11.

48 marks the conclusion of the Fourth Book of the Psalms.

PSALM CVII.—This psalm presents itself to us as a general treatise on the ways of Providence, in disciplining the sons of men with difficulties and perils, from which a door of deliverance is often wonderfully afforded them. In the last stanza, which differs in structure and apparently in drift of reasoning from all the others, some commentators have found an especial allusion to the return of the Jews from the Captivity in Babylon ; which to me is by no means obvious.

4. *And found no city or home.*—As the verse is divided by the Masoretic accentuation, we should construe, They wandered in the wilderness, in a desert of road, they found no city of habitations—whence the rendering of the authorized version, which for "desert of road" gives, a solitary way. But if the word derekh, way, be construed as part of the second hemistich, we have the sense expressed by the Septuagint, They wandered in the wilderness, yea, the desert—a path to a habitable city found they none.

33. *He turneth the main rivers.*—This clause, like those with which the preceding stanzas open, apparently serves to introduce another case in which God's moral government is illustrated by the vicissitudes of the affairs of mortals. "Look," says the psalmist, "where Jehovah has visited a nation with ruinous dearth, by causing the sands of the desert to overspread the kindly soil—" or he means, haply, in letting the land run to waste for want of tillage, because the inhabitants have been slaughtered or carried away captive in warfare,—"even here doth he often restore plenty and fertility." [Compare Luther's translation, which has caught, I think, the import of the passage, though freely accommodating the grammatical structure.]

39. *Again when they are 'minished.*—These words appear to intro-

duce a new example, though the preceding stanza is not completed with the regular burthen. Jehovah, it is here alleged, allows nations also to be afflicted by misgovernment, say the yoke of foreigners, or by other disasters and calamities, yet will he, in the one case, overthrow the tyrants, in the other, as we may infer, find other means of relieving the sufferings of the people.

Psalm CVIII.—This is a compilation from two psalms ascribed to David, viz., Psalm lvii. 5 to 11, and Psalm lx. 6 to 12, and was probably transcribed at a comparatively modern period, with a symbolic adaptation of old forms to new events.

Psalm CIX.—v. 6. *The fiend at his right-hand.*— The Hebrew word Sātān may, with equal propriety, be applied to a human or a spiritual antagonist; and between these renderings the authorities of the Rabbins, Jarchi and Aben Ezra, are divided in the present passage. I prefer the latter, however, from its correspondence with the concluding clause in next verse, [let his prayer be turned into sin] which must mean, as De Wette judges, his supplication towards God, and from the obvious antithesis in verse thirty-one.

8. *And in his functions.*—So the authorized version—after the Septuagint—Let another take his office—compare the application in Acts, i. 20, to the office or "episcopacy" of the false apostle. "But as this representation," says De Wette, "appears too special, it is perhaps better, with the Syriac version, &c., to understand, his worldly wealth, as the word p-qūdhāh must be rendered in Isaiah, xv. 7.

Psalm CX.—This psalm is treated of as though relating to the Messiah by our Lord Jesus in Matt. xxii. 41, &c. "How, then, doth David call him [the Christ or Messiah] Lord—saying, The Lord said unto my Lord?" not that it fully appears, whether these words imply an authoritative interpretation of the passage, or merely a reference (for the sake of introducing a discussion) to the received opinions concerning its meaning. [But compare Hebrews v. 6, 1 Cor. xv. 25, and Acts, ii. 34.] I believe, with De Wette, that the author of the psalm, notwithstanding his hyperbolical language, wrote only in reference to a contemporary King of Judah.

1. *Jehovah to my lord hath said.*—The licence, hitherto adopted in conformity with ecclesiastical custom, of rendering the word "Jehovah" by "the Lord" [Adhōnāi, ὁ Κύριος] has been abandoned in the present psalm, to which it was thought to give a somewhat perplexed appearance. The prevalent structure of the verses, and the quantity of matter contained, were thought favorable to a version in the common metre.

3. *With holy pomp*—i.e., in ornaments of holiness, pontifical vestments. But this expression not seeming appropriate to a description of young men arming for the battle, De Wette and other commentators would substitute the reading of several manuscripts, b-harrēy qōdesh, on the holy hills, *i.e.*, of Jerusalem, for the similar words—b-hadrēy qōdesh ; compare Jerome's translation.

Ibm. Thy young men's mustering as the dew.—In support of this explanation, compare the metaphoric language of 2 Sam. xi. 12, Job. xxxviii., 8 and 29. [De Wette.]

5. *The high Lord.*—For the simple form Adhōnī, my Lord (v. 1), we have here the quasi-plural Adhōnāi, which in Hebrew usage is only applicable to Jehovah. Here, therefore, the poet addresses himself to the royal priest, whom he has hitherto spoken of in the third person ; it describes him in a different position, not sitting to the right of Jehovah, but having Jehovah on his right-hand ; for he was before depicted as the honored guest or viceroy in the palace of the Holy One, but now as the warrior combating under his protection. It is less clear whether the next verse applies directly to Jehovah, or to his anointed ; the latter is probably the subject of the last verse. I fear I may have hurt the feelings of many of my readers by not putting a more theologic construction on this psalm. It is so easy from the standpoint of modern orthodoxy, to understand it as a Miltonic dialogue between the Father and the Son, or an elegant dramatic illustration of the creed of St. Athanasius. And so, indeed, it may be found handled by Professor Keble. But the Hebrew who wrote this had not so learnt to refine on the doctrine of God's unity from the formulas of Byzantine theologians ; he would have shrunk from imagining him under the form of a man on earth, still more of *two* men.

Psalm CXI.—An alphabetic psalm; two letters being represented in each verse except the 9th and 10th, but in these three together. But the opening words, Praise ye the Lord, *i.e.*, "Hallelujah," must be regarded as a *title*.

2. *Whose pleasure they compose.*—I read with Kimchi, the Chaldee and Syriac translators, and the authorized version, chaphescyhem, the delighters in them, for chephseyhem, their pleasures [or purposes].

Psalm CXII.—This is also an alphabetic (Hallelujah) psalm, of similar construction with the preceding, of which several phrases are repeated in it, but applied, it would appear, with less propriety, whence De Wette considers it the work of an imitator.

5. *He prospers well.*—In the Hebrew, *t*ōbh ish, which Kimchi considers equivalent to ashrēy ish—blessed is the man—citing a similar expression from Jer. xliv. 17. For "a good man" [authorized version and old translations] the idiom of the "sacred language" would have required ish *t*ōbh [Rosenmüller]. The mention of his lending and giving is introduced, not only to show the man's generous dispositions, but the means which Providence puts at his disposal—the reward rather than the merit. To the same purport must the subsequent phrase be interpreted, He shall maintain his cause in [the] judgment.

Psalm CXIII.—The word Hallelujah, Praise ye the Lord, forms a title as in the preceding psalm. Perhaps the same word at the end should belong to Psalm cxiv.; how can it make either a verse by itself, or an integral part of verse 9?

Psalm CXVI.—v. 1. *I am well pleased.*—See the Prayer Book translation; the passage is similarly explained by Jarchi and Aben Ezra, and among modern commentators by De Wette and Rosenmüller.

3. *The snares of death.*—Compare Psalm xviii. v. 4.

8. *The Lord my soul from death.*—Compare Psalm lvi. 13.

11. *Deceivers are all men*—*i.e.*, the help and faith of mankind fail me, unhappy are those who trust them. "Cease ye from man, whose breath is in his nostrils; for wherein is he to be accounted of?" [Isaiah ii., 22.]

PSALM CXVIII.—This psalm appears, like the following, to be nothing else than a cento of accredited devotional phrases (collected from various sources, as will be indicated in the notes upon the several verses), and loosely strung together, for the purpose, perhaps, of being interwoven with liturgical recitations, upon a day of thanksgiving or commemoration. This view is consistent with the citations from the poem that occur in the New Testament, as in Matt. xxi. 9, where the people shout before our Lord, as he enters the holy city, "Hosanna [save now;] blessed he who cometh in the name of the Lord" (see v. 25 and 26), which had probably become an adage.

1. *Praise ye the Lord*, &c.—Compare Psalms cvi., cvii., and cxxxvi., in which last the finest use appears to be made of this expression, which, to judge by Ezra, [c. iii. v. 11,] must have formed a common burthen for devotional poems.

2. *Speak, O Israel*.—With the parallel expressions, "Israel, house of Aaron, and fearers of the Lord," compare Psalm cxxxv. 19 and 20.

6. *Fear what flesh can do to me*.—Compare Psalm lvi. 11. The rest of the paragraph is composed of a kind of expressions very common in the Psalter.

PSALM CXIX.—An alphabetical psalm, in which each letter is repeated eight times at the beginning of a verse. The poem is also characterized, like the Sestinas of Petrarca, by a systematic repetition of about eight words in each stanza; which rule, and the numerous exceptions to it, may be pretty clearly traced in the authorized version, except that the two nearly synonymous terms, Dābhār and Imrāh, are both rendered, Word; to mark the distinction, I have generally, where the context permits, given Promise for Imrāh, according to the general application of the term. For Piqqūdhīm I have used Ordinances; the word Precepts, used in the authorized version, having evidently acquired a different application since the epoch of our translators, as is still shown by its use in legal and municipal language; no one would now talk of God's precepts, for the expression would imply no peremptory authority. The other words I have translated in the usual manner, Testimonies, Statutes, Commands [or Commandments], Judgments, Law, the distinctions not being very clear; but see notes on verse 119 and verse 132. The psalm is a collection of maxims, devotional expressions, and "forms of sound words" suited to men in various positions and circumstances.

3. *Do from his paths not swerve.*—For Derekh path, it has been conjectured that we should read Dābhār, word, otherwise this verse has no characteristic word, and the whole stanza lacks two of the series.

26. *I have owned my ways.*—*i.e.*, set before thee in prayer my whole condition.

32. *If thou a large heart make me.*—*i.e.*, an understanding heart, in modern parlance, *mind* or *brain*; compare 1 Kings, v. 9.

57. *It is my portion.*—Literally, as the verse is construed by Rosenm. and others, in accordance with the accents, It is my portion, O Lord, (I have said) to keep thy words; not as in the authorized version, Thou art my portion, O Lord; I have said that I would keep.

70. *Their heart is fat as brawn.*—*i.e.*, callous and senseless, as in Isaiah vi. 10.

83. *I parch like flagons hung in smoke,*—"Which are thence," De Wette explains, "dry and shrivelled." The wine-skins were probably dried over the fire, to be subsequently filled with liquor.

119. *I love thy covenant hence.*—Properly, testimonies; which generally, according to Kimchi, means in this psalm the ceremonial observances which God instituted; here the expression seems referrable to the promises that accompanied, and were commemorated by these institutions.

131. *I ope my mouth and gasp.*—An expression of vehement desire.

132. *As is thy judgment.*—Literally, As is judgment [Mishpot]. The word may be taken, as the Chaldee renders it, in the sense of custom, in accordance with Gen. xl. 13, and Jos. vi. 15; we may also understand, "as is equitable;" compare v. 149.

T

172. *My tongue shall sound thy promise.*—On the Hebrew compare, with Rosenmüller, Exodus, xxxiii. 18.

PSALM CXX.—This psalm and the fourteen following bear the common title Shīrēy hamma"alōth or " Songs of the Goings up," of which various explanations have been attempted. I am inclined to understand it as referring to the return of the Jews from the Captivity, (as they came in sections, first during the reign of Cyrus, under Joshua and Zerubabel, and next under Ezra, and during the reign of Artaxerxes ; see Ezra i. and ii., 7 and 8), not that these proceedings form exactly the subject of all these poems, but that they may all have been written at the period indicated; even those that bear the names of David and Solomon being, if the titles are not so far altogether spurious, adaptations or *rifaccimenti* of ancient pieces, (see Psalms cxxii., cxxiv., cxxvii., cxxxi., and cxxxiii.) The style and rhythm of these psalms, and, in particular, the elegant repetitions and novel combinations of the leading phrases in most of them, are very characteristic.

1. *In hour of woe.* — " This psalm," observes Rosenmüller, "seems referrable to the times immediately following the Captivity, when the people, though no longer detained in foreign countries, had to complain of the envy, the calumnies, and stratagems of the Samaritans, and the other people around Judæa, who opposed the restoration of the Jewish state and worship, and left no stone unturned to hinder the rebuilding of the city and Temple."

2. *What shall God give to thee.*—This verse may be construed, What shall he [understand the Lord] give and add to thee, O tongue of perfidy? [Compare the authorized version and the comments of Venema, and C. B. Michaelis], or again, What shall the tongue of perfidy give and add to thee—which is explained, Wherein shalt thou, O enemy, be profited by thy falsehood which thou utterest;—compare the Chaldee version, Luther, Geier, and Rosenm.

5. *To dwell with Meshech*, &c.—The word Meshech applies properly to a Caucasian tribe (Gr. Moskhoi), and Kedar [Qēdhār] to a nomadic Arabian race. In the present passage, the terms are apparently transferred to some rude nations, among whom the exiled Jews were conversant.

Psalm CXXI.—1. *I lift mine eyes up toward the hills.*—Namely, those that stand round about Jerusalem.

6. *Nor moon by night.*—The moon was made "to rule the night," whose frosts and dews are accordingly considered as her ministers.

Psalm CXXII.—This psalm is ascribed to David, but to judge by the mention in verse 5 of the thrones of the house of David cannot have belonged to so early a period. There is some difficulty, too, in referring it to the times of the Return from Captivity, in which, of course, there was no king in Judah. But as " thrones of judgment" are mentioned, not royal thrones, we may, perhaps, understand the expression of Zerubbabel and his assessors, inasmuch as he was invested with some authority over the returned Jews, and was by birth the heir of David. Verse 3 of this psalm presents a modernism in the form of the relative pronoun, and verse 1 a Syriacism in the construction of the participle and verb auxiliary.

3. *As a city, where in good accord men dwell.*—Literally, As a city well bound together in itself. Of which words the most material explanation is furnished by Chrysostomus, who says, " He asserts the continuity of the edifices and the stability and compactness, and that there was no empty space in the midst thereof, but it was all compact, coherent, and continuous," and so on ; I omit, *propter egestatem linguæ*, the succeeding epithets of the eloquent Hellenic father. Our Prayer-Book, with more refinement, but less clearness, gives " built as a city that is at unity with itself." And indeed the poet possibly intimates, that the dwellings were not jealously separated from one another, nor extravagantly unequal in dignity, so that they looked like the homes of peaceful and independent citizens, not as where a fastness of foreign mercenaries is environed by the hovels of an alienated and impoverished peasantry.

Psalm CXXIII.—" The poet," observes De Wette, " speaks first in his own name, and then [v. 2] in that of the nation, as in many of the elegiac psalms we find a transition from the personal to the universal style, or *vicê versâ*. That the people of Israel are referred to, and that the enemies are heathens, is sufficiently manifest.

PSALM CXXV.—This psalm was composed under heathen oppression, and in a period when a part of the Israelitish nation were apostatizing ; perhaps, as Tiling and Rosenm. suppose, at the time of the re-establishment of the Jewish State, when many of the people allowed themselves to be seduced by the Samaritans. (Nehemiah, c. vi. and xii.)

3. *For o'er the just man's lot.*—That is, as De Wette understands, the momentary disastrous condition of the state, under the sceptre of the wicked, (*i.e.*, heathens), shall not, thanks to the protection of Jehovah, endure for ever.

Ibm. Lest haply even they.—" Lest, overcome by the grievousness of their sufferings, they should forsake the ways of piety to follow the example of bad men."

PSALM CXXVI.—As the Jews did not return from exile simultaneously, but in two or more separate migrations, (see Ezra c. ii. and viii.,) so here the first arrivers give thanks for their own repatriation, and proceed to pray for the success of the remnant that is to follow them.

4. *Like southern floods in flow.*—Like torrents in hot countries which are dried up in summer, but appear again in the rainy season.

PSALM CXXVII.—A psalm attributed to Solomon, yet included among the Shīrēy hamma"aloth ; it may, perhaps, be a restoration or modification of an ancient poem.

PSALM CXXIX.—v. 1. *Up from my youth have they.*—Referring to the oppressions which Israel had suffered, as under the Egyptians and Philistines, in the earliest periods of their history.

3. *The ploughers on my back.*—A euphemism for the scourgers.

8. *God bless you, or the Lord you speed.*—The verse, perhaps, imitates, as we are told in the Chaldee version, both the greeting of the passers-by, and the answering salutation of the reapers.

Psalm CXXX.—v. 4. *Therefore shall men thee fear.*—They shall not, as in desperation, cease to reverence thee, and to take warning from thy judgments.

Psalm CXXXI.—v. 1. *Myself in things too high or hard.*—The verse does not necessarily refer to difficult speculative inquiries, but much rather to worldly ambition; were it otherwise the Psalmist's words would disparage the books of Job and Ecclesiastes, which introduce us to such anxious questionings respecting the moral government of the world, and the rational object of its existence.

2. *Like a child newly from his mother weaned.*—Helpless and dependent—as we should imagine even the sucking-child, had he here been mentioned — but having more consciousness of his position. It seems too great a refinement to say that the weaned infant represents a person whose desires are controlled and pacified towards all objects that he should not covet.

Psalm CXXXII.—This psalm seems to refer to the dedication of the first Temple, as a work which Solomon was allowed to execute for the sake of David, his father, and for which the latter had made anxious preparations. In structure it has no apparent connexion with the other Songs of Degrees.

5. *Till for the Lord I find a home.*—This refers to David's bringing up the ark of the covenant, lately recovered from the Philistines, to the Tabernacle in the city of David, 2. Samuel, vi.

6. *In Ephrath.*—Probably put for Ephraim, compare 1. Samuel, i. 1, and 1. Kings, xi. 26.; (for in Bethlehem, which is also called Ephrathah, we find no occasion on which the ark was left), and this for Shiloh, in the Ephraimitish territory, where the ark was kept before Samuel's time.

Ibm. And the place in Jaar we found.—Literally, in the field of Jaar, (Ya"ar) [the wood], which seems to mean Kirjath Jearim, near which city the ark was abandoned by the Philistines, 1. Samuel vi.

8. *Come up to thine abode.*—This verse and the following are quoted in the prayer of Solomon, 2. Chron. vi. 41. &c.

9. *Thy Priests with righteousness be clad.*—For *righteousness* the author of Chronicles substitutes salvation, which word had probably a like effect in the context; so that we may understand, Let thy priests wear that appearance of content and confidence, which may intimate that they are under the protection of thy gracious judgments.

PSALM CXXXIII.—*Like Hermon's dew, like dew down Zion's hill.*—The words "like dew," appear necessary to be supplied to give a satisfactory signification—for how could the dew of Hermon, so remote a mountain, descend upon the hill of Zion. [Kimchi and Jarchi.]

PSALM CXXXIV.—A psalm for watches in the Temple. According to De Muis, quoted in Geier's commentary, it is a dramatic poem, in which, verse 1—3, a more reverend Levite [dignior e Levitis], admonishes the others of their duties; to whom they, in verse 3, reply by way of thanks, invoking for him the blessing of Jehovah.

PSALM CXXXV.—This psalm strikes us as a kind of anthem compiled for liturgical purposes, (and that with taste and judgment, but without much original effort,) from the preceding and subsequent psalms, and from psalms cxv. to cxviii., as will appear from the references.

5. *For sure the Lord is great.*—Compare psalm xcv. 3.

6. *Whate'er the Lord sees good.*—From psalm cxv. 3; the appropriation is continued in verse 15.

7. *The clouds he marshals forth.*—Compare Jer. x. 13 and li. 16.

8. *He that in Mizraim.*—Compare the following psalm, verse 10, etc.

19. *But do ye bless, O Israel.*—compare the commencement of Psalm cxvii.

PSALM CXXXVI.—A psalm admirable for the simple majesty of its form. The verses seem most naturally to group themselves in threes, except that at the end we have only two left to connect together, and that between verse 21 and 22, there is no decided break. The burden of the psalm " for his mercy [is] for ever," seems to have been a favourite one in the Hebrew liturgies ; see Ezra, iii. 11.

Psalm CXXXVII. — v. 1. *By Babel's waters.*—The supposed speakers, says De Wette, were no longer suffering a rigorous confinement or hard treatment, but had some comforts and pleasures occasionally offered them, by which they might have been tempted, if their national feelings had been less intense, to forget Jerusalem in their mirth.

In accordance with this view it may be supposed that the phrase, by the waters of Babel, was associated with gardens, or pleasant meadows, by the side of the Euphrates, and other rivers, where the people may have congregated to make merry and to hear music. But the psalm was perhaps written when Babylon had fallen into the hands of her destroyers, and when the Jews saw accomplished the vengeance they had coveted.

3. *While our hearts dull sorrow kept.*—This is far from a literal translation, but I must excuse it by the unsatisfactory state of our knowledge of the full force of the word Tōlālēynū, in the authorized version "those who wasted us," in others, " those who made us lament," "who led us captive," &c ; these, it is said, required of us a melody,

7. *Remember Edom's sons.*—On the hostility which the Edomites had shown to the Jews in the time when their city was overthrown, compare Jer. xlix. 7—22, Amos, i. 11—12, and Obadiah.

Psalm CXXXIX.—A psalm ascribed to David, but of which the language is apparently too modern.

5. *Thou dost before me stand.*—So the authorized version, " thou hast beset me behind and before." The Prayer-Book gives, " thou hast fashioned me behind and before ; " but the subject which such words would refer to, is not introduced till verse 13.

9. *If I the wings of morn.*—i.e., if I traversed the whole

course of the sun and the daylight, even to the furthest west, (for this quarter, to the Hebrews, is always represented by the sea), even so should I be always in thy presence.

13. *Sure! thou hast wrought my frame.*—The Hebrew verb is more regularly translated, Thou hast possessed—so the Vulgate, "Quia possedisti renes meos;" and our Prayer-Book, "For my reins are thine," but the interpretation, here adopted is also suitable in Gen. xiv. 19., Deut. xxxii. 6, and recommended by the Arabic etymon. [Rosenm.]

Ibm. Hast tissued me.—With thews, skin, &c., [Kimchi] ; so understand "*covered.*"

15. *From thee were hidden not my bones.*—The last word may be allowed, De Wette thinks, even to express the Hebrew "ōsem, [commonly taken strength or substance,] even without reading in lieu thereof "aṣāmīm, bones.

Ibm. Patterned in earth full deep.—A euphemistic metaphor.

16. *My limbs in thy book set.*—This clause is commonly interpreted, In thy book were they all written, [in the] days [when] they were fashioned, and [when there was not] one of them ;" the words "they all" being taken to refer to the recent limbs and organs, of which a notion is suggested by the preceding word "embryon." On another exposition, see De Wette.

17. *O God, how fathomless.*—Literally, how hard, obscure. In the authorized version, How precious also are thy thoughts unto me—but the above interpretation is justified by De Wette from the use of a similar word in Dan. ii. 11.

19. *Ye men of blood, away.*—Having hitherto emphatically asserted, as with reference to himself for an example, how bare and open are men's thoughts and ways before "the God of the spirits of all flesh," the psalmist leads us hence to consider that He will surely punish, as He can discern, the impious, and that He will judge between the oppressor and the innocent ; before this power he denounces his opponents, whether they were heathens or apostates in his own nation.

Psalm CXL.—This psalm, titled as David's, breathes complaints of slanderous or perfidious and violent enemies, like those who were around Saul, including Doeg and the Ziphites. Herein Rosenm., however, judges that the Hebrew people, restored to their own land from the Babylonian territories, and personated by one man, complains of the envy and calumny of the Samaritans and the surrounding nations, and against them implores God's succor; which view makes the "Scripture of less private interpretation."

Psalm CXLI.—This psalm also is titled as David's, but presents like difficulties with the preceding. The speaker, in De Wette's opinion, is a Jew, who sees his countrymen cruelly persecuted, and is tempted by their enemies to join a party of renegades from among them. Many verses in the poem appear perplexed and equivocal; let us glance at those from which most light is opened. The poet, in verse 7, sees the bones of his countrymen lopped and strewed on the earth like billets—an emblem, to all appearance, of cruel [Antiochian?] persecution. He does not, I think, in verse 6 invoke a judgment upon these national enemies—as if you translate, Let *their* judges [the heathen powers] be overthrown in stony places, [Prayer-Book version]; for he has not yet spoken of the atrocities of fanaticism, but only of the perfidious blandishments by which it sought to make renegades. These words may be literally rendered, Their judges were dashed down into the hands of the rock—and we may fairly deem, with Ewald, that the term, Their judges, is explained by the following verses, and applies to the heads of the chosen people. Otherwise, the expression, in the place it occupies, would not breathe the forbearance which the psalmist in verse 3 implores Heaven to inspire him with; it would furthermore be absurd to conceive, that men just hurled, as from heights Tarpeian, should listen to words of mildness—as I suppose the Hebrew to mean—or of triumphant pleasure, as De Wette takes it. Some commentators interpret these words of judges overthrown from the heights of honor or office, and so humbled, that they are henceforth fain to hearken to the proffers or ovations of their former victims; but the Hebrew expression has not, I think, the blandness of this conception.

3. *A watch before my mouth.*—The psalmist, as one of those tempted to become renegades, prays, I think, not merely for caution by which he may parry inveigling proffers without committing himself to wrong concessions; but further for a spirit of prudent and gracious mildness, that he may not embitter the minds of his country's potent enemies.

5. *If me the righteous strook.*—" The sense is," says De Wette, " I bear willingly from friends any unpleasant treatment for my reformation; but the wickedness of the enemies can I not bear."

Ibm. And flinch not, though to fall again it were.—*i.e.*, the stroke or rebuke; but on this passage, which has much obscurity, see the same commentator.

Ibm. Nay, but my prayer.—Literally, But my prayer is in their evils, by which commentators understand, My prayer is against their wickedness; *i.e.* of the heathens; but Ewald, more conformably, I think, with the context and the tenor of the psalm, [as appears at the conclusion mainly,] gives, My prayer is regarding their [Israel's] distresses.

6 *When down the rocks are thrown,*—See, on these verses, the introductory note.

PSALM CXLII.—A psalm entitled Maskhîl of David, when he was in the cave, as if relating to the adventure of cutting Saul's skirt. As De Wette remarks, the poem seems to have no particular connexion with this occasion, and the title may have been founded on a misconception of the word Masgēr, keep or dungeon, in the concluding verse.

PSALM CXLIII. — Has many resemblances to preceding psalms, especially to Psalm lxxxi.

PSALM CXLIV.—This psalm is attributed by its title to David; though verse 10 seems to show that it was written when both he had reigned and many kings after him. It is obviously compiled from Psalm xviii. and other originals.

1. *Who teacheth my hands war.* — Compare Psalm xviii. 34.

3. *Lord, what hast thou in man?*—Compare Psalm viii. 4.

4. *Man is like nothingness.*—Compare Psalm xxxix. 6, 7, 12.

5. *Come down and lower the skies.*—Compare Psalm xviii. 10, Psalm civ. 32.

13. *In the mead.*—So De Wette, not "in our streets"—for the streets of Salem are not now contemplated as grass-grown, so that flocks can have no seemlier areas to multiply themselves in. "Art thou not she that was full of stirs, a tumultuous city, a joyous city?"

PSALM CXLV.—This psalm is styled Davidical, but is in language and sentiment comparatively modern; the words of David in Psalm xxx. 1, may have afforded an impulse to the author. It is an alphabetic poem, but written with more freedom, fluency, and lyric feeling than the generality of that class. The Hebrew text has no verse corresponding to the letter Nūn, but the omission [after verse 13] is plausibly supplied by the Septuagint.

3. *Great is the Lord.*—Compare, with De Wette, the opening of Psalm xlviii.

8. *The Lord is ruthful, tender.*—Compare, with De Wette, Psalm lxxxvi. 15, and ciii. 8.

13. After this verse the Septuagint inserts—πιϛτὸς κύριος ἐν τοῖς λόγοις αὐτοῦ, καὶ ὅσιος ἐν πᾶσι τοῖς ἔργοις αὐτοῦ, which may be readily translated into Hebrew, using ne'emān as the first word to supply the letter Nūn.

15. *On thee, Lord, wait the eyes of all.*—Compare Psalm civ. 27.

PSALM CXLVI.—The following psalms, till the end of the Book, bear the title of Hallelujah—praise ye the Lord. They are fitly placed at the conclusion, as hymns of triumphant thanksgiving; the Septuagint attributes the three first to Haggai and Zechariah, and the style is suited to the music of a highly cultivated templeworship. The text of the present psalm does not appear to require explanation, and many of the verses, which are adapted from other psalms, will be readily discovered by the reader.

PSALM CXLVII.—v. 1. *For to give praise is meet.*—Compare Psalm xxxiii. 1.

3. *He heals the broken-hearted.*—Principally referring to the exiles of the preceding verse; so verse 6 applies to these and to their national oppressors.

9. *The raven's brood.*—Compare Job, xxxviii. 41, and with the next verse compare Psalm xxxiii. 10, 17.

PSALM CXLVIII.—v. 4. *Water which art over heaven.*—I believe the word water, according to Hebrew usage, to include vapor generally, whether in the shape of visible steam, or of cloud, or of moisture lost in the atmosphere, see Psalm xviii. 11.

PSALM CL.—In these six lines I have ventured to employ a quantitative hexameter, but partly anapaistic, as in Greek lyrical models.

www.ingramcontent.com/pod-product-compliance
Lightning Source LLC
Chambersburg PA
CBHW030818230426
43667CB00008B/1273